The Boom in
Contemporary Israeli Fiction

Edited by

ALAN MINTZ

The Boom in
Contemporary Israeli Fiction

BRANDEIS
UNIVERSITY PRESS

Published by

University Press of New England

Hanover and London

BRANDEIS UNIVERSITY PRESS
Published by University Press of New England, Hanover, NH 03755
© 1997 by the Trustees of Brandeis University

Printed in the United States of America   5 4 3 2 1
CIP data appear at the end of the book

Published with the support of the Jacob and Libby Goodman Institute for the Study of Zionism and Israel.

"Magic Realism in the Israeli Novel" by Robert Alter originally appeared in *Prooftexts* 16:2 (May 1996). Reprinted by permission.

The Tauber Institute for the Study of European Jewry Series

Jehuda Reinharz, *General Editor*
Michael Brenner, *Associate Editor*

The Tauber Institute for the Study of European Jewry, established by a gift to Brandeis University from Dr. Laszlo N. Tauber, is dedicated to the memory of the victims of Nazi persecutions between 1933 and 1945. The Institute seeks to study the history and culture of European Jewry in the modern period. The Institute has a special interest in studying the causes, nature, and consequences of the European Jewish catastrophe within the contexts of modern European diplomatic, intellectual, political, and social history.

The Jacob and Libby Goodman Institute for the Study of Zionism and Israel was founded through a gift to Brandeis University by Mrs. Libby Goodman and is organized under the auspices of the Tauber Institute. The Goodman Institute seeks to promote an understanding of the historical and ideological development of the Zionist movement through an exploration of the seminal issues in the history of Zionism and the State of Israel.

Contents

The Boom in
Contemporary Israeli Fiction

ALAN MINTZ

Introduction

HEBREW LITERATURE, which began with the Bible, has had a very, very long history. Modern Hebrew literature, which began with the Enlightenment, has been around for two centuries. Against this time line, the Hebrew novels and short stories written in Israel over the past twenty-five years might seem like callow and unproven recent arrivals. Yet, in fact, the opposite is true. Readers and critics share the heady realization that they are living through an explosion of literary creativity and that many of the works written during this period not only do not pale in comparison to their strongest precursors but are in fact likely to be studied with close attention in the future.

The point, of course, is not to fix the value of reputations or speculate in the bourse of literary immortality, but to indicate the excitement and sense of moment that have attended the arrival of new works of fiction in Israel since the mid-1970s. Fresh writers have appeared on the scene and older writers have developed in new ways. The field has also become more crowded. It used to be that a literate Hebrew reader would have to satisfy his or her appetite for fiction largely by reading novels translated from European languages. Each year a few novels written in Hebrew would demand attention and give pleasure, but they did not make for a steady diet of satisfying reading. By the 1980s the trickle had become a steady flow. Not only were there many more conventionally "serious" works of fiction, but there were also many more attempts to write "genre" novels in Hebrew: detective novels, thrillers, romances, historical novels. These are the kind of works that had previously been imported in translation and now have served to fill out the literary system.

More and better works of fiction also created a new audience for fiction. This had something to do with a general shift from poetry to prose. During most of this century, throughout the waves of immigration from Europe and the struggle for nationhood, the Hebrew-reading public has carried on a love affair with poetry. Poems were declaimed by national figures at public ceremonies and carried in the rucksacks of anonymous soldier-farmers. For Jews who were only one generation removed from study of the Torah and observance of the commandments, the writing and reading of poetry, as a private communion or a communal sacrament, served as a kind of substitute piety. The national preoccupation with poetry has been on the wane for some time now, however; one is tempted to point to Yehuda Amichai (b. 1924) as the poet whose widely accessible and widely read work signaled the end of an era. Wonderful poetry continues to be written in Israel, but, in a way that parallels the fate of poetry in most Western democracies, the poetry scene is scattered and unsure of itself. New commanding poetic voices have not emerged, and poets find themselves marginalized in the arena of public culture and pressed into a defensive position concerning the prerogatives of their craft.

Why this turn to prose? This is one of those questions that naturally come to mind but about which few satisfying answers can be given. No research protocols or analytic frameworks I am aware of can shed much objective light on this subtle yet fundamental phenomenon in culture. We are left with speculations, and the speculation I would offer, though it is hardly original, centers on the capacity of prose fiction to give adequate representation to the way in which the individual self is entangled with other selves in the world of social relations. In the decades after independence, the Israeli reality became more diverse and less ideologically driven. Whole sectors of the population became established economically at the same time as social, ethnic, and religious cleavages deepened. The move away from labor socialism at the polls and state ownership in the economy were not simply outgrowths of shifting political currents, but causes and effects of a deeper change. The construction of the self in Israeli society became less dominated and organized by a national collective myth, and the "story" of the individual became many stories enacted in many arenas with many possible outcomes and many possible interconnections. To be sure, poetry can—and Israeli poetry does—offer abundant insights into these changes, especially through a strong tradition of political verse. But it is my conjecture that prose fiction has proved better suited to comprehend the interwoven strands of this complex society in transformation and give an account of "how we live now."

The new audience for Israeli fiction is in part a creation of a publishing industry that operates very differently now than it did in the past. Since the 1920s and 1930s, when the basic institutions of the Yishuv were set up, books of poetry, essays, and fiction were generally put out by publishing houses connected to political movements, with varying degrees of insistence on the "political correctness" of the published works and their authors. Private houses, such as Schocken, were a rarity; these were either vanity presses or cooperative ventures by small circles of avant-garde writers. Beginning in the 1970s, large commercial publishing houses entered the scene and introduced more of a free-market model based on profitability and consumer demand. Even the older, movement-based publishers were quickened by this entrepreneurial spirit; as ideological constraints weakened, the desire to connect with wider audiences led to a greater flexibility of publishing arrangements and to many joint ventures with commercial houses.

The publishing marketplace in Israel has come to resemble in many respects the way books are sold and promoted in America. There is a culture of best-sellers in which a few books get read by a great many people and benefit from concentrated media attention. This means that there are some writers who are receiving substantial royalties (in Israeli terms), and, while I know of no writer who lives solely from writing serious fiction, money has become a new factor. There is a greater investment in the promotion of books and the manipulation of their reception in the press. A handful of powerful editor-professors attempt to shape the tastes of the serious reading public, and many boundaries are crossed between the academy, the publishing houses, and the media. The "Americanization" of publishing in Israel, in short, has all the merits and demerits of the model it has copied. Undeniably, it has had the general effect of quickening the climate within which fiction is written and read, and of engendering excitement about new talents. The best books do not always sell the most copies, but sometimes they do, and the larger number of works that manage to get published creates a wider field of critical play and possibility.

In this connection, it is worth noting that the audience of Israeli fiction is located not only within Israel. There are, to be sure, hundreds of thousands of Israelis who have left Israel and settled in other countries, primarily the United States; like Israelis in their homeland, most do not consume serious literature, but some do. More to the point, there is a significant audience for Hebrew fiction translated into other languages, mostly (but not exclusively) English and European languages. Interestingly, despite the size of the American audience and the large scale of its Jewish community proportional to other countries, Israeli novels sometimes do better in French, German, or Italian than in English. In any case, commercial successes are rare; critical succès d'estime much less so. If the diffusion of Israeli literature in translation is not broad, these works often do make an impact in intellectual and critical circles. This notice contributes to an awareness of the presence of Israeli literature on the international literary scene. Amos Oz, A. B. Yehoshua, Aharon Appelfeld, and Yehuda Amichai are among the Israeli writers who are acknowledged as significant figures of world literature.

What ends up being translated is not always what is most popular or highly regarded in Israel. Getting translated has to do with a combination of factors: commercial publishing considerations, cultural politics, and the degree of the author's determination to make it happen. Amalia Kahana-Carmon, the important New Wave writer whose work took a pronounced postmodernist turn in the 1980s, has always declined to allow her work to appear in English or other languages, presumably because of her belief in its untranslatability. In the end, the most important factor lies less inside Israel and more in the way in which Israel and its culture are perceived and thought to be relevant in the minds of foreign intellectuals and the national culture they are part of. How Israeli literature in translation is read in different lands—what is chosen for translation, the sales and diffusion, the critical notices, the features that are foregrounded—in short, everything we associate with the phenomenon of reception is a fascinating subject that awaits exploration.

Does the existence of an international audience change the way in which Israeli writers go about their writing? Certainly writers with major reputations who have had previous works translated must be somewhat mindful of the fact that they are not likely to be read by Israelis alone, although this is an awareness that is hard to separate out and measure. Aharon Appelfeld, the prolific author of Holocaust literature in Hebrew who has seen much of his work appear in translation, does in fact seem to see himself as an international Jewish writer. This is evidenced, in part, by the fact that he has sometimes published the original Hebrew text of a work in Israel *after* the translation has appeared abroad. In general, however, most Hebrew fiction is intended to be an internal exchange between Israeli writers and Israeli readers, and a give-and-take between citizens of a nation who all largely share the same fate and live under a similar set of cultural and historical circumstances.

From its beginnings in the eighteenth century, modern Hebrew literature has always seen itself as discharging an oppositional mission in relation to the established community, a role that carries on the prophets' commitment to be what Ezekiel called a "watchman to the house of Israel." But because Israel is a country constantly under scrutiny by the world, its internal affairs, from the raucous behavior of its politicians in the Knesset to the protests of the disadvantaged in development towns, cease being solely internal. Such is the case with literature as well. Novels that are written in Hebrew and meant to have their impact in a single cultural system are read in translation—eavesdropped upon, as it were—by outsiders to that system. Artists may aim their work at a target audience and even encrypt their messages in a code known only to that audience; yet once the artwork is released into the world, the artist has little control over its dissemination and interpretation. Knowing this to be the case, no serious Israeli artist, I think, would or should feel constrained to write differently. But there remains a certain ironic loss of innocence in this knowledge of the complexity of cultural reverberations.

One of the main claims for the broader significance of Hebrew literature lies in its success in creating a rich secular culture in the face of antagonistic pressures, and in doing so in a way that is instructive relative to both European literatures and other Middle Eastern societies. In contrast to Western societies in which the process of secularization unfolded over the course of several centuries, the Jews emerged from the medieval religious culture of their ancestors much more recently and much more suddenly. This transformation, moreover, took place under extreme conditions of persecution, revolution, and displacement. That under these circumstances a significant number of extraordinary works of modern literature should get written in a revived classical tongue (a story unto itself) is impressive enough. Most important, however, is the fact that literature and the institutions of literary culture became a principal mode of encountering and mediating modernity. Between the claims of religious tradition and the headlong imitation of Western values, the national movement managed to nurture a literature that could appropriate elements of the past in secularized form and then use them in the service of creating a viable civic society. This is especially true in the case of the novel as an institution, which began a continuous line of development in Hebrew in the 1850s and reached the degree of variety and complexity described in this volume. It is not the uniqueness of this achievement that is the point as much as the paradigmatic status of Israeli literature as an instance of enriched rather than impoverished secularization.

It is only natural that a large part of the audience for contemporary Israeli literature in translation is, and will likely remain, American Jews. One wishes the audience were larger. Given the large number of American Jews and their generous book-buying habits and given the generally high quality of Israeli literature, it is surprising that more Israeli fiction is not translated and that which is sells only respectably at best. The paradox is just another facet of a selective and ambivalent relationship to Israel on the part of American Jews. Although support for Israel is a widespread sentiment in the American Jewish community, it is a considerably smaller number of Jews whose support is expressed in active involvement in Israel's affairs and in inquisitive curiosity about the workings of Israeli society. The difficult and problematic knowledge of

Israel provided by reading Israeli literature—the nature of serious contemporary literature in all societies, as we have said—is the kind of de-
mystifying knowledge that many American Jews would sooner not have.
The construction of American Jewishness is often dependent upon an
idealization of Israel that focuses on the heroic struggle for statehood
and the resistance to annihilation. There are whole genres of American
popular fiction—Leon Uris's *Exodus* the most famous among them—that
rework these themes and seem to keep many Americans supplied with
what they feel they need to know about Israel. It is to be hoped that,
with the maturing of the relationship to Israel on the part of American
Jewry, attentiveness to Israeli literature will play a greater role in the
enterprise of mutual understanding between the two communities and
will become, at the very least, a norm for literate Jewish leaders.

The Boom in Contemporary Israeli Fiction covers the years 1973–1993. It is
interesting that in Hebrew literary historiography it has long been the
custom to demarcate creative periods by significant historical events
rather than by inherent aesthetic developments such as the first appearance of a genre, technique, or theme. This is a practice that says
much about the close connection between the historical vicissitudes of a
nation and the evolution of its literary history. In marking off the twenty
years between 1973 and 1993, we have departed from this custom only
in making one rather than both dates the years of significant armed
conflicts. The year 1973, of course, evokes the Yom Kippur War; the
year 1993, however, marks the famous handshake between Yassir Arafat
and Yitzhak Rabin, the official end to the Intifada, and the beginning
of the peace process. All such attempts at periodization, to be sure, are
at some level acts of interpretive intervention that bear a purely heuristic relationship to the ongoing and crisscrossing flow of human activity.
Nonetheless, there is something to be gained from positing a correlation during these years between developments in the social and political
arena and developments in serious literature.

    Although the 1973 war ended in a victory for Israel, there was little
of the euphoria that had marked the aftermath of the Six-Day War in
1967. Instead, there ensued a sense of aloneness in the world and a feeling of vulnerability at home that was deepened rather than mitigated
by the occupation of the West Bank and Gaza. The Territories became
the breeding ground for radicalized nationalism fueled by a resurgent
Islam; the Intifada, the loosely organized terror against Israeli soldiers
that emerged later on, deeply scarred the morale of the Israeli public. The political identity of that public also underwent an abrupt shift.

The Labor Party, which had dominated political life since before the state was created, was voted out of office. The rout was a sign, among other things, that Jews who had emigrated from Arab lands had not only reached a demographic majority in Israel but had now made their numbers count in the political process. The ascendancy of the Likud meant the dismantling of some of the central institutions of labor socialism and the privatization of state-run industries. In the new free-market economy, the disadvantaged did worse while the middle classes enjoyed a steady rise in their standard of living and in the availability of consumer goods. Speculation in the stock market with its attendant risks became an endeavor for individual investors as well as institutions.

Israeli society in general became more cosmopolitan and westernized; many Israelis traveled abroad, especially young people who had recently completed their military service. Hundreds of thousands of Israelis left for good, emigrating mostly to America in search of better opportunities. During the same years, large numbers of Russian Jews (and non-Jews) and smaller numbers of Ethiopians settled in Israel, creating at once a renewed sense of Zionist mission and a massive economic and social burden. On the religious scene, the moderate Orthodox nationalists who had been part of the Zionist enterprise since its inception lost ground, both politically and demographically, to ultra-Orthodox groups that promoted separatist interests. The control of domestic relations by religious law helped to spur the emergence of a nascent women's movement and promote feminist reflection in pockets of the society. A momentous shift took place as well in the relations between Israeli Jewry and Diaspora Jewry, which since the days of Ben-Gurion had been characterized by the unambiguous hegemony of the Israelis. The Jewish communities of the Diaspora, especially in America, rejected the notion that their communal lives lacked value and vitality and existed only to provide material and human resources to Israel's development, and took steps to place the relationship between the two communities on a more equal footing.

This is a hurried overview of complex historical forces, but it is enough to suggest the ways in which the self-conception of Israeli society has broken down and been reshaped over the past twenty-five years. Central to that self-conception, which was consolidated during the Ben-Gurion years following the establishment of the state in 1948, were the values of Labor Zionism and its pioneering lineage: work on the land, solidarity with comrades, state-supported social welfare, a nationalist interpretation of Jewish history expressed in the school curriculum, a devaluing of Diaspora values in general and Yiddish culture in particular, and the encouragement of a secular, native Israeli culture. Unofficial but implicit in this ethos was a parallel set of hierarchies that privileged male over female leadership in many areas of politics and culture and extended a similar sense of entitlement to citizens of Ashkenazic background over those from Arab lands or of Sephardic heritage. Religion was also meant to remain a marginal presence that required some concessions but made no substantial claim on the identity of the state. Holocaust survivors were encouraged to suppress their experiences and their stories and assimilate into the nativist spirit. And free enterprise and individual ambition were regarded as necessary evils in a democracy that esteemed solidarity to the commonweal.

Before us, then, is a set of oppositions—male/female, Ashenazic/Sephardic, religious/secular, Eretz Yisrael/Diaspora, collectivism/individualism, native Israelis/Holocaust survivors—whose rigidities were disturbed if not set aside during the period between 1973 and 1993. The crucial role played by Israeli literature, especially fiction, in these years was to interrogate these oppositions and lay them open to scrutiny. Literature performs this task either by giving voice to the suppressed term in the binary opposition or by ironizing the privileged term and, in general, by complicating the relationship between the two. One of the images used by critics to describe this moment in Israeli literature is the breakdown of a single story into many stories. In this image, there existed a Zionist master story or plot that preoccupied Hebrew literature from the settlement period until the 1970s. This was, with many variants, an account of the national enterprise and the struggle of individuals to create their lives within it. At the center of this story was a male protagonist of European descent, unconnected to religion but connected to the national struggle, whose outlook had been shaped, either sympathetically or antagonistically, by the values of the youth movement or military service or the institutions of the new state. In the great change that followed, the one story became many stories; the dominance—as well as the representational sufficiency—of the master plot was broken and forced to yield to the stories of those who had until then been kept on the margins. Like all models, this account of Hebrew literary history is an idealized story in itself that disregards numerous antecedents and ancillary developments; nevertheless it possesses a kind of gross truth that puts large cultural shifts into perspective.

The critical studies that make up this volume approach these changes from three different, and at times overlapping, angles: minority discourse, that is, writing by or about ethnic groups that had not previously been the subject of literary representation; women's writing and the re-examination of gender codes; and magical realism, the fantastic and postmodernist narrative techniques in the writing of fiction.

The whole notion of minorities in Israeli society is one that is at odds with the official Zionist ideal of "ingathering." Rather than being seen as ethnic groups or minorities, the Jews who came to Israel from many countries around the globe were meant to be absorbed into a new society in Zion that represents a departure from life in the many and varied diasporas. In actuality, however, the culture of the Yishuv and later the state was based largely upon the norms of a single society: the socialist Zionism that had emerged in Eastern Europe; it was often into that culture that Jews from other lands were, willingly or unwillingly, gathered. Over time the Israeli Jews whose families had settled in Israel for ideological reasons became themselves a minority, yet the institutions of the state and its literary culture continued to bear the impress of the Eastern European socialist stamp.

Jews from North Africa and the Middle East—together loosely called Sephardim—had long been presences in the Old and New Yishuv, but it was not until the upheavals occasioned by the War of Independence in 1948 that great numbers arrived in Israel. The immigrants from Eastern lands were extremely diverse in their backgrounds. Some came from the secularized urban professional classes of Cairo, Damascus, and Bagdad; others were shopkeepers with a traditional religious outlook; and still others came from small towns and villages that had hardly been touched by industrial life. Only a small number were Zionists in the modern ideological sense of the term, and the great majority experienced their sudden arrival in Israel as an enormous and unanticipated upheaval. While the Zionist leadership took a romantic and ethnographic interest in the varied and distinct folkways of this exotic population, Eastern Jews were urged to integrate themselves into the dominant civic culture of the new state. After the hardships and indignities of the transit camps hastily set up to absorb this mass immigration, some did succeed in assimilating into Israeli society, while others, who had been settled in outlying "development towns" that never developed, slipped into a chronic underclass.

Creating a voice and projecting it within the literary world of the newly adopted country required taking on the challenge of Hebrew. Most of the writers from Ashkenazic backgrounds had either been born into Hebrew-speaking families or had been educated in Hebrew-oriented schools before coming to Palestine. Intellectuals from Eastern lands, by contrast, were at home in Arabic, and sometimes French or Berber or Turkish. Being suddenly transplanted into a Hebrew-speaking culture presented aspiring writers with the enormous challenge of learning to create in an adopted language. Some clung to Arabic and were marginalized; others went through a difficult gestation period and began to write in Hebrew. The first works produced by Sephardic writers dealt with the humiliations of transit camps and were written in the tradition of social outrage. By the period covered in this volume, Sephardic writing had evolved into a nuanced examination of the complexities of acculturation into Israeli society. The most recent fictional efforts have reached beyond the temporal and spatial boundaries of Israel to reevoke in highly imaginative terms the Jewish life of Bagdad and Damascus before the establishment of Israel and the "ingathering" of Eastern Jewry. The works of Sami Michael, Shimon Ballas, Eli Amir, and Amnon Shamosh moved the Eastern voice toward the center of Israeli literature.

Though not an ethnic minority, survivors of the Holocaust and other Jews who came to Israel as displaced persons also constitute an identifiable group whose voice gained literary expression only belatedly. The specter of political passivity—the contemporary perception of European Jews going to their death "like sheep to the slaughter"—clashed sharply with the heroic myth at the core of Zionism. During the first twenty years after the Holocaust, the survivor was often represented in Israeli literature as morally tainted in contrast to the brave and hardworking sabra. Until the Eichmann trial in 1961 provided a showcase for Holocaust testimonies, survivors were not encouraged to tell their stories—to themselves, as well as to others. Aharon Appelfeld, who began to publish short stories in the 1960s, has been the most imaginatively powerful writer to focus on the Holocaust. Apart from Appelfeld's fiction, the single most important work to address the Holocaust is David Grossman's *See Under: Love* (1986), an ambitious postmodernist novel that employs a variety of storytelling techniques to explore the persistence of the tragic past. Although the novel's central character is a son of survivors, Grossman himself is not, and as such he joins an increasing number of younger Israeli writers who have approached the subject of the Holocaust despite having no direct experience of it.

The minority that by nature stands most apart from the national consensus is made up of Israeli Arabs. Their language of literary expression is of course Arabic and not Hebrew, although there is the distinguished example of Anton Shammas, who has written a beautiful novel, *Arabesques*, in Hebrew. Given the intensity of political differences, it is unlikely that there will be a major contribution to Hebrew literature by Arab writers, although the possibility always remains open. As a subject for Jewish writers in Hebrew, the representation of Arabs has played a significant though not central role in Hebrew literature. The image of the Arab most often served as a screen upon which writers projected the hopes and the fears and the moral dilemmas of the Jewish settlers in Palestine. In Yitzhak Shami's novella "Revenge of the Fathers" from the 1920s, for example, the Arab is portrayed as the instinctual native son of the land; this was an ideal that the Zionist student pioneers from Eastern Europe could aspire to but not immediately embody. In S. Yizhar's story "The Prisoner," which was written during the 1948 War of Independence, the forlorn, anonymous Arab prisoner serves as a touchstone for the Jewish narrator's struggles with his conscience. In Amos Oz's 1968 novel, *My Michael*, Arab twins from the female narrator's childhood occupy her adult fantasy life and mirror her erotic and aggressive obsessions.

The publication of A. B. Yehoshua's first novel, *The Lover*, in 1977 marked a turning point in the representation of the Arab. Naim is a teenage boy from an Israeli Arab village in the Galilee who works in a garage owned by an Israeli Jew named Adam and who in the course of the story becomes entangled with Adam's family. The novel is composed entirely of monologues, and Naim has his monologues along with the other characters. But when he first speaks, a third of the way through the novel, it has the force of a stunning debut. It is the first time in Hebrew literature that an Arab character is given his or her own voice and allowed to articulate an inner life that is not largely a projection of a Jewish fantasy or dilemma. Although Yehoshua's *The Lover* was indeed a breakthrough, it would be an exaggeration to say that it opened a floodgate of efforts in this direction. There are exceptions like Itamar Levy's *Letters of the Sun, Letters of the Moon* (1991), a novel that is told entirely through the consciousness of an Arab boy in a village in the Occupied Territories. In the end, however, the Arab remains very much an other, a flickering presence in Israeli literature.

The role played by women in modern Hebrew literature has been an equivocal one. While there have been a number of important women poets in the first half of the century (Rachel, Elisheva, Yocheved Bat-Miriam, Esther Raab, Leah Goldberg), in fiction there has essentially been the lone example of Devorah Baron, whose short stories are only now receiving wide critical attention. Like other revolutionary ideologies, Zionism's proclamations concerning the equality of women were true more in theory than in practice. In the core myth of Zionism, it is the figure of the male soldier-farmer that occupied center stage. Women are assigned supporting roles; they are participants in this new historical endeavor, but rarely as leaders. In the gendered language of Zionism, the partners in this new grand passion are, on the one side, the Land, as both mother and virgin bride, and on the other, the heroic Hebrew (male) pioneer, who has returned to possess the Land or to be received back into its bosom. Although flesh-and-blood women were essential to the settlement of the country, they were often marginalized by the prerogatives of the Great Mother, the land itself.

It is a sign of the enormous changes in culture and society that by the 1980s women writers were among the most visible and creative voices in Israeli fiction. These include Savyon Liebrecht, Ruth Almog, Michal Govrin, Dorit Peleg, Judith Katzir, Orly Castel-Bloom, and Ronit Matalon. What prepared the way for this belated explosion? The key precursor in women's writing is Amalia Kahana-Carmon (born in 1930), whose first collection of stories, *Under One Roof*, was published in 1966. Kahana-Carmon belongs, together with Oz, Yehoshua, and Appelfeld, to the New Wave in Hebrew fiction that used modernist techniques to interrogate the ideologically laden social realism of their predecessors. Yet whereas Oz and Yehoshua directly engage the Zionist narrative by writing about the kibbutz and war and peace, Kahana-Carmon, like Appelfeld in his own way, writes more subversively by sidestepping the Zionist narrative altogether. Just as Appelfeld writes about Holocaust survivors to whom the heroic posture of the Jewish state is irrelevant, so Kahana-Carmon writes about the inner lives of women as a zone removed from the passions of the national story. Influenced by the style of the Hebrew Chekovian writer Uri Nissan Gnessin from early years of the century, Kahana-Carmon focuses on the inner space of subjectivity where language, fantasy, and desire come together. Yehudit Hendel and Shulamith Hareven are women writers of Kahana-Carmon's generation —though they began to publish later than she—whose fiction directly engages the Zionist narrative. Their work features heroines whose spirit and pluck might have carried them in feminist directions if their lives had not been overtaken by the claims of historical emergency.

Less noticed but of equal significance is the interrogation of gender that has been conducted in fiction written by men. The Zionist revolution was as much about a new construction of masculinity as about anything else. Beginning in the late nineteenth century, Hebrew writers undertook an unsparing critique of the East European Jewish male, the archetypal denizen of the shtetl, as ineffectual, overintellectual, effeminate, passively sensual, and wife-ridden. The theorists of Zionism presented the new movement as a kind of therapy for these sickly Diaspora bodies and minds. The new "muscle Jew," in this scheme, would remake the Jewish male both inside and out. How successful this therapeutic regimen was in practice is difficult to assess, but it is clear that as a masculine ideal it is very much the model for the young men who populate works by writers, such as S. Yizhar, who came of age during the War of Independence in 1948.

When Amos Oz and A. B. Yehoshua began publishing in the 1960s, their work was addressed to the issue of ideology itself and the role it played in suppressing or ignoring the exigencies of human needs. From the 1970s onwards, it is possible, I think, to detect a shift of focus from a preoccupation with ideology to an exploration of masculinity. This can be seen most clearly in Yehoshua's novels *Five Seasons* (1987) and *Mr. Mani* (1990), which concern male characters who have either taken on feminine characteristics or who seek access to the female mysteries of reproduction. The most conspicuous exploration of these issues takes place in the work of a writer who burst upon the literary scene in the 1970s and died shortly after the publication of his major work. That work is the epic novel *Past Continuous* (1977) by Yaakov Shabtai, which broke new ground in a number of areas. In tracing the daily movements of three men through a series of futile experiences culminating in the suicide of one of them, the novel evokes the vacuum of despair that came after the ideological passions of the generation of the founders of the State. Integral to this entropic slide toward death is a clutching for the remnants of machismo and the muscular myth of Zionist settlers. Shabtai's and Yehoshua's works have initiated among younger writers of both sexes an intense awareness and exploration of the constructed and deconstructed nature of gender in Israeli society.

The third broad category of innovation in Israeli writing between 1973 and 1993 lies in the rethinking of fiction itself. As a modern secular literature, Israeli writing has always been influenced by currents in Europe and America. The so-called Palmah Generation writers from the 1950s were deeply influenced by the canons of socialist realism. The New Wave writers of the 1960s and 1970s were influenced by the high modernism of Faulkner and Kafka. Many of the Israeli writers discussed in this volume were influenced in part by the techniques of magic realism and postmodernism. Yet, whereas in the first two instances there is a considerable lag between the time of the European influences and their eventual adoption in Israel, in the more recent case the gap is much shorter. Rather than being a belated enactment of European development, the radically innovative novel *See Under: Love* by David Grossman, for example, is already a participant in an emerging international postmodernist style. The significant question posed by the new Israeli literature, as is the case with any literature that is written at a remove from the traditional centers of culture, is how these "borrowings" are naturalized within the internal traditions and concerns of Israeli culture.

Five areas of fictional experimentation are worth noticing. The first is the use of the fantastic or magic realism, which can be defined as the suspension of one or more of the laws of nature within an otherwise realistically conceived fictional world. Grossman's *See Under: Love* is the chief but not lone example, and it is not coincidental that these nonrealistic procedures have been mobilized to deal with the event that tampers with received categories of meaning: the Holocaust. In his novel *The Blue Mountain* (1989), which deals with the pioneers who settled the Galilee, Meir Shalev makes limited but effective use of magic realism to convey—and simultaneously deflate—the enormous energy and willfulness of the mythic settlers.

A second feature is deliberate derivativeness expressed in the borrowing and recycling of previous literature and other cultural materials. In Grossman's *See Under: Love*, for example, Bruno Schulz's writings are quoted extensively, the juvenile literature of Jules Verne and Karl May is returned to repeatedly, and different historical styles are imitated wholesale. This last practice, the ventriloquizing of discourse from different historical periods, is the very principle around which Yehoshua's *Mr. Mani* is constructed. In earlier periods of Hebrew literature, the relationship to the past centered on the use of allusion, a phrase or a metaphor embedded in the work's contemporary fictional discourse that activated associations from earlier, and usually classical, Jewish literature. In the postmodernist practice, however, the unit of reference is often much larger; rather than a point of concentrated meaning in which past and present texts momentarily engage one another, a postmodernist text may itself be made up of large swatches of earlier works or of playful imitations of them. Moreover, the materials borrowed are likely to come not from the classical tradition but from popular genres of writing and from the materials of everyday life and popular culture.

A third tendency is a movement away from ideology toward storytelling. In some of the key texts of this period—Grossman's *See Under: Love* and the novels of Meir Shalev, for example—such momentous developments as the settlement of the Land of Israel and the Holocaust are used as the stuff of storytelling and mythmaking rather than as events of moral-historical meaning. The shift from history to story is a supremely self-conscious move that becomes thematized within the novels themselves. The subject of Grossman's Holocaust novel is the gravest event of our century, yet its engagement with the event itself is minor relative to the immense preoccupation with the difficulties of writing about it and the extravagant fictions spun from its thread. For many writers, Yaakov Shabtai especially, the failure of ideology and the weakness of the spirit allows for a margin of hope or resolution only on the plane of art rather than within the mire of human affairs. But this is not the sacred art of high modernism with its priestly aspirations. The notion of art and the commitment to it among these Israeli postmodernists are at once as serious and less solemn. The playful and manipulable aspects of the artifice of their art are expressions of a commitment to experiment with the possibilities of narrative and a willingness to lay bare the mechanics and devices of their efforts. The boundary between low hijinks and serious experiment is not infrequently crisscrossed by many writers.

A fourth aspect of fictional experimentation is the great interest evinced in recent Israeli writing in taking the novel apart and putting it back together differently and variously. These experiments take place at three different levels. The first is the actual discursive fabric of the novel as it presents itself to the reader reading the words on the page. At one extreme is the extraordinary—and, for most critics, extraordinarily successful—effort of Yaakov Shabtai in *Past Continuous* to make the novel into a single paragraph composed of a minimum of sentences. Shabtai's narrative loops back and forth in time and connects the fates of several extended families creating a sense of continuous duration at the level of reading that is missing from the experiences of the characters. At the opposite extreme are the works of Yoel Hoffman (*Bernhardt* and *Christus of the Fish*), which neutralize the epic aspiration of the novel by chopping it up into tiny pieces. A diminutive paragraph may appear alone on a page, representing a bubble of consciousness; and on some pages there may be nothing at all. Some of the most successful experimentation manipulates the materials that compose the novel. We may not realize how conventionalized are our expectations as readers of novels until we come across an example of the genre, as is the case with Grossman's *See Under: Love*, in which each of the novel's four sections is written in an entirely different literary style and based on a different genre model. In A. B. Yehoshua's *Mr. Mani*, each of the five chapters features the speech of one person in an extended dramatic dialogue with another; the questions and answers of the other person are unvoiced but implied; furthermore, the whole of each "half dialogue" is introduced and followed by several pages of biographical and historical background supplied with a tone of factual discursive detachment.

Finally, Israeli writers have also been fascinated by what can be done with, and to, point of view. Amalia Kahana-Carmon is identified with an earlier literary generation, but her recent writings have a distinctively postmodern temper. The narrator in her *Above in Montifer* (1984) is a woman who has subjugated herself to a man and tells her story from the vantage point of extreme abasement and obsession. The narrator in Itamar Levy's *Letters of the Sun, Letters of the Moon* is a probably retarded Arab growing up in a village on the West Bank under Israeli occupation;

his radically limited view of the world around him serves as a technique for undoing stereotypes and making strange the ostensibly familiar and threatening. Dorit Peleg's *Una* (1988) and Yoav Shimoni's *Flight of the Dove* both split the narrative point of view in two and develop each line of sight in different ways.

As in any era of intense experimentation, time will determine which works will endure. There is a potential in postmodernist practice for narcissism and trivialization, and it often depends on the will and the gifts of the individual writer as to whether a work transcends the effects of technique and creates the aura of a work of art. In the meantime, Israeli fiction continues to thrive, providing us all the while with challenging writing and an incomparably insightful glimpse into the experience of Israeli society.

Magic Realism in the Israeli Novel

UNTIL THE PUBLICATION in 1986 of David Grossman's spectacular second novel, *See Under: Love,* the very conjunction of magic realism and the Israeli novel would have seemed like a contradiction in terms. Since then, the face of Israeli fiction has assumed new, at times surprisingly antic, features, and there have been abundant and exuberant transgressions of the conventions of realism of varying kinds. But it is important to keep in mind that any manifestation of fantasy in Hebrew fiction has to be made against the heavy weight of a dominant tradition of intent realism that goes all the way back to Hebrew writing in nineteenth-century Russia.

It is exemplary of the governing impulse of Hebrew fiction that when Mendele (S. Y. Abramovitch, 1835–1917) adopted Gogol as an important literary model, he drew exclusively on Gogol the satiric realist, excluding Gogol the fantasist. A nose is a palpable Jewish nose in Mendele, drawn by the novelist to loom over tangled beard and greasy caftan, and by no means meant to detach itself from its realistic physiognomic moorings and to go strolling through the shtetl streets. Characteristically, when the next generation of Hebrew fiction writers rebelled against Mendele and his followers, it was in the name of a grittier, more immediately mimetic realism: they rejected his coy, learned playfulness, and, even more, they rejected the symmetries, the beautifully crafted traditionalism, and the dense allusiveness of his prose. The most powerful practitioner of this early twentieth-century anti-*nusakh* realism was Y. H. Brenner, and it is deeply instructive about the later course of Hebrew fiction that he should have been taken up by young writers and critics in the 1960s, and repeatedly since then, not exactly as a formal model but as an ultimate touchstone of uncompromising literary authenticity. The first wave of writers who spoke Hebrew as a native language, the Generation of 1948, had cultivated their own kind of rather drab, morally and ideologically serious realism, at least in part influenced by the Hebrew translations of Soviet Socialist Realism on which many of them had been nurtured in the socialist youth movements during the 1930s. The New Wave writers of the 1960s then found in Brenner an indigenous Hebrew model of

realist intentness, and displacing the norm of realism was never much
at issue, despite the experiments of the early A. B. Yehoshua (in his first
collection of stories, *The Death of the Old Man*) with dreamlike and sur-
realist narratives. Yehoshua's career in fact bears witness to the strong
centripetal pull of realism on Hebrew writers. After his dalliance with
the fantastic macabre in *The Death of the Old Man*, he moved through the
symbolic novellas of *Facing the Forest*, where much was spooky or psychologically strange but nothing violated the laws of nature, to a series of
four novels in which, despite the psychological weirdness of some of the
characters, every effort is made to honor the contract of realism.

There were, of course, expressions of fantasy in Hebrew fiction before the mid-1980s, but by and large these were marginalized by critics,
readers, and even by the community of writers. Yehoshua's early stories
drew directly on S. Y. Agnon's dreamlike fictions in *The Book of Deeds*,
but despite the large claims made for this collection by the critic Ba-
ruch Kurzweil in an effort to strengthen his account of Agnon as a
radical modernist recording the acute spiritual disjunctions of modernity, readers have tended to see these stories, and the more pervasive
neo-gothic strain in Agnon, as secondary to his real achievement. It is
symptomatic that so many critics should insist on the status of Agnon's
crowning achievement, *Just Yesterday* (1945), as an "epic" of the Second
Aliyah, even though they are perfectly aware that substantial portions
of the novel are devoted to the perspective of a ratiocinating dog, who
proves to be the book's most reflective character. In another direction,
Yitzhak Oren has long explored science-fiction and metaphysical-fiction
hypotheses in his stories, and precisely for this reason, he has remained
on the margins of Hebrew fiction. It is also well to remember that even
after 1986, as some younger writers began to give fantasy a much freer
rein, the momentum of the realist tradition in Hebrew prose has scarcely
diminished. Yehoshua Kenaz's painfully unblinking representation of
geriatric humanity, soiled sheets and all, in *The Way to the Cats* (1991),
scored an impressive succès d'estime; and *Victoria* (1993), Sami Michael's
panoramic account of the life of Baghdad Jewry early in the century,
with all its folkways and physical constrictions and familial convolutions,
became a runaway best-seller. When one speaks, then, of magic realism
in the Israeli novel, what is being described is not a dramatic turning
point or the defining direction of a whole new generation, but simply
one trend among other new trends and persisting old ones. What should
be noted is that it is also a trend that would have been unimaginable in
the Hebrew novel just a few years ago.

But what is magic realism? The chief provenance of the term, of
course, is Latin American fiction, and the name, actually borrowed from

a rubric introduced by art historians of the 1920s, was first given general currency by the Cuban novelist Alejo Carpentier in the 1950s (*lo real maravilloso*). By now, the term has been so overused and so loosely used that a good many critics and writers are sick of it. Thus, Michael Kerrigan, writing in a recent issue of the *Times Literary Supplement* (November 5, 1993), begins a review with this sardonic observation: "For some time, Magic Realism has been brewed under licence in North America and Europe [and, now, we might add, in the eastern Mediterranean]. Latin writers have come to bristle at the very mention of the term, and more sophisticated critics abroad have in their turn assumed a more disdainful attitude." The burden of what follows will be an attempt to determine whether the term designates a coherent literary phenomenon that might be distinct from other fictional deployments of fantasy, and to see, through a scrutiny of a few recent Israeli examples, what might be the attractions and the pitfalls of this mode of fiction.

Not all fiction with fantastic elements is magic realism, and we will avoid at least some confusions by not following the loose practice of some critics who tend to label any fantasy fiction written in the later twentieth century as magic realism. What kinds of writing should be excluded? In general, I would say that when a writer constructs a fantastic fictional world that is merely extrapolated from or thematically analogous to the world of familiar experience, and that does not seriously pretend to be a direct representation of it, the "realism" component of the term is not sufficiently present to justify the label. As it stands, J. L. Borges's famous story "Tlön, Uqbar, Orbis Tertius" could be plausibly characterized as a piece of magic realism because its fantastic world, where totally different concepts of identity, being, causation, and time obtain, is circumstantially anchored in a real Buenos Aires where two scholarly friends scrutinize a text, purportedly published in New York in 1917, which is "a literal but delinquent reprint of the *Encyclopedia Britannica* of 1902." Had Borges plunged us immediately into Tlön's realm of disorienting otherness without the realist frame, the story would be a metaphysical fantasy but would not qualify as magic realism.

Thus, fiction that seems pervasively dreamlike, that has the sense of arbitrariness and constant unpredictability of the surreal—repeated violations of causality and temporality, unmotivated spatial displacements, and so forth—stands outside the category of magic realism. *The Book of Deeds* and most of the stories in *The Death of the Old Man* therefore do not belong to this mode of writing. To put this another way, when the fantasy is free-floating, when the constraints of history and social institution and the laws of nature exert little gravitational force, the realism component of our double-barreled term does not apply. For both similar and opposite reasons, science fiction must be excluded. Similar, when science-fiction worlds are blatantly based on premises about the constitution of reality contrary to those of our own world—say, intelligent beings shaped like pea-pods who communicate telepathically—for this formula yields magic without the realism. Opposite, when the future fiction scrupulously observes the empirical principles observable in our familiar world while equipping its characters with high-powered extrapolations of current technologies, which yields an odd kind of realism without the magic.

A second category of the fantastic that must be excluded from magic realism is the introduction of fantastic sequences that are realistically motivated within the fiction as dreams, hallucinations, and free associations. There has been a good deal of this in recent Hebrew writing because of the pervasive interest in the quirkiness of the inner life of the characters. Here is a characteristic moment in *Christus of Fish* (1991), an experimental fiction by Yoel Hoffman:

What did she think when she washed her big body? Here are the arms? Here's the navel to which the blood vessels came from Eva Weiss's womb? Here are the heels? And perhaps she set sail in her bathtub ship under the crescent moon and her flesh gleamed in the light of another sidereal frame, more distant, until (in a kind of cosmic x-ray) the filigraine of the network of nerves was revealed.[1]

With the verb "set sail" (*hifligah*), the narrator's imagination goes soaring from the here and now, which in the previous lines is given a strong bodily definition, into the far-flung realm of "another sidereal frame" (*gerem shemeymi aher*) in which the physicality of Eva Weiss's daughter is transmuted into a weird and evocative poetic image, the network of the nerves as a filigraine seen in cosmic x-ray. But it is, after all, the imagination of the narrator that manifestly does this work of fantastic transposition. Nothing in the actual chain of narrated events or in the constitution of the fictional world is transformed by the fantasy, which is a free-associative movement clearly triggered by the metaphoric conception of the bathtub as a ship. Fictional realists have always recognized that consciousness imposes all sorts of fantastic structures on reality—think, for example, of the prominence of phantasmagoria and hallucination in Flaubert's *Sentimental Education*—but distorting along fantastic lines the contours of what the fiction presents as objective reality is quite another matter.

What is the characteristic strategy of distortion one encounters in magic realism? Let me suggest that there must be some sort of persuasive, minutely represented realistic frame within which the elements of fantasy are played out. That frame will involve an attempt at the faithful representation of at least some, and perhaps all, of the following: history, politics, social institutions, the family, and the ineluctable aspects of biological existence. All of these tend to be perceived, as they are typically perceived in realism *tout court*, as constrictions, limits, inevitabilities, as manifestations of a realm that is intractable or perhaps even menacing. Within this frame of realist constrictions, certain laws of physical reality are suspended. Although the break with realist necessity is often flamboyantly obtrusive, it is also delimited in one way or another so that it does not destroy the frame of realism, so that it does not impart a sense that all elements of the represented world are arbitrary and unpredictable. One could say that the violation of the laws of nature in a magic-realist fiction is carried out in a lawlike manner: history, society, and the human body continue to exert their relentless compulsions while some hypothesis—or a network of such hypotheses—contrary to what we know of reality is played out in the fictional world as though it, too, manifested a law of nature, like gravity, the irreversibility of completed events, and mortality. In Günter Grass's *The Tin Drum*, Oskar, the protagonist, successfully implements a decision to remain physically fixed at the age of four. This willed arrested growth is of course contrary to what we know empirically about bodily processes, but it is used as a narrative vantage point from which the horrors of the Hitler years are seen all the more sharply, themselves uncompromised by fantastic distortion. Salman Rushdie's *Midnight's Children* works with the fantasy-hypothesis that all children born at midnight on August 15, 1947, when Indian independence was declared, can communicate with each other telepathically. This antirealist narrative datum in no way diminishes Rushdie's representation of the virulence of religious strife in this period of historical upheaval or of what he sees as the sinister and oppressive character of Indira Gandhi's rule.

There seems to be no generally accepted convention for how the fantasy-hypothesis is delimited formally. It may be one narrative thread that runs continuously through all the others, as in *The Tin Drum*. It may recur intermittently—I suspect this is the most common practice—or it may be sequestered in one or more sections of the larger narrative, producing the effect of a realist frame with magic insets. David Grossman's last two novels provide an instructive set of illustrations of the repertory of possibilities for inserting and delimiting fantasy-hypotheses in magic realism. In *See Under: Love*[2] the first of the four sections of the book is entirely realistic. (Instructively, those Hebrew readers who disapproved of the conjunction of magic realism and the Nazi genocide tended to like this section even though they were unhappy with the rest of the book.) In the second section, the Polish Jewish writer Bruno Schulz,

who was actually murdered in the ghetto of Drohobycz by a German officer, as the novel itself reminds us, metamorphoses into a salmon, and a
global fantasy takes over the narrative. In the third section, which corresponds more to the practice of Gunter Grass, there is a single antirealist
hypothesis, that Anshel Wasserman cannot be killed, while the documented historical horrors of the death camp—the lineups, the random
shootings, the gas chambers—are represented in all their ferocity. The
last section of the novel incorporates a fiction within a fiction, involving the invented heroes of Wasserman's adventure stories, and so here
a whole network of fantasies can be spun out. The framework of these
fantasies, however, remains the grim historical reality of the systematic
mass murder of European Jewry, even in this section undiminished in its
hideousness. By contrast, in Grossman's next novel, *The Book of Intimate
Grammar* (1991), realism, following a child's point of view in a manner
reminiscent of the opening section of *See Under: Love*, is the predominant
mode, though there is one extended sequence (the demolition of Edna
Blum's apartment, to which we shall return) in which we progress by
gradual stages from realistically represented obsession to the enactment
of fantasy. If the "Bruno" section of *See Under: Love* illustrates one end
of the spectrum of magic realism, where the fantasy-hypothesis begins
to take over reality, the opposite end is exemplified in Gavriela Avigur-
Rotem's highly engaging first novel, *Mozart Was Not a Jew* (1992). The
novel as a whole is a realistic family saga about two Jewish families from
Russia who settle in Argentina early in the century. One of the children
has telekinetic powers, but this magic-realist feature surfaces only a few
times, plays no important role in the plot, and seems almost a small gesture of literary deference to the Latin American context of the novel.

It remains to be seen why novelists should find it attractive to sus-
pend certain of the laws of nature, either intermittently or pervasively, in
fictions that otherwise address historical and cultural realities with considerable urgency. I will propose some tentative answers to that question
by scrutinizing a few instances of Hebrew magic realism from the late
1980s and early 1990s. First, however, I would like to avert another possible confusion by stressing that the fantasy component in this mode of
fiction is never intended to raise an issue of "decidability" between a realistic and a fantastic fictional world. There are a few eminent instances of
stories of another sort that teeter on the brink between realism and fantasy, where in the end the reader cannot decide which way to construe
the fiction. The most famous case of this sort is Henry James's "The Turn
of the Screw," in which the assumption that the governess is delusional
and the contradictory assumption that she is actually seeing ghosts seem
equally viable hypotheses for reading the story. In the Hebrew tradition,

a roughly similar instance occurs in Agnon's "Betrothed," where the wraithlike appearance of Shoshana at the end of the race of maidens on the beach has been construed by some readers as a natural event (the woman stricken by sleeping sickness arises from her torpor and comes out to claim her betrothed) and by others as a supernatural event, in which the young woman is a kind of *revenante* claiming Jacob Rechnitz for the realm of the dead she seems to inhabit. Such fictions of hovering decidability are quite different from magic realism. Smadar Shiffman, in a recent article on Meir Shalev's *The Blue Mountain*[3] (1988), invokes both "The Turn of the Screw" and "Betrothed" and tries to define a difference in Shalev: "Unlike Todorov and some of his followers, I would like to suggest that this blurring [of reality and fantasy in a writer like Shalev] is conceived of as immanent to the represented world, not as something that theoretically at least, could be clarified and decided."[4] This is fair enough, but as Shiffman proceeds, she is nevertheless still caught up in Todorov's notion of a readerly "hesitation" about the character of the world represented in the fiction. She thus can claim that Shalev "leaves us suspended in a world that is neither marvelous nor realistic," a world "filled with so many incredible elements that we can hardly avoid questioning its reality."[5] This formulation strikes me as misconceived. At any rate, it does not jibe with my own reading experience of Shalev or of other magic realists. There are, of course, numerous things that happen in *The Blue Mountain,* and again in Shalev's second novel, *Esau*[6] (1991), that we know could not happen in the realm of experience outside fiction. But, in keeping with what I have observed about the deployment of lawlike and delimited fantasy-assumptions in magic realism, I don't think there is any sense of suspension between alternatives and I don't think we are encouraged to question the reality of the represented world.

Esau represents a historical reality in which, for example, hideous acts of violence are perpetrated on the Jews of Palestine in the Arab attacks of 1929, as in fact was the case. It is also one of the givens of the novel that a woman who is raped and has one breast cut off in the attacks should continue to produce milk in her remaining breast until old age and should serve as wet-nurse to generations of children. Although Tia Dodoch's eternally engorged breast does not at all correspond to the laws of female physiology, it seems to me that as readers we accept it as how things work in the novel—as we accept Oskar's arrested growth or the telepathy of the Midnight Children—without any diminished sense of the actual atrocities of 1929, the social evolution from Mandatory Palestine to Israel a decade after statehood, and the inexorability of aging and physical decay, all of which are quite seriously represented in the novel.

We read even the most scrupulously realistic novels with an awareness of
their double status as faithful representations of the world outside literature and as literary inventions. Emma Bovary may be an utterly plausible
image of a certain kind of bourgeois housewife who might be encountered in a hundred provincial towns in mid-nineteenth century France,
but our granting the persuasive power of the character as realist representation is simultaneous with our understanding that she is a figment
of Flaubert's imagination. In magic realism, there is a tacit modification
of the implicit contract between novelist and reader: the writer's freedom of fictional invention, always assumed by the reader, is extended to
encompass certain willful suspensions of the limits that we know are imposed on human existence. These willful suspensions, as I have argued,
do not necessarily compromise the realistically represented world of the
fiction or ask us to call it into question. Rather, it is as though the novelist were saying: let us assume a world exactly like our own, with precisely the same historical and moral dilemmas and existential burdens,
in which, however, something like permanent lactation or telekinesis or
invulnerability to bullets can occur; how might the antirealist element
serve to throw the realistically represented world into sharper focus?

Let me begin with an example to which I have already alluded: the
invulnerability of Anshel Wasserman in *See Under: Love*. Each time a German puts a Luger to his forehead and pulls the trigger, all that happens
is that Wasserman hears a little buzzing in his ears and the bullet completes its harmless trajectory through his head by ricocheting off one of
the walls. Some literalist readers have been quite offended by this invention of Grossman's, feeling that it is frivolous and perhaps even immoral
to play around in this way with a moment in history when millions of Jews
were in fact appallingly vulnerable to Nazi bullets, blows, and poison
gas. On the level of narrative mechanics, Wasserman's invulnerability
makes possible a compelling plot development. Because he can't be
killed, though he desperately wants to die, he enters into a bizarre anti-
Scheherazade pact with the camp commandant, whereby he will present
an episode of his adventure stories each night to the commandant, who
will reward him for his performance by attempting to shoot him. Thus
Nazi mass murderer and Jewish victim are locked together in a weirdly
engrossing relationship, as could almost never have happened in historical reality. This relationship, however, allows the novelist to explore
the submerged humanity of the executive of genocide—surely something that it is worth trying to understand—which Wasserman ends up
using to subvert and destroy him. To be an agent of genocide, as many
analysts have observed, requires a certain reordering of consciousness
so that the assembly-line murderer can perpetrate unspeakable atroci-

ties as a regular work routine without compunction. Different modes of consciousness are brought into play when the mind is engaged in imaginative literature, and the confrontation of the two orders of consciousness in the strange collaboration of the Hebrew storyteller and the death camp commandant is deeply instructive.

Beyond this enabling of a revelatory relationship, the fantasy-hypothesis of Wasserman's invulnerability leads us to ponder a troubling dilemma about destruction and survival. Wasserman wants nothing but death for himself because after he has witnessed the murder of both his wife and his only daughter, life has become intolerable. Since the fate of fictional characters is always implicitly exemplary as the fate of actual persons is not, except by interpretive coercion, Wasserman's magic-real predicament also points up the quandary of real Jews, and of the Jewish people collectively, in the face of genocide. Alongside the murdered millions, millions survived, but with the continuing awareness of having lost everything and perhaps everyone, of having seen things that the mind can scarcely bear to think about. On the collective level, the Jewish people has stubbornly survived, and has experienced the dramatic rebirth of national sovereignty in Israel—just as before the Nazi era it managed to survive the onslaughts of the Crusades, the Chmielnitzki massacres in the seventeenth-century Ukraine, and the pogroms of the Black Hundreds. The standard Zionist version, with evident reason, celebrates the miracle of Jewish survival. The anti-Scheherazade of Anshel Wasserman suggests a darker side of the consciousness of survival that need not be programmatically affirmed but that should not be evaded: Is survival worth the candle after everything to which we have been subjected? After such knowledge, might not the blankness of extinction be a welcome alternative to the continuing anguish of survival? It is the necessary task of imaginative literature to contemplate disturbing ambiguities that cannot be accommodated by the pragmatic frameworks, and the mind-sets they require, of quotidian existence. David Grossman, by endowing his protagonist in lawlike magic-real fashion with a physical constitution that includes an invulnerability to bullets, is able to probe certain aspects of the abysmal historical experience that is his subject. There are obviously other legitimate ways to approach the subject fictionally, but quite a few writers in different countries seem to have concluded that when history becomes abysmal and drastically violates the assumptions of conventional morality, the nature of historical experience may be more adequately represented by abrogating some of the laws of nature within the fiction.

Let us now consider a central magic-real invention in a much more playful novel, Meir Shalev's *The Blue Mountain* (the original Hebrew title,

Roman Russi [A Russian Novel], invokes the dimension of parody as the
English title does not). Shalev, of course, is not dealing with anything so
disturbing as genocide, but the exuberant and often quite hilarious playfulness of his book does not detract from the deadly seriousness with
which he represents the contradictions of the Zionist enterprise, the
human costs it exacted, and the ephemerality of all ideological projects
under the dissolving aspect of eternity. (This last perspective is haunt-
ingly evoked in the prehistoric cave discovered by the old schoolteacher
Pinness.) The most notable of the novel's delimited suspensions of the
laws of empirical reality is the story of Ephraim and his bull, Jean Valjean. Ephraim, serving as a commando in the British army during World
War II, is so hideously disfigured in an explosion that when he returns
to his native village in the Galilee, he has to keep his face covered with
a mask. The disfigurement drives him to become a recluse, and in fact
the people of the village are very leery of him. Ephraim then acquires
a calf that becomes his sole bosom-companion, and he carries the calf
around with him on his shoulders wherever he goes. Jean Valjean grows
to a full-sized bull weighing 1300 kilograms, and Ephraim continues to
carry him around on his shoulders, though he is not otherwise endowed
with supernatural strength. The bull meanwhile proves to be the prize
stud of the region, inseminating cows far and wide. Eventually Ephraim
and his bull run off to join a traveling circus. We get a report of his disastrous coupling with the circus's Rubber Lady, and then he disappears
from the horizon of the novel's action, leaving only a trail of vague
rumors about his continuing peregrinations.

This fantastic story has an obvious literary genealogy. In antiquity a
tale circulated about a certain Milo of Crotona, a champion athlete,
who took upon himself the physical discipline of walking around with a
calf on his shoulders, gaining strength each day as the calf grew until he
was able to carry the weight of the full-grown bull. This bit of legendary
anecdote is spliced with an allusion to more recent literature: the bull
is named after the outcast convict hero of *Les Miserables*, while Ephraim
plays the role of Quasimodo, the hunchback of Victor Hugo's other
most famous novel. There is, finally, also a hint of biblical allusion: Jean
Valjean is referred to as Ephraim's "pet calf," or literally, "the calf of his
delight" ('*egel sha'ashu'av*), which points to a famous verse in Jeremiah
(31:20) in which the name of Ephraim figures: "Is not Ephraim a dear
son to me, a child of delight [*yeled sha'ashu'im*]?" The calf is thus the object of tender love for Ephraim as Israel is for God in Jeremiah, and the
wretched outcast Ephraim ought to be the object of God's tender love,
but He is conspicuous by His absence in the novel.

The allusiveness of Shalev's brand of magic realism accords nicely with the flaunted awareness in both his novels that the deployment of fictional invention takes place against a dense background of antecedent literary tradition. (Magic realism does not necessarily imply literary self-reflexivity, but the two easily come together.) But beyond the sheer pleasure of playing an elaborate literary game, what is this fantastic business about a man carrying one-and-a-half tons of bull doing in a novel that is intently concerned with the Zionist effort to create a new kind of community on the soil of the Land of Israel?

A recurrent principle of much magic realism is that the physical universe of the fiction is in part governed by psychological rather than physical laws. Thus, in the Mexican novel *Like Water for Chocolate* (1989) by Laura Esquivel, a young woman's pent-up passion, ignited by one of her sister's magic recipes, produces a literal explosion, causing the wooden shower-shed in which she is standing naked to burst into flames. (The novel, by the way, unlike its popular film version, actually introduces each episode with a real Mexican recipe, which functions as a ballast of quotidian physical reality for the book's high-flying fantasies.) The underlying idea is not to present the psychology of the characters analytically—as, say, Proust does—or to represent psychological processes mimetically—as does Joyce—but to extrude psychodynamic forces by extravagantly externalizing them. In *The Blue Mountain*, Ephraim's status as pariah is confirmed, grotesquely but effectively, by the necessity he feels to take up the calf as his sole companion. His disfigurement has imposed upon him an absolute sexual isolation. The grown bull, fertilizing all the cows of the region, serves as a sexual alter ego for the celibate Ephraim and at the same time as a zoological analogue to Ephraim's cousin Uri, the village's irrepressible cocksman. The maimed ex-commando's terrible separation from the possibility of sexual connection is then forever sealed when his attempted coupling with the Rubber Lady, whose preternatural flexibility seems to promise a world of perverse pleasure, is interrupted by Jean Valjean and turns into a ghastly uncoupling. Ephraim now runs away from the circus as he had run away from the village, and thus he turns into another legendary archetype, a Wandering Dutchman eternally driven from the habitations of men and the ministrations of women by a terrible curse.

The most fantastic aspect of Ephraim's relationship with the bull is of course his ability to carry around this superhuman weight. The narrator explains that it was not strength but despair that enabled Ephraim to carry the bull. This psycho-physical explanation makes sense in the hybrid world of the novel. Real history inflicts real wounds in this novel. Ephraim, after all, loses his face fighting for the British in World War II, like real Palestinian Jews who sometimes paid a terrible price, or the

ultimate price, as volunteers for combat duty. Similarly, the grenade
that kills both the narrator's parents is hardly a fanciful invention of
magic realism, for such acts of Arab terrorism were repeatedly carried
out against members of the Zionist community from 1936 through to
the armed struggle for statehood. Though we obviously understand that
no one in that same historical reality of Palestine in the 1940s carried
around a ton and a half on his shoulders, the externalized representation of the concentrated power of utter despair is genuinely wrenching.
The acuteness of the character's suffering is not undercut by the fantasy
but, on the contrary, is made palpable by it.

All this nevertheless remains, a reader may reasonably object, very
bizarre. But it seems to me that bizarreness is precisely the thematic
point. The Zionist enterprise, which is the historical subject of the novel,
was the most successfully implemented of all the different ideological
projects undertaken by Jews grappling with modernity. But ideology is
by design systematically rationalist. It comes with a set of causal expla-
nations for why things happen in a certain way in history and with a
pragmatic plan for shaping the course of future events according to its
understanding of the nature of historical process. Shalev's novel raises
questions in a variety of ways, both realistic and fantastic, about the
ideological confidence of the Zionist enterprise, suggesting instead that
history may be more unmanageable, perhaps even more abysmal, than
the Zionist founding fathers were willing to imagine. At the same time,
his upbeat ending makes clear that it is by no means his intention simply
to invalidate Zionism. The fantastic fate he invents for the disfigured
Ephraim is grotesque, uncanny, a manifest violation of conventional
notions of how things happen in the real world. The man with a mask
on his face and a bull on his shoulders becomes an image of everything
that communitarian Zionism, operating on its hopeful ideological premises, cannot assimilate. Our children, after all, were supposed to turn
into strong, beautiful, confident avatars of a new kind of Jew, as in a way
Ephraim was before his wounding—and not into inconceivable monsters
of loneliness and despair. The grotesquely transformed Ephraim is still
a human being, a son of the village, and the townsfolk's horrified withdrawal from him, which leads to his self-banishment, is a kind of primal
sin of the community, as both the narrator and his embittered grandfather recognize. The fantasy-hypothesis by which the character becomes
Quasimodo with the huge bull Jean Valjean on his shoulders exposes the
inner contradictions of the community, its inability to cope humanely
with the irruption of unanticipated horror into its collective life.

My last example is a sequence of magic realism working at the border of realism. David Grossman's *The Book of Intimate Grammar* is, as I

have already noted, in most respects a realistic novel. Indeed, it seems to me one of the most compelling representations of the emotional and physical anguish of early adolescence in recent fiction anywhere. There is, however, one long episode, occupying nearly a quarter of the book and occurring more or less in its middle, that begins realistically but by stages builds into a set of actions that verge on the fantastic. Edna Blum, a single woman in her thirties who has an apartment in the same housing development as Aharon Kleinfeld, the young protagonist, and his family, comes to Aharon's father with a business proposition: she would like to make some structural modifications in her apartment, and knowing him to be good with his hands, she proposes, for a generous fee, that he undertake to knock down an interior wall. His wife is immediately suspicious of the whole business—with good reason, as the events prove. Mrs. Kleinfeld grudgingly agrees to the deal, but with the stipulation that she will be present to keep an eye on what is going on (she will then bring along her son). Even in the early stages of the project, bizarre features begin to emerge. Edna Blum makes a point of feeding her demolition man each time he comes, favoring thick sandwiches with lots of spicy meat. The wife, not about to have any of her conjugal prerogatives usurped, makes sure to serve him a heavy meal before each of his stints in Edna's apartment. The two women in this way enter into a weird competition over the man, with obvious implications of claims to sexual possession, by vying to stuff him to the gills.

As the demolition gets underway, its heavy erotic charge for Edna Blum is made vividly clear. Aharon's father stands amid the clouds of flying dust in sleeveless undershirt and workshorts, his body glistening with sweat, his muscles rippling, as he swings the sledgehammer, pounding again and again into the gradually disintegrating wall, while Edna watches his every motion, mesmerized. "Three days. The innards of the wall were torn open step by step; and Edna scarcely moved from her place, half-sitting, half-prone, clinging to the thin, primal terror that pulsed through her, touching a pleasure too sharp to bear."[7] The breaking down of the wall patently becomes a surrogate for the sexual act to the evidently virginal Edna. When the industrious Mr. Kleinfeld finishes taking down the wall, she proposes, for a still more extravagant sum, that he go to work on a second one. (By this point, the irate Mrs. Kleinfeld vows that she will not set foot again in Edna Blum's apartment.) He agrees, and then, predictably, she proposes a third wall after the second, and then a floor. The mad pact continues until her entire small apartment is reduced to a scene of utter devastation, with nothing left to knock down. Here is how she looks at the end of the process, now bereft of all hope:

Only Edna had begun slowly to turn to stone as she stood. She felt how the stone was pouring into the soles of her feet, rising to her knees, to her thighs, to her parched sex which the stone filled and enveloped. She still managed to reflect how Mr. Kleinfeld would now have to hew delicately and carefully in order to extricate her from the envelope of marmoreal stone that had formed over her desolate breasts, but her heart, her lips, her brain had already turned to stone.[8]

The stone, of course, is purely metaphorical and not literal, as it would be in a blatantly magic-realist fiction. But, especially coming from David Grossman, the writer who had turned a man into a fish and had invented a child who lives a life-span in a day, is this really an instance of magic realism? There is no fictional rearrangement here of any law of nature: a hired sledgehammer, pounding day after day, would in fact reduce an apartment to rubble, as the novel reports. Let me suggest that a reader's perception of the pressure of fantasy in a narrative is partly determined by the norms of realistic representation established in the narrative as a whole. The extended account of the destruction of Edna Blum's apartment within the world of *The Book of Intimate Grammar* is rather like the insertion of a long episode from Yehoshua's *Facing the Forest* in his somberly realistic *Five Seasons*. Throughout the novel, the rules of the child protagonist's psychological "grammar" are observed with the most persuasive precision: there is scarcely a thought or a gesture that does not seem utterly plausible, motivated with manifest verisimilitude. The social milieu and the historical moment—life in a *shikkun* (housing development) toward the end of the second decade of statehood—are also evoked with the most meticulous attention to realistic detail. The Edna Blum episode begins in a way that seems perfectly continuous with the realism of the preceding narrative: there is nothing implausible in her proposing to hire a muscular neighbor to take down a wall in her apartment, even if her intentness and her readiness to overpay him may lead us to wonder about her motives. As the demolition proceeds, however, with the rhythmically battered apartment coming to seem more and more an extension of Edna Blum's body, madness takes over, and it is not easy to situate it between the alternatives of acted-out psychosis (realism) and fantasy turned into fact (magic realism). One can of course explain Edna as a frustrated woman whose erotic obsession becomes monomaniacal, causing her to disregard all sane considerations of self-preservation, not to speak of propriety. And in fact, after the dust from the last hammer blow settles, she is carted off by her parents, apparently for psychiatric care. At the same time, one must keep in mind Mr. Kleinfeld's persistent complicity in the madness, which cannot simply be explained by the profit motive and threatens to violate plausibility for an otherwise sane character. This whole Yehoshua-like sequence stands out in its bizarreness against the norms of the surrounding novel. Even without any abrogation of physical laws, it feels very much like that extrusion of psychology into external acts and objects which is a characteristic feature of magic realism. What Grossman gains by switching fictional gears is an amusing, dismaying, compelling dramatization of submerged psychological impulsions. The mixture of zany inventiveness and mimetic seriousness is precisely the kind of special pleasure, which will be relished by some but not by all, that magic realists offer their readers.

The reasons why this mode of fiction should now appeal to some younger Israeli writers are multiple, and some may remain obscure. It is also not altogether clear whether such loosing of the steeds of galloping fantasy in the fields of realism may not prove to be a mixed blessing. No doubt, Israeli magic realism is in part a predictable pendulum swing in Hebrew literary history, a new generation of writers defining itself against the dominant norms of its predecessors by vigorously adopting an antithetical mode of fiction. An active interest in foreign models, both Latin American and European, must also be conceded. There are, as several critics have noted, more than a few elements of *A Hundred Years of Solitude* in *The Blue Mountain*, and there are ghosts of Garcia Marquez, Grass, perhaps also Rushdie flitting around in the strange world of *See Under: Love*. But "influence" is always a matter of finding in other literatures formal strategies or thematic emphases that answer the special needs of one's own ideological, cultural, and historical predicament.[9] Earlier I proposed that magic realism is fantasy working within, and against, a realm of constriction and intractability. Israeli reality since the 1950s has repeatedly been felt by writers to be precisely such a realm, though their typical response to it until the last few years did not involve fantasy.

Israel, we should recall, is a tiny state hemmed in by enemies, which makes it rather different from other tiny states, like Denmark and Holland. Or perhaps it might be more pertinent to say that Israel is a tight little island, at once Jewish and Western, surrounded by a bloc of states that are culturally other and that, at least until very recently, have been unwilling to recognize Israel's existence in any way that Israelis could sense as a confirmation of their belonging to the region. Within its tensely drawn perimeters, Israeli society long sought to be ideologically regulative for its members. Moreover, as a small society where everybody seems to know everybody else, from high-school class to army service to power structures—see, for example, Irit Linor's pop fiction *Two Snow-Whites* (1993)—it combines universalist aspirations with, as Israelis sometimes say, the provinciality of the shtetl. In the first generation of Statehood writers, this cultural predicament is characteristically reflected in

representations of the coercive or at least restrictive peer group. S. Yizhar's *The Days of Ziklag* (1958) is the grand culmination of this kind of
Hebrew fiction. Within a few years, Hebrew writers, as I had occasion
to observe long ago,[10] began to play out scenarios of flight or escape in
their writing; the exemplary instance of Dalia Ravikovitch's well-known
poem, "The Blue West," has its elaborate analogues in a wide variety of
Israeli novels. One might say that after fantasies of flight beyond the
horizon in the generation that came to prominence in the 1960s, some
younger Hebrew writers are experimenting with imaginative flights of
another sort in the very representation of the national here and now.

Every mode of fiction has its own pitfalls, and it is not my intention
to argue for the superiority of one over the other. Let me conclude with
a brief contrast between two novels, one realist and the other magic-
realist, that cope imaginatively with the constrictions of Israeli existence,
exhibiting different virtues and different potential problems. Amos Oz's
A Perfect Peace[11] (1982), which still seems to me his best novel since *My
Michael*, spells out the scenario of flight. In the first sentence, we are
informed that the protagonist, Yonatan Lifshitz, has decided to leave
his wife and the kibbutz on which he was born to make a new life for
himself somewhere else. The kibbutz is of course the tight little island
within the tight little island, the apogee of constrictiveness and ideological coercion in Israel, especially as it is seen in the fiction of Amos Oz.
Yonatan Lifshitz feels an intolerable burden of expectations of performance placed on him by his father, by the kibbutz, by the movement,
by the nation, and he wants out. In the event, his attempted escape is
not in search of a new life but is rather a gesture toward suicide, crossing the border into Jordan on the way to Petra, on foot and alone, from
which, however, the novelist rescues him and returns him, reconciled,
to the kibbutz. Oz's representation of the familial, social, and political
constrictions of kibbutz life is minutely observed, often with a shrewd
satirical eye, and seems quite convincing. After such entrapments, Yonatan's flight has its psychological satisfactions, and the whole sequence
of escape to the desert badlands is gripping. The danger of this mode
of fiction is that the fantasy of flight, in the fictional enactment, may
become melodramatic, or that the opposition between escape and belonging may be worked out too schematically, though I think that Oz
manages to avoid both these traps in *A Perfect Peace*.

The magic realism of Shalev's *Esau* responds to the constrictiveness
of the Israeli condition in an opposite way. The narrator has already
made good his escape, having lived much of his adult life in America,
from which he returns on an extended visit to the Israeli village where
he grew up, to his father, to his twin brother, and to his brother's now

devastated wife, who was the girl he loved as an adolescent. The impulse of physical flight is defused here because it is an already accomplished fact that is only a background to what goes on in the novel. Most of the fantasy-hypotheses played out here have to do with the body—that eternally lactating breast, a priapic erection that persists over the years. These fantastic bodily processes stand in dialectic opposition to the novel's stress on aging and physical decay, which, together with the claustral social world of the small Israeli town, are the prime instance here of the realm of the intractable.

Esau is an odd mixture—odder, I think, than *The Blue Mountain.* It begins with a kind of narrative prologue, set in the nineteenth century, and subtitled, "A Fabricated Story About People Who Did Not Exist." This section is extravagantly literary in a self-reflexive mode, abounding in borrowings from and explicit allusions to Rabelais, Fielding, Sterne, Nabokov, and others. Although no physical laws are violated here, the narrative is a continuous chain of weird and bizarre events, involving a pilgrimage to Palestine by a young German duke who is seized and womanhandled by a band of exotic females, and emerges from his night of captivity physically lacerated, with micrographic inscriptions tatooed on his penis. On his return to Germany he commits suicide, joined in the act of self-destruction by an adolescent female cousin who has vowed never to do the same thing twice.

This narrative prologue draws us into the world of *Esau* in a spirit of zany, grotesque playfulness, and after two readings of the novel, I am not sure that it isn't at least in part a mistake. The novel after the prologue confronts the dilemmas of life in the family (Israeli subspecies)—parental discord, misplaced love, sibling strife, and so forth—with existential seriousness. The play of fantasy in the midst of this seriousness often has a heightening effect of externalizing psychological themes and highlighting existential questions in ways akin to those we observed in our earlier examples from Israeli magic realism, including Shalev's previous novel. Beyond mimesis, the fantasies are also fun, and there is certainly nothing wrong with fiction's providing fun for the reader. The inherent danger of fun through fantasy, where there is no reality check, is self-indulgence. There are moments in the narrative prologue when the playfulness seems merely goofy, and as a result the threat of exuberant invention spilling over into silliness is never quite dispelled in the body of the novel proper. *Esau* does in fact set its tale of familial convolutions in a vividly realized Israeli world of local color, tangled human contradiction, and harsh historical necessity; and, on the whole, the deployment of fantasy helps to define that world more sharply. The delicate balance, however, between realism and fantasy that is maintained

in *The Blue Mountain* sometimes wobbles a little here. This is still the
world of shared historical and cultural experience, despite all the fantastic elaboration, as is the case in the strongest magic-realist fictions;
but there are moments when we begin to wonder whether we are on
the verge of getting lost in a fun house of merely literary games. The
new Hebrew magic realism has clearly been associated with a moment of
energetic renewal in the Israeli novel. The great danger is that it could
turn into a set of mannerisms in which fantasy is a crazy mirror reflect-
ing the writer's study, not an instrument to probe history, culture, and
the eternal frailties to which flesh is heir.

Notes

1. Yoel Hoffman, *Christus shel dagim* (Jerusalem: Maxwell-Macmillan-Keter,
1991), Section 166 (no page numbers). The translation of this and subsequent
Hebrew texts is mine.
2. David Grossman, *'Ayen 'erekh: 'Ahavah'* (Tel Aviv: Sifrei Siman Kriah, 1986).
3. Meir Shalev, *Roman russi* (Tel Aviv: Am Oved, 1988).
4. Smadar Shiffman, "Meir Shalev and the Fantastic in Israeli Literature,"
Prooftexts 13:3 (September 1993), p. 260.
5. Ibid., p. 262.
6. Meir Shalev, *Esav* (Tel Aviv: Am Oved, 1991).
7. David Grossman, *Sefer hadiqduq hapnimi* (Tel Aviv: Sifrei Siman Kriah,
1991), p. 157.
8. Ibid., p. 209.
9. This idea is studied in illuminating detail in Chana Kronfeld's *On the Margins of Modernism* (Berkeley and Los Angeles: University of California Press,
1996).
10. In the chapter "A Problem of Horizons" in my book *Defenses of the Imagination* (Philadelphia: Jewish Publication Society, 1977).
11. Amos Oz, *Menuhah nekhonah* (Tel Aviv: Am Oved, 1982).

ANNE GOLOMB HOFFMAN

Bodies and Borders: The Politics of Gender in Contemporary Israeli Fiction

THE WORK OF a number of recent Israeli writers gives evidence of a rich engagement with issues in modern Jewish history. I shall be examining the literary responses of Yaakov Shabtai, A. B. Yehoshua, and several others to a cultural inheritance that includes an ideologically loaded conception of masculinity. These (male) writers take apart a construction of masculinity as public, visible, and clearly defined. Through absorption in a thematics of body and gender, their fiction turns away from the public staging of masculinity and moves instead to explore modes of experience that are less bound by fixed conceptions of self and other. Furthermore, these writers explore the ways in which conventional distinctions between male and female enter into large-scale political issues of boundary and national identity. Through literary play with borders and identities on the level of both the individual and the collective, these writers challenge a history of images that fix gender into shifting sets of political alignments.

In order to understand the politics of gender in recent Israeli writing, we have to go back in time to nineteenth-century Europe and the rise of racial antisemitism. In fact, the scope of my work concerns the responses of modern Jewish writers to ideologically motivated images of the body, in light of a history of negative racial stereotypes. Under the guise of science, classifications of race provided the framework for a system of differences in which language, physiology, and gender played a part. Antisemitic stereotypes demonstrate that the Jewish "body" played a crucial role in the enterprise of fashioning a concept of degeneracy that would integrate mental, moral, and physical attributes and allow for definitions of nationality that could claim scientific legitimacy. (I put "body" in quotation marks to emphasize that our knowledge of the body is always a construction, the product of the systems of thought that shape our view of the world, whether we are aware of them or not.[1])

The cognitive activity of stereotyping uses crude simplifications of the body that enter into distinctions between self and other, insider and outsider. Sander Gilman has demonstrated the strong visual component in the development of European stereotypes of gender, race, and pathology. In terms of our focus, it is important to note that nineteenth-century racial science placed the Jewish male in the category of the pathological and the feminine. Indeed the stereotype of the feminized male Jew provided a necessary antitype to the idealized conceptions (myths) of national identity that were taking shape in Europe and to the racial ideologies that supported them.[2]

Recent work on the politics of identity can help understand how body image enters into large-scale conceptions of group identity. Judith Butler develops a critique of identity politics, that is, of the claim by a group to an identity that is its fixed and unchanging essence.[3] Her work demonstrates the dependence of identity on a conception of the body as bounded and bordered. Furthermore, she argues that coherent and bounded identities develop out of the repression of an abjected other, an excluded "outside," a "threatening spectre."[4] In order to lock itself into place, identity requires its excluded, denied, or abjected other. Butler's analysis can be applied to romantic myths of nationality in nineteenth-century Europe, which drew upon the negative image of the feminized male Jew in order to sustain fictions of the idealized virility of the dominant group.

If we look into the history of the human sciences, we find the intersection of physical anthropology (out of which racial science developed) with linguistics and philology, fields whose quests for the origins of languages led them into conceptions of nationality and eventually race. (Historically speaking, the result was a disastrous confusion of language, race, and nationality, from whose effects we are still recovering.) In the mythic construction of difference, we find that certain racial groups are characterized as virile and active in contrast to others described as passive and effeminate. The mythic construction of "Aryans" and "Semites" offers the most striking instance of this. Taking note of the "mixture between romanticism and the new sciences" in the nineteenth century, George Mosse has shown us how new studies in physiognomy, anthropology, and philology interacted with romantic myths of national origin to produce conceptions of racial difference in which Jews and blacks provided the necessary foil to their Aryan counterparts.[5] Mosse elucidates the role of a cult of manliness in developing ideologies of nationalism.[6]

Now to turn to Jewish responses to these developments in European politics and culture: As a movement to redefine Jewish national identity and aspirations, Zionism constituted a response to European nationalisms and to scientific racism which classified Jews as racial inferiors. Part of the impetus for Zionism came from the disappointment of Jew-

ish expectations of acceptance and integration following the Enlightenment and the gradual Emancipation of Western European Jews. Despite
real progress in the area of civil rights, the failure of Emancipation to
bring about genuine equality can be attributed, at least in part, to the
tenacity of deeply rooted anti-Jewish attitudes in Europe, attitudes that
took on new life with the rise of antisemitism and "scientific" racisms in
the latter part of the nineteenth century.[7] (This amounts to an updating
of old prejudices from theological to pseudoscientific terms.) The rise
of Jewish nationalism can be understood both as an acknowledgment of
the intractability of European antisemitism and as an attempt to reverse
antisemitic stereotypes by formulating a positive conception of national
identity.

Thus, as part of a collective effort, Zionism appropriated the negative
image of the male Jew and transformed it into the positive image of the
"new Jew" or the "muscle Jew."[8] In the broadest sense, Zionism can be
understood as an attempt to revolutionize Jewish identity and to develop
a distinctive national culture.[9] Zionism can be seen as an "erotic revolution" that sought to "transform the Jewish body itself" through "the
creation of a virile new Hebrew man," an ideal that shaped the emerging culture of modern Israel. Crucial to this transformation, David Biale
notes, is a conception of the "physical body as a mirror of emotional disease" and of the individual body as a "microcosm for the national body
politic."[10]

The success of the transformation, along with a keen sense of the
constraints imposed by the image of the "new Jew," can be found, in
a variety of ways, in the literature of the early State, a literature that
offers us images of sons who struggle to come to terms with a national
patrimony. Indeed, the Biblical *akedah*, the sacrifice of Isaac, forms a
prominent theme in the writing of the generation that came of age with
the formation of the State of Israel, communicating the discomfort of
"sons" with burdens they nevertheless accept as their own.[11]

Recent Israeli writing responds to an ideologically charged inheritance by challenging popular constructions of masculinity and interrogating their relationship to larger issues of collective identity. From turn-
of-the-century Europe to Palestine and the establishment of the State of
Israel, the arena of the Jewish confrontation with modern culture shifts
from the scene of European modernism in the first part of this century
to the intense explorations of cultural identity and politics that are to
be found in recent Israeli writing.

I would like briefly to refer to the work of two writers, turn-of-the-
century European Jews, to illustrate the internalization and reformu-

lation of antisemitic stereotypes. The writings of Otto Weininger and Max Nordau give evidence of different facets of a crisis in Jewish identity. Both present clear and unambiguous arguments, each of which is diametrically opposed to the other. In the work of each writer, we can observe the theoretical formulation of a response to deeply rooted problems of Jewish life in Europe. Weininger's response, it can be argued, is untenable in its self-negation, while Nordau's makes a substantial contribution to the development of an ideology and a new conception of nationhood.

Perhaps the most striking feature of Weininger's 1906 book, *Sex and Character*, is its extreme receptivity to negative stereotypes of Jews and homosexuals.[12] Weininger argues for a Platonic idea of masculinity that corresponds to the notion of "ideal type" taking shape in moral anthropology and ethnography. Women, Jews, and homosexuals provide the necessary antitypes against which this "ideal type" can be seen. Jews are like women insofar as they lack any essence and can only imitate the true masculine. Thus Weininger identifies masculinity with consciousness and develops a concept of genius as the product of a masculine transcendence and mastery of time.

Nordau shares with Weininger (and their contemporaries) the acceptance of a normative masculinity that fuels a system of differences and boundaries. But that is where the similarity ends. When he proposes a cure for the situation of the Jews in Europe, Nordau argues that this is both a Christian and a Jewish problem. As Nordau constructs it, "Judaism," in nineteenth-century Europe, is a disease or pathological condition shared by Jews and Christians alike, a blight on their existences that can only be dealt with by allowing the Jews (who are not degenerate, but whose circumstances may make them appear to be so) to develop in their own land.[13] Nordau's essays on Zionism delineate a "muscle Judaism" that he links to the active male Judaism of the ancient world. Post-exilic Judaism is for him the story of martyrdom. Operating in his construction of Jewish history is the contrast between Jewish suffering, identified as passive and by implication feminine and Jewish "athleticism," explicitly identified as masculine and active.

Nordau accepts European stereotypes of Jews as degenerate and the association of Jews with urban life and disease, but ascribes that pathology to circumstances, rather than to heredity or race. Thus his writing reflects both an internalization of antisemitic stereotypes and a vigorous challenge to them. It was Nordau, working closely with Theodor Herzl, who conceptualized a new *Muskeljudentum*—a muscle Judaism—in an effort to transform the negative image of the ghetto Jew into the image of the "new Jew," the "muscle Jew." In fact, Nordau's friendship with Herzl offered a popular Jewish image of male friendship on the model of the fraternal organizations then in vogue.[14]

The extent of Nordau's internalization of antisemitic stereotypes can be seen in his description of the physical features of ghetto Jews; their eyes, for example, have narrowed and taken on "sly" expressions, because of the enclosed, sunless environments they have inhabited. Here, the Jewish body exhibits a negative sign of difference, acquired in Lamarckian fashion over centuries of life in exile. It is in relation to another mark of difference, however, that Nordau's writing makes its most interesting move. As part of his program for a new *Muskeljudentum*, Nordau proposes a return to an ancient model, but with a difference. The identifying mark of the male Jew is his circumcised penis. Unlike the Hellenized male Jew, however, the "new Jew" will not try to conceal this mark of race, but will display it proudly. Nordau argues for a virility that will recover the strength that the Diaspora Jew has lost; he attempts to sustain this conception by transforming the symbolic wound into an assertion of identity and power.

As it evolved, the project of Zionism became to transform Jewish life through the establishment of a national homeland and the renewal of the Jewish body through labor on the land. Focusing on this historical theme, we see that the Zionist "negation of the Golah" and development of the image of the "muscle Jew" carry signs of an internalization of the image of the feminized Jewish male of the Diaspora.[15] Moving forward in time, we can read recent Israeli fiction in terms of its responses to Zionist ideology and the development of the State, and, in particular, to the stereotypes of gender and body that enter into images of national identity. Like any ideological formulation, the Zionist image of the "new Jew" requires a certain amount of repression and simplification. In contemporary writers such as Yaakov Shabtai and A. B. Yehoshua and several others, we see that the repressed underside of the virile image of the new Jew is not projected onto an other who is external to the self, but rather is held within and returns to disrupt the neat outlines of conscious identity and the political assertion of that identity. The effect of the fiction of these writers is to disrupt ideologically loaded conceptions of masculinity.

In a literature characterized by the fertility of its historical imagination, the work of two writers in particular stands out. Yaakov Shabtai produced two remarkable novels in his brief career, *Zikhron devarim* (*Past Continuous*) and *Sof davar* (*Past Perfect*), each of which summons up popular conceptions of masculinity in order to subvert them from within. Over recent years, the fiction of A. B. Yehoshua has deepened its engagement with Jewish history and identity by interrogating the dominant historical narratives and seeking alternative conceptions of gender, narrative, and history. While this study takes the fiction of Yehoshua and Shabtai as its focus, I will comment in closing on recent developments in fiction by Amos Oz, David Grossman, and S. Yizhar, and for a bit of gender difference, Orly Castel-Bloom.

Yaakov Shabtai's first novel, *Zikhron devarim* (1975), translated as *Past Continuous*, is an extraordinary text that consists of one long paragraph.[16] It moves in and out of the consciousness of characters who live in Tel Aviv in the early seventies, focusing primarily on the obsessive and self-limiting concerns of a trio of male characters—Caesar, Goldman, and Israel. Shabtai's elaborately orchestrated sentences highlight the interdependence of these three male characters, members of the same generation, drawing our attention to their participation in a shared dilemma of masculinity.

We watch the ongoing and unsuccessful efforts of three men to establish their masculinity through commerce in women's bodies, or the exchange of emblems of masculinity whose binary opposition to femininity threatens to break down. Consider this portion of an exemplary sentence which offers a close look at how the "system" works:

Caesar . . . went on admiring [Eliezra] and telling Goldman and Israel that she had invented sex, and giving them accounts of her exploits in bed, but Goldman confided in Israel that as far as women were concerned he had nothing but pity for Caesar, since he, Goldman, had no doubt that Caesar derived almost no pleasure at all from his sexual relations, which had certainly undergone a process of standardization by now and become mechanical and boring, the truth of the matter being that Caesar was a compulsive fucker, suffering from a production-line "fucking complex," which, with his father fixation and castration complex, drove him to keep on proving his virility because he was really so unsure of it, whereas Eliezra was a frigid woman trying to act the part of a nymphomaniac in order to establish some kind of relationship with others, which was exactly what neither of them were capable of, according to Goldman, neither Caesar nor Eliezra, who refined their techniques of lovemaking and increased their enjoyment from day to day, using all kinds of aids and appliances, looking at pornographic pictures and reading erotic literature as they copulated, and observing themselves in the mirrors which Caesar had fixed to the ceiling and three sides of the couch so that he and Eliezra could see themselves making love to each other and also so that he could photograph them in the act from the various perspectives provided by all these mirrors, which drove Israel, who had left his place by the wall and started crossing the road, crazy, because the moment he opened his eyes he saw himself reflected and wherever he looked he was confronted by his own image, which would not let him be, but he said nothing about this to Caesar, and glancing at the hairdresser—who had finished curling her hair and making up her face, which now looked like the mask of fresh, young woman's face—entered the lobby, which was full of pleasant scents of soap and cosmetics, and went upstairs to the studio, where he found a note hastily penned in Caesar's handwriting on the lid of the piano in which he apologized for taking so long, mentioned the summer and the funeral by way of reminding Israel that weariness, heat, and sorrow increased the sexual urge, added that life was full of problems but everything would work out in the end, and signed off with a drawing of a camel with a flower sticking out of the end of its huge sexual organ. (113–15/85–86)

This excerpt from one sentence in the novel demonstrates the inter-twined masculinity of its three main characters. Goldman and Israel feed off Caesar's tales of his amorous activities, tales which provide the ongoing substance of their relationship. Indeed Caesar occupies center stage in a mirrored studio that expresses his dependence on an audi-ence that consists of two men, Israel and Goldman, who share in his fantasies of sexual exploits. Israel stands in the street waiting for Caesar to raise the shutter, a signal by which Caesar communicates the end of his lovemaking and permission for Israel to reenter the studio. But while Israel may occupy the child's position in relation to Caesar's sexu-ality, he is also the silent partner in Caesar's lovemaking, the necessary third to corroborate Caesar's use of the feminine commodity.[17]

What we have here amounts to a virtual enactment of what French theorist Luce Irigaray terms a "hom(m)o-sexual economy": men engage in the exchange of women as commodities, their manifestly heterosexual interactions masking the homosexual underpinnings of the system.[18] Caesar plays a pivotal role in the novel's grammar of masculinity, insofar as the hyperbolic extravagance of his sexual exploits suggests a hyped-up masculine norm. At the same time, the masculine posture exemplified by Caesar is so exaggerated that it disrupts its "own" masculine order and turns back upon itself. This is self-inflation to the point of rupture.

In fact, the novel demonstrates the breakdown of a system that sus-tains masculine subjectivity by defining it as that which is not feminine. A series of striking visual images, found at the start of the novel and repeated later on, betrays the anxiety that underlies the cultural con-struction of masculinity. First off, we are given Caesar's photos of nude women (6/8), tacked up on the walls of his studio. The display of these objectified images of women provides a striking reminder of the func-tion of the female body as object of the male gaze. Next, intensifying the effect of this specularization of women, Caesar displays a set of porno-graphic pictures to Israel (10/11). This piling of image upon image frames and repeats the subjection of the woman's body to the male gaze. Caesar uses the pictures to confirm his masculinity by comparing the size of his penis to those in the photos. The lens of the camera, the eye of the voyeur produce the effect of a hyper-representation, which is heightened further by the mirrored ceiling over Caesar's bed in the studio—suggesting the endlessly self-reflective and repetitive scenes of sexuality through which Caesar seeks to identify himself, and the others, Israel and Goldman, seek to know themselves through him.

At the same time, along with these emblems of masculinity, the opening pages of the novel yield also an image that suggests both the diametric opposite and the complement to Caesar's ideal of an aggressive sexual identity. Israel's contribution to Caesar's picture gallery is a reproduction of El Greco's *Saint Francis* that suggests an alternative sexuality in its depiction of the feminized man, the son's submission to the father, the position of self-abnegation. In the contrast between Caesar's hyperphallic pictures and the masochistic posture of Saint Francis, the reader may sense the fluctuation, within the claustrophobic space of the novel, between alternative constructions of masculinity.

The reproduction of the painting of Saint Francis is a striking visual cue that suggests culture's appropriation and elevation of what Freud calls the "negative Oedipus complex," or the son's wish to be the woman (to occupy the feminine position) in relation to the father. The negative Oedipus is the counterpart to the positive Oedipus complex that involves the son's wish to take the father's place. While normative definitions of masculinity focus on the "positive Oedipus complex" (and its resolution in the son's identification with the father), Freud tells us that both positive and negative versions of the Oedipus complex may form part of the child's experience.[19] The *Saint Francis* reproduction functions as a visual cue, to suggest the other side of the son's relation to the father.

In *Three Essays on a Theory of Sexuality*, Freud notes that the conflict of the generations expressed in the Oedipus crisis is the source of the possibility of progress; that is, the narrative of "progress" finds its source in the resolution of the Oedipus complex that incorporates the son into the social order, while allowing him to oppose or even outdo his father.[20] In contrast, Shabtai's novel assembles the same narrative ingredients that Freud's model suggests, but places them in fixed positions, from which our three male protagonists are unable to dislodge themselves. The novel shows these "sons" to be stuck in an Oedipal impasse in relation to the father, from which there is no outcome. The narrative impasse of *Past Continuous* discloses unresolved Oedipal needs, so that the three male protagonists can only continue to engage in anxious defenses of masculinity against the threat of castration, as well as the ongoing struggle against the wish to be the woman for the father. This novel ends catastrophically with Goldman's suicide, the mortal illness of Caesar's son, and Ella's turn away from Israel and her son. As devastating as they may be, however, these outcomes merely confirm the impasse of masculinity that is signalled at the start of the novel by the series of striking visual images I described.

The "sons'" anxious defenses of masculinity are linked, in the larger context of the novel, to a breakdown of the intergenerational structure that shapes the historical narrative of Zionism.[21] This intergenerational dilemma or impasse is exposed through the text, as the sentence itself becomes the mirror in which the collapse of structure makes itself visible. Here is the novel's opening: "Goldman's father died on the first of April, whereas Goldman himself committed suicide on the first of January" (3/7). From April 1 to January 1, the death of the father and the suicide of the son define the temporal structure of the novel. Within that frame, the many characters in this crowded novel supply accounts of themselves that go back in time beyond that April first marker, and forward beyond the January first closure as well. These recollected events go back to Europe and Russia and include narrative histories of *aliyot* to Eretz Yisrael. On the scaffolding of the present (April 1 to January 1), we gain access to the past. The novel sets up a tension between its oppressive temporal scheme of paternal death and filial suicide (nine months), on the one hand, and the broader historical compass of the rise of the State of Israel, on the other (forty years, approximately).[22] But with the collapse of the narrated events, most obviously in Goldman's suicide, but really in the catastrophic nonproductivity of all three male protagonists, the larger historical span of recollected events is implicated.

The moment in the narrated present of the novel that supplies the structure of the sentence is made to open out to include or at least to indicate the larger history of the State. However, because it is the nonproductive moment in the present that forms the primary structure, the effect is to reduce that larger historical span to the structure of the sentence, rather than the other way around. The claustrophobic atmosphere of this novel is in part a product of this oppressive structure, which appears even to have history in its grips. To the extent that the novel implicates larger structures, that larger historical frame collapses into the particular syntactical and temporal scheme of the novel, beginning with the father's death on January first and ending with the son's suicide on April first.

While the opening sentence supplies the temporal frame that signals the breakdown of an intergenerational model of progress, that collapse makes itself felt within sentences as well, down to particular lists of nouns or objects. Thus, for example, the bookcase in Goldman's father's apartment is described as "crowded with books by Berl Katznelson and Ben Gurion and Bialik and Brenner and Shalom Aleichem" (47/38–39). A properly emblematic structure, Goldman's father's bookcase holds the names of the fathers, proper nouns that serve as the signifiers of the socially constituted ideologies of Zionism, as well as the more general context of modern Jewish culture. The son's bookcase supplies the contrast and counterpart to the father's. Along with the other miscellaneous contents of his bedroom, Goldman's bookcase holds books on Kabbalah and rabbinics, Taoism, psychology, including the Jungianism of Erich Neuman (169–70/125–26). We learn also that, testifying to his interest in astronomy, he has read and reread Kepler's family horoscope (340–41/247) and third-person autobiography (342/248), and has translated an excerpt from Kepler's *Somnium* (382/277). (Kepler's *Somnium* [Dream] was published posthumously by his son in 1634; suggestive of a family romance, it chronicles an interplanetary voyage.[23]) Through his readings, Goldman seeks to find a way out of a relationship to the father that is bound up with a particular historical trajectory. These collected titles provide graphic evidence of his effort to unify the individual with the cosmic. Nevertheless, as lists of names without accompanying verbs, these collections of nouns lack predication and collapse in a heap.

While the father's bookcase marks the decline of a particular narrative trajectory, the effect of these lists and catalogues is to suggest a view of history as discontinuous clutter, in which individual items fail to take root in larger causal structures. Thus an impasse on the level of character extends into the larger span of history, insofar as collections of ideologically loaded signifiers fail to produce a story of meaningful action in the public domain. While those signifiers invoke history, they lack the causal structure or predication necessary to historical narrative.

And yet, how is this collapse of history within the frame of the novel to be understood? The novel absorbs its historical referents, employing them as signifiers in the dilemma of masculinity that is its subject. Thus the dynamics of the narrative amplify our understanding of the development of modern Israel by taking us beyond the normative masculinity of the historical record, disclosing dimensions to the historical process that may otherwise go unnoticed. Recording without commenting on the thoughts and actions of its characters, this intricately detailed narrative offers to its reader access to dimensions of subjectivity, including its infantile determinants, that often escape attention, whether on the level of the individual or the collective.[24]

Shabtai's second novel, *Sof davar* (*Past Perfect*), published posthumously in 1984, picks up where *Past Continuous* leaves off, in its depiction of brittle interactions, fantasies, and flirtations.[25] *Past Perfect* follows its protagonist, Meir, in his marriage, attempts at extramarital flirtation, and work in Tel Aviv, through the death of his mother and a trip to Amsterdam (during which he keeps trying unsuccessfully to find the red-light district), and then back to Tel Aviv. There, in a startling break with conventional realism, the last section of the novel seems to show Meir going back into the body of a woman to an archetypally female landscape, from which he is reborn as an infant in the very last lines of the novel.

As I read it, this is a novel about spatial relationships. *Past Perfect* plays with the concept of territorial demarcations or boundary lines on the levels of the individual, the nation, and ideology. It introduces shifts in relation to space that can be located on several maps: (1) the infant's mapping out of body image or a crude sense of self in relation to the mother: this is the determination of boundaries between self and other, out of which individual identity takes shape; (2) the more easily recognizable map of Europe, America, and the Middle East on which the street maps of Tel Aviv, Amsterdam and London are to be found; (3) the quasi-metaphysical map that differentiates Zion from Golah, homeland from Diaspora. Learning the difference between self and other, male and female, requires establishing boundaries, as does the delineation of territory that defines nations, or on an even broader scale, the metaphysical differentiation of Zion from Golah. The plot of *Past Perfect* comes out of the destabilization of relations among these three maps.

Gender becomes part of the picture here, insofar as we tend to associate masculinity with a more bounded sense of self and femininity with more flexible or permeable ego boundaries. Theorists of various persuasions would agree that the establishment of normative masculinity requires the negation of a relationship to the preOedipal mother that is fluid and unbounded.

Past Perfect gives novelistic expression to the undoing of a masculine economy through the experience of its central character, Meir. Shabtai triggers our attention with obvious signifiers of the popular construction of masculinity, such as the books Meir browses through in a Tel Aviv bookstore — *Behind the Male Myth* and *The Joy of Sex* (48, 61/46, 56), as well as the stereotypically masculine activities of minor characters in the novel whose activities amount to crude clichés: the taxi driver who's slept with a thousand women (18/21); the Turkish mover, a man who is described as resembling Marcello Mastroanni and moving with the elegance of Jean Gabin (22–24/24–26).

Meir's attention oscillates between the outward movement of attraction to women (which belongs to the cultural economy of sexuality) and an inward pull to his own bodily processes, early ties to the mother, and death. As Meir experiences slippage of his orientation in space and in relation to his own body, the delimitation of the world of the narrative unravels as well. One map displaces another: the map of the mother's body, whose boundaries are indeterminate, takes the place of the socio-political map, encompassing America, Europe, and Israel, on which modern Jewish history is inscribed. This shift becomes inescapable in the last section, where we no longer have one set of coordinates, or one recognizable plane of geography, but it is happening throughout the first three sections of the novel. As a result, conflicts between approach to and avoidance of the female body take up a lot of the novel's energy; much of the activity of the novel derives its impact from the primitive dramas of body image found in the early stages of ego development.

In *The Ego and the Id*, Freud observes that "The ego is first and fore-most a bodily ego" and furthermore, that its structure forms in reaction to the impact of experiences of loss. Here Judith Butler takes us back to the radical nature of Freud's insights through her emphasis on the shaping of identity out of the "sedimentation" of a cumulative history of experiences of the body.[26] If Freud shows us how the ego forms as a kind of crust at the point of contact between inner and outer worlds, Butler uses that insight to stress the factor of repetition of experiences through which the contours of the self are established over time. Shab-tai's novel put that process of separation and individuation into reverse gear, producing a comedy of the undoing of ego boundaries. In effect, Meir goes through an adult approximation of infantile experience—as if the novel were to allow us to imagine the infant's autoerotic absorp-tion in the body from the self-conscious perspective of an adult.

But this rich and abundantly detailed psychology of the protagonist serves as the vehicle, by means of which the reader is brought into con-tact with larger movements in the world of the fiction, shifts in political geography that exceed the dimensions of any one character's psychol-ogy. Most striking here are the ways in which the fiction links issues of gender and sexuality on the level of the individual character—Meir—to large-scale issues of nationality, territory, and ideology. Disturbances on the level of individual character correspond to the symptomatic disrup-tion of the narrative universe as a whole, undoing the polarized oppo-sition of male and female, and transgressing the borderlines of gender and identity.

This cosmopolitan novel uses the map of city streets to chart shifts and movements that are both psychological and political. Meir is a crea-ture of Tel Aviv: its street names yield a sense of place that supports indi-vidual identity, by rooting it in a sociohistorical continuum. As he makes his way through the city and feels the presence of his grandmother, his wanderings weave a unique fabric whose threads consist of maternal presence, the urban scene, and street names, loaded signifiers that carry the names of people and activities involved in the establishment of the

State of Israel. For example, in the course of two pages, Meir traverses Frishman, Sirkin, Bograshov, Shderot Ben-Zion, Kikar Habimah, Ibn-Gevirol, Kikar Ha'iriyah, Dizengoff, and Emil Zola. It is when he crosses Gordon that he imagines his grandmother turning the "corner of Smolenskin in her brown felt slippers and in her gray housedress and her big grown wool scarf around her shoulders, coming to greet him with a radiant smile full of understanding and good will" (8–11/12–14). The radiant grandmother is associated not only with a particular neighborhood, but with a nostalgic vision of the Labor Zionist past.[27] In fact, the pervasive citation of street names in the Tel Aviv sections of the novel invokes a synoptic vision of modern Jewish history; Meir's walks constitute a map that invokes the history of the Zionist settlement of the land of Israel.

Past Perfect is explicitly a post-1977, post-Likud novel, whose anatomizing of masculine desire is linked to the breakdown of the ideology of Labor Zionism.[28] In this respect, the reader's first association to the phrase, a "return to the land," is most likely to be to the ideology of labor. *Past Perfect* revises or supplements those associations, so that "return to the land" acquires a significance closer to the sense of Freud's interpretation of the *unheimlich*—the experience of the "uncanny" or "unhomelike"—which derives from repression of a relationship to the original *Heim* or home, that is, the mother's body.[29] The construction of national identity in terms of a relationship to the land discloses itself to be the uneasy product of a system of relations that sustains distance and difference from the female body. In *Past Perfect*, Shabtai gives narrative expression to the disintegration of a political-social map (Zion vs. the Golah) that is shown to depend upon a tenuously maintained set of differences and distances between male and female.

Meir effectively experiences the world through the mother, insofar as her presence anchors him in space and defines its contours for him. But the novel shows us that this mother is both the source of all security and the starting point for a pervasive insecurity that destabilizes the foundations of the fictional world. Suggestions of destabilization can be felt throughout, beginning in the first chapter, with the mother's recurring expressions of discontent with the reality of Israel in the late 1970s and her loss of the Zionist dream. Dreaming of an idyllic setting in Gibraltar where she once took a vacation, the mother refers repeatedly to Israel as the "real Golah." Although she tries to dissuade an American friend from leaving Israel to return to Miami, she voices a repeated critique of the shift from Labor to Likud: "Who would have imagined that that Begin would rule here? Ben Gurion and Berl Katznelson would turn over in their graves" (56/51).

Inasmuch as the mother forms part of the street map of Tel Aviv and the history of the State of Israel, her death is the particular stimulus that upsets a system of differentiations. With her death, spatial relations are no longer the same, as her body is nowhere and everywhere: Meir sees her floating in a dark room, then as a faint presence floating over northern Tel Aviv (137–38/114–15). He imagines an alternate space, a "land both boundless and clearly defined" (146/121), just after he sees a vision of her neatly combed, holding her copy of *To the Lighthouse* (145/120–21).[30]

Shabtai plays his own literary games as he invokes Virginia Woolf's Mrs. Ramsay, the maternal center of *To the Lighthouse*, whose death destabilizes a carefully constructed domestic universe. At the same time, the death of Meir's mother becomes the subject of a metaphysical farce, as neighbors and family gather to discuss whether or not to respect her wishes that her body be given to science and the remains cremated. " 'Where will she be? Where?' 'It's a scandal. What will become of her body? . . . A person has to be buried somewhere.' 'There has to be a grave, a person has to have a grave' " (120/101).[31]

In contrast with *To the Lighthouse*, which gives place to the mother, after her death, by incorporating the mythic image of Demeter into an English landscape, Shabtai's novel crosses Europe and returns to Israel, as it traces the undoing of the boundaries of a gendered subjectivity on the map of nations.[32] On that map, the Amsterdam of chapter 3 signifies the forbidden sexuality that Meir seeks and fears. To Meir, Amsterdam is the place of sexual dirt—sex shops and prostitutes in windows—that promises the realization of his fantasies. Instead, of course, we have the grotesque comedy of Meir's Kafkaesque experience of Amsterdam: in place of prostitutes in windows, he encounters Israelis who ask him in Hebrew for directions to the red-light district.

It is in the novel's last section that Meir falls off the map definitively, murmuring "This is the place," as he feels himself swallowed up into the body of an older female physician who has seduced him (252–53/207–8). That "place" is no longer Eretz Yisrael, but the body of the woman to which he has returned. This is not allegory, but a comedy of spatial shifts and disorientations, the pathos of a man (an Israeli "everyman," one critic called him[33]) whose moorings have gone awry. In this last section, differences disappear and with them go the demarcation lines of gender, body, and nationality.

The landscape of the concluding section resonates strongly with suggestions of an archetypal femininity.[34] In Shabtai's novelistic fantasy, the maternal body figures as the lost, but primal source of infantile pleasure, as Meir moves into a postpolitical landscape of absolute freedom, where the state has withered away and all desires find satisfaction (265–

66/218–19). Fear and anxiety fade away, as his body opens like a ripe and juicy fruit (268/220). Faced with an irresistible vista of lush hills, he removes his clothes in order to roll down them over and over (271/222). Meir reaches a grove of trees that he names the "curly forest" (276/226), and he experiences a pleasure beyond pleasure.

Feminist theory on both sides of the Atlantic assigns positive value to loosening or blurring boundary lines, to greater flexibility or permeability of borders. However different their approaches, theorists such as Nancy Chodorow and Carol Gilligan, on the one hand, and Hélène Cixous and Luce Irigaray, on the other, speak for modifications in the conception of identity as a stable, bounded configuration and point to the hyperconstructedness of masculinity as a problem in culture. "Writing belongs to woman," claims Cixous, in the sense that "woman has greater access to the other within her." Cixous responds to the rigid economy of patriarchal culture with the project of *l'écriture féminine*, the effort to write the body, loosening the boundaries of the ego, valorizing the indeterminacies in the feminine sense of self.[35]

In a manner that resonates sympathetically with these aspects of feminist theory, *Past Perfect* loosens territorial demarcations so as to show parallels on the levels of individual, nation, and ideology, the maps to which I referred. The text associates masculinity with distinct borders and masculine action with aggressive appropriation of territory—be that the female body or the claim to a national homeland. Thus, the collapse of boundary lines in this novel can be read as a challenge to territorial claims and an assertion of the value of permeability.

Maps keep things separate and assign names to them, and indeed the politics of identity requires that borders be secure. Differences are never neutral, but rather form part of hierarchies, in which one term is privileged over another. Insofar as it gives fictional form to the undoing of a system of hierarchized differences, *Past Perfect* forms part of a literary response to some of the issues and oppositions that have shaped modern Jewish history. Indeed both of Shabtai's novels form part of a significant literary initiative, insofar as the fiction prompts an interrogation of ideological constructions of body and gender, to probe a stereotype of masculinity that may have served in its time to counter negative images, but came in turn to impose burdens of its own.

While Shabtai's fiction works its way out of an oppressive masculinity, the fiction of A. B. Yehoshua engages the dynamics of gender and sexuality on an interpersonal level that resonates with implication for the history of the nation. Yehoshua's fiction invites the reader to think about mod-

ern Jewish history in light of relationships within families, a perspective
that brings to the scene of history an awareness of instinctual drives and
the workings of repression and repetition. The effect is to displace the
manifest record of public events through the disclosure of dramas of unconscious motivation. Yehoshua's fiction works a double effect: on the
one hand, it acknowledges such deep components of our experience of
narrative as the need for secure definitions and coherent accounts of
origins and differences, while, on the other hand, it prompts us to confront the denials and forgettings that go into the maintenance of those
ostensibly stable constructs.

   Molkho (1987; tr. *Five Seasons*) is a novel that takes its protagonist
through five seasons, each a section of the book, which follow the death
of Molkho's wife after a long illness.[36] Each season or section initiates
expectations of a plot of male desire in which Molkho fails to fulfill the
role of the lover that he has fantasized for himself. Instead, the novel
prompts an interrogation of gender categories and the consequences of
gender distinctions for narrative. It does so through preoccupation with
varieties of femininity, a thematics of the body, and the recurrence of
body parts in the text, not to mention the feminization of the protagonist, Molkho.

   In his stolid, unheroic manner, Molkho opens himself up to the feminine, observes its varieties, and notes it in himself, resisting all the while
masculine prototypes of action. The novel is self-consciously organized
into sections that go nowhere; they take a tour only to end up back
where they started. This double movement—both provoking and frus-
trating the reader's expectations—gives Yehoshua's novel an intriguing
position in modern Hebrew fiction, a literature that abounds in male-
authored texts that focus on ideological conflicts, demands for action
in the public domain, and the dilemmas of sons in relation to paternal
inheritances. While Yehoshua's novel acknowledges an agenda of masculine concerns, it also signals its ambivalence, marking out a movement
away from the sphere of public action to more private concerns and a
concomitant preoccupation with the body.

   The novel is set at the time of Israel's 1982 withdrawal from Lebanon,
a collective reversal of direction that receives only incidental notice
in the novel. Nevertheless, the reformulation (or reversal) of character and plot that marks this novel resonates with implication in terms
of that *national* crisis of direction. The reader's sympathetic response to
the novel may be first engaged by the texture of mundane and bodily
experience, but that microcosmic focus never loses its reference to the
larger political-social world.

   At the start of the novel, the eerie figure of the early morning bicycle rider, whose appearance punctuates the wife's death, inaugurates the play with gender that marks this text. Molkho sees the bicycle rider first as male, then female, then male (11/17–18), and associates the figure with death, as if it carries "remnants" of his wife (21/25–26). (Late in the novel, when he remembers the bicycle rider, he prefers to think of it as female [291/270].) In its suggestive recurrences, the bicycle rider constitutes a liminal figure, signalling entry into a magical space where binary oppositions between life and death, male and female are undone. These binarisms are culturally constructed oppositions that shape perception; their confusion in the figure of the bicycle rider draws the reader's attention to the beginnings of a process of decomposition in the novel.

Through the novel, Molkho "reads" the signs of a relation to a primitive body as they disrupt the more "active," explicitly "masculine" interactions that are thrust upon him. He experiences an infatuation with a young girl in a remote settlement in the Galil and, as he follows her on a mountainous path, imagines devouring her buttocks. Later, seated in the one café of the village, he orders the special of the day, to find himself served an enticing stew, in which organ meats of indeterminate origin float in a savory sauce. All of which, along with other instances of body play, suggest primitive stages of development where body outlines are indeterminate and the mouth is the primary locus for interaction with the world.

Late in the novel, Molkho sits naked in an armchair in a Vienna hotel room, gazing at himself in the mirror. Not only has he gained weight, but he notices breasts sprouting on himself (301/282). This comic feminization can be read as something of a counterpart to Yehoshua's choice of a protagonist who is of Sephardi origin, a reflection of Yehoshua's own cultural heritage to which he had not before devoted major focus.[37] Feminization extends the exploration of otherness that the choice of ethnicity begins. Issues of ethnicity and gender coincide in this novel to produce a text that challenges some Israeli stereotypes concerning the role of the Ashkenazi population in the development of the State and the dominance of that group in its political structure, along with the more general association of masculine with active and feminine with passive.

Molkho traverses a map that ranges from Israel to Paris to Berlin (East and West). It is in the last section of the novel, on the East Berlin street that he imagines to have been his wife's childhood address, that Molkho enters what the text describes as the cancerous red cell of an old elevator, imaginatively reliving his wife's girlhood. The increasingly explicit imagery of cells, organisms, and enclosures throughout the novel reaches its fullest expression here in references to "the small red cage" and the "malignant cell" of the elevator cab (345–46/331–32).[38] This East Berlin elevator cab is encrusted with the imagery of a demonic cancer, the cancer that is here understood as the return to the body with a vengeance.

When Molkho rings the bell of a randomly selected East Berlin apartment to ask about Dr. Starkmann, his wife's father, who killed himself fifty years earlier, we understand the moment to amount to enclosure in a deathly circle (346/332). Unfortunately, the English translation omits the following description of Molkho on the doorstep, at the threshhold of return: "this was the moment that he would be able to slip back into his home" (*lahamoq hazarah leveyto*). The "home" here, Yehoshua's wording suggests, is the original home or *Heim* of which Freud writes in his essay on the uncanny. Interpreting the sensation of the *unheimlich* or the "uncanny" in terms of its apparent opposite, the *heimisch* or "familiar," Freud refers to the womb as the original *Heim*, from which we all emerge. (With this bit of deconstructive play, Freud goes on to note that the feeling of the *unheimlich* may be evoked by reminders of the original *Heim*, the womb.[39])

That the point of deepest return for the Sephardi protagonist should be his wife's birthplace in East Berlin raises questions about the function of place in narrative geography. Place in *Five Seasons* has significance in a geography of the body, as well as on the map of world politics, as the play with body and body parts in the novel has the effect of disrupting the neat boundaries of adult identity, blurring distinctions between male and female. On the political-cultural level, Molkho's journey to Berlin brings the Sephardi protagonist to the birthplace of his Yekke wife, using her personal history, as well as the city's divided status, to remind the reader of Germany's Nazi past. This play of culturally loaded signifiers evokes the violent contradictions of modern European history, in a manner that is attuned to the ambivalence of Jewish participation in European culture.[40] Through Molkho the character, the novel introduces a new perspective on that cultural complex: it positions its Sephardi protagonist as the naive explorer whose journey highlights those contradictions by contrast to his very innocence of them.

This question of the place of the Sephardi brings a welcome complication to the Israel-Diaspora issue. In effect, the novel works against cultural binarisms, from the male-female split so generally pervasive, to oppositions that reflect stereotypes that have structured the history of modern Israel. The connection can be made here between Yehoshua's fiction and his more polemical essays, which argue for the chance for normalization that Israel offers to the neurotic relation of the Diaspora

Jew. To the credit of the fiction, however, it cannot be reduced to the theses of the essays. Yehoshua may set up dichotomies that resonate with political and cultural values, but the elements of the fiction resist simple identification in terms of those values. Despite the novel's use of the political geography of East and West Berlin, not to mention the landscape of Israel to which Molkho returns, the narrative resists generalization to the level of national politics, although it derives some of its power from that collective frame of reference. Thus, Molkho's homesickness (*Heimweh*) can be read as the culmination of regressive trends on the level of the individual, rather than in terms of a generalization to the collective.

The conclusion of the novel returns to language of "active" and "passive," associated with the opposition between male and female, but with a difference. Molkho indicts himself for passivity and repeats the necessity "to love," but the action of his sentence remains unresolved (358–59/346). Syntactically, it has nowhere to go. While he acknowledges a new feeling of "freedom," there is no indication of the direction it will take. The conclusion echoes ironically with the language of gender, but the nouns and verbs, subjects and objects of the gendered plots of amorous activity have lost their moorings.

While the book's five seasons may each offer a new female object to Molkho's male desire, each discloses instead the seemingly regressive journey back into the bed and the body of the woman. *Five Seasons* plays out a comedy of the diffuse body—the lost, archaic body, which seems to surface in bits and pieces (literally), here and there. Not quite the delegitimation of the Oedipal narrative, nor yet the affirmation of the pre-Oedipal, Yehoshua's novel testifies to an alteration of the text that it cannot quite assimilate.

The effect of the novel is to alter a specular narrative economy in which woman is the object of the male gaze, by admitting to the text signs of a relation to the body that transgress, exceed, and call into question gendered dichotomies. Nevertheless, far from envisioning a space free of such dichotomies, *Five Seasons* retains its links to an identifiable social world in which masculine and feminine continue to name a hierarchized set of oppositions.

We know that Yehoshua wrote *Five Seasons* in intervals, as he was working on *Mr. Mani* (published in 1990), but if we read one text alongside the other, what is the result?[41] I have suggested that each of *Five Seasons*' five sections initiates and frustrates a plot of masculine desire; along with the eruption of body parts into the text and the recovery of an archaic relationship to the maternal body, the novel plays with dichotomies of East and West, Sephardi and European. As such, *Five Seasons* complements *Mr. Mani*'s more direct engagement with the substance of historical narrative.

Mr. Mani suggests a fable, or more precisely perhaps, an antifable of gender and nationalism. To explain what I mean by antifable, let me call to mind Freud's speculative tale, his fable as it were, of the tyrannical father and the primal horde, as related in *Totem and Taboo, Moses and Monotheism,* and elsewhere. This psychoanalytic myth provides an account of the origins of human society whose narrative elements—father, sons, hatred, aggression, and love—are those that comprise the conceptual universe of classical psychoanalytic theory. Freud's tale of origins establishes an Oedipal scenario in which masculinity takes shape.[42]

Mr. Mani can be read as a reformulation or a disruption of a myth of the male hero. The novel takes a counter-direction, as it moves backward in time through five sections, each of which is located at a historically significant moment. Its reverse chronology, the omission of the auditor's response to each of its five speakers, and the confused and confusing repetitions within and among the sections all suggest narrative strategies aimed at disrupting and complicating simple models of identity or action. The *kivun negdi* or counter-direction of the Manis is to go against the consolidation of sexual, religious, or national identities and against the aggressive defense of those identities. *Mr. Mani* is thus a historical novel in that it engages the *errors* that are an inevitable component in the construction of historical narrative. Not only does it reformulate or disrupt a myth of the male hero, it extends its subversive critique to the large-scale consolidations of nationality that took place in Europe toward the end of the last century. The whole thrust of Yehoshua's fiction is to work against totalizing concepts, which form the basis for fictions of identity that claim absolute difference between self and other.

Contact with members of the Mani family in each generation disrupts the ideological assumptions of the speaker-narrator in each section of the novel. The speakers are themselves the subjects of the narrative, despite their disclaimers. Yehoshua's half-dialogues impose upon us as readers all the false starts, hesitations, and repetitions that characterize the utterances of each of the five speakers. We are made to imagine the responses (or failures to respond) of each of their auditors; our sympathies shift not only from speaker to auditor, but also to the figures who populate each speaker's tale. The dialogic possibilities multiply, if we begin to consider the number of angles from which one can approach this text.

With Hagar's imagined life in her womb, Yehoshua initiates a thematics of the female body that recurs in a variety of transformations through the novel's five sections. Thus the second section of the novel (set in

Crete, 1944) brings us the discourse of Egon Bruner, the young German soldier who offers a theory of the purifying womb of culture to his grandmother and to us as readers. Both Hagar and Egon are in error, but their errors are productive in reorienting our reading by indirection to the inevitability of distortion in any effort to understand and to narrate. Furthermore, Egon's wrongheadedness acquires powerful resonances, as we think about his theory of the "womb of civilization" in light of the history of ideologies of race and nationality.

With his plunge from the airplane into the "blue womb" of the Mediterranean (88/95), "from the belly of the plane to the void of the world" (101/107), Egon Bruner restages the encounter of German with ancient Greek, the scene of an appropriation of a "landscape" in service of a narrative of national identity. For Egon that *nof* or landscape is "the place from which our Europe was born" (84/91) and he recounts his plunge into the *rehem*, the womb of culture, of which his teacher, the old classicist Koch, taught him.

As Egon stumbles into the "legendary labyrinth" of Knossos (94/100), he feels close to the Führer and to his old teacher Koch in understanding their common search for the ancient origin (*hamakor hakadum*) from which they construct the possibility of the birth of a "new man" (95/101).[43] It becomes evident that, despite his claim to correcting an old error—the move of German culture toward the east, as opposed to south and "back into the bluish womb of the Mediterranean" (115/119) —Egon's effort to purify German barbarism through immersion in classical culture merely repeats the error in another idiosyncratic variant. Much of Egon's theorizing can be traced to elements of nineteenth-century ideological trends such as the German conception of the *Volk* and the romantic view of Greece as the pure childhood of Europe.[44]

Egon's theorizing uses images of the body that are intelligible in terms of infantile sexuality, as well as in the context of large-scale political movements. Thus, for example, Egon describes his effort to "go out once and for all outside of history whether from the front or from the rear" (*'im melifanim ve'im me'ahor*) (93/99). His vocabulary—"belly," "womb," "from the front or from the rear"—suggests a primitive map of the body that verges on the cloacal. Through this vocabulary of the body, Egon's discourse mixes elements of infantile sexuality into his vision of national redemption.[45]

Egon speaks of recovering the "culture that is before culture" (*hatarbut shelifne hatarbut*) (116/120), that is really his own appropriation of a female ground in service of a narrative of national salvation. Indeed Egon's vocabulary, particularly with respect to gender, carries with it resonances reminiscent of Freud's efforts to write about the pre-Oedipal phase of development. Freud suggests something like the notion of a "culture before culture," in the sense that the Oedipal crisis remained in the foreground of his theorizing, while he acknowledged, at least for girls, the importance of the more shadowy pre-Oedipal period that lies behind it. Freud writes, "Our insight into this early, pre-Oedipus phase in girls comes to us as a surprise, like the discovery, in another field, of the Minoan-Mycenaean civilization behind the civilization of Greece."[46] Drawing on his favorite metaphor of archaeology, Freud uses the distinction between the Minoan-Mycenaean and classical Greek civilizations to mark the distinction between the pre-Oedipal (the shadowy domain of attachment to the mother) and the Oedipal. Freud's metaphors trace graphically his approach to (and avoidance of) the unknown territory of the archaic maternal body, a region remote from his experience and consequently from his theorizing.

Yehoshua's use of a German speaker who refers repeatedly to Minoan civilization as a precursor to Europe may well serve to remind us of the historical context in which Freud developed *his* analogy between the psychoanalytic and the archaeological. Egon Brunner's plan for national redemption through return to an archaic womb reflects nineteenth-century European appropriations of classical culture in service of myths of racial purity and national identity. That revisioning of classical culture was fueled in part by such developments as Heinrich Schliemann's purported excavations of Troy in 1876 and the excavations of Sir Arthur Evans in 1900 at Knossos to which *Mr. Mani* explicitly refers.

The spellbinding tale of Yosef Mani, his head protruding from an urn like that of a wise snake, mingles the story of archaeologists (*sippur hahofrim*) with the story of what they uncovered (*sippur hanehparim*) (102/108). Yosef Mani's account of Sir Arthur Evans (1851–1941) and his discovery of Minoan civilization (so named, by Evans, after Minos, the designer of the labyrinth) may stimulate the reader's awareness of the use of an archaic prehistory to provide a foundation for the emergence of European culture.[47] Cumulatively, the effect of this layering is to remind us that historical narrative is shaped by the bias of its practitioners. Yehoshua finds his own narrative path to a critique of the racist bias of nineteenth-century classical scholarship, insofar as Egon's theory suggests a parody of the German appropriation of elements of classical civilization in support of a myth of racial purity. The novel prompts us to go even further to observe that the activity of narration itself involves the appropriation of unknown territory that may resist incorporation into a narrative frame.

In Egon's Minoan journey into the labyrinth, he is guided by the figure of the Jew, the wise serpent in the urn, who lectures "with enthusiasm on an early civilization lacking guilt and fear" (118/122).[48] (Putting on Yosef Mani's glasses leads Egon to the experience of seeing things as if from the wrong end of telescope: yet another signal of the "perspectivism" that is so important to the novel.) The labyrinth itself suggests the challenge of mastering a body—earth—that is identified as feminine.[49] Thus, in Yehoshua's version of the Daedalean myth of the maze as historical comedy, it is the Jew who leads Egon back into the body of the mother, in order to achieve the rebirth of Germany out of its Mediterranean womb. In search of a solution to the catastrophe of modern Germany (e.g., 116/120), Egon seizes upon Yosef Mani's notion of the Jew who has negated himself and finds in it an instructive model for his own perverse project—purification of "the bluish womb [*bet hareḥem hakehalḥal*] to which we [Germans] are returning" (123/127). In Egon's reasoning, "race" (*gezaʿ*) is a metaphor for nature (*tevaʿ*), which is the essence of "human and national character" (124/128).

The idea of an essential Germanic character was central to the ideology of the *Volk*, as it developed in Germany in the nineteenth century.[50] We should remind ourselves, in this respect, that nineteenth-century nationalism drew upon new forms of scientific racism—including racial antisemitism—to supply the necessary counterparts or antitypes to positive stereotypes of national identity.[51] Using Hitler's warning of the necessity of ferreting out "the Jew within each one of us," Egon classifies the Jews as "laboratory animals" on whom Germans can test out what they are as yet afraid to carry out on their own flesh; they offer an opportunity for the German to find out "if it's worthwhile to return to the point of origin and to become again *man, new man* who has negated the shell of history, that stuck to him like ugly scales" (128/131). In Egon's scheme of national salvation through a return to origins, the Jew figures as the atavistic creature, a scaly monster on the path to a master race. Thus Egon functions for a while as a tour guide, whose goal is not so much to take visitors through the labyrinth as it is to show them a "possible goal" for Europe in the example of the Jew who has negated himself (130/132–33).

With the flight of the members of Yosef Mani's family, Egon becomes possessed by the idea of finding them, lest they "continue to befoul our pure, blue womb" (137/139).[52] This notion of a womb befouled, of the Jew as the contaminant of a pure body, underscores the link between Jew and body; Egon's myth of Aryan redemption though classical culture rests on a metaphorized womb. In this schema, the Jew, not surprisingly, retains an association to the body, which is resistant to the move of metaphor. The notion of "negating" the Jew that so engages Egon positions the Jew as an ongoing component in the construction of cultural myth — a fleshly other associated with a primitive relationship to the body.[53]

The conjunction of the Jew and the feminine in the excavation (or appropriation) of an archaic past is a particularly striking feature of this section of *Mr. Mani*. Here, feminist inquiry into Freud's writing may help in understanding the workings of gender in the metaphors that shape the exploration of "unknown territory." Commenting on Freud's use of the term "Minoan-Mycenaean" as an analogy for the girl's pre-Oedipal attachment to her mother, Sarah Kofman argues that Freud imposes an order of priority on material that resists that move toward a cultural hierarchy. She reminds us that the historians of Freud's day saw Minoan-Mycenaean culture as

a simple *preface*, external to Greek history; in the same way, the preoedipal period was seen as merely a preamble to the Oedipus complex . . . [But] whether one takes the preoedipal period to be a preface to the Oedipus stage or as the first chapter of its history, . . . the gesture of dominance remains the same: in both cases one loses the specificity, the radical strangeness of the totally other, one overcomes the astonishing "surprise" that the discovery of feminine sexuality elicited if one reinstates it within the process of a history that *must* lead to the Oedipus complex in every case.

While Kofman is concerned to show how Freud's writing evades the radical otherness of feminine sexuality, her analysis of his historical analogy also draws our attention to a mode of structuring a relationship to the mother's body that is deeply embedded in culture. Not only does "Freud's heroic model" continue "to be Oedipus," as she puts it, but his use of the historical and cultural ordering of the Minoan-Mycenaean as preface to the classical Greek supports the linear narrative of the Oedipal hero.[54] It is the use of this Oedipal model to shape historical narrative that Yehoshua's novel challenges.

Freud's use of the Minoan-Mycenaean analogy posits a suggestive link between the archaeological effort to retrieve buried origins and the impulse to recover an archaic maternal body. This old association of femininity with the land leads to an interpretation of nationalism as a reinvention of origins that appropriates the mother's body, using stereotypical associations of masculine with active and feminine with passive. From this perspective, putatively historical tales of origins that are used to bolster assertions of national identity have the function of structuring a relation to an archaic female body. *Mr. Mani* is a historical novel in that it engages the errors that are an inevitable component in the construction of historical narrative.[55] Through a reading of recurring errors, the reader becomes aware of the repeated return to the site of the female body that produces the never-to-be-completed or stabilized theorizing of the womb.

The thematics of the womb makes its most striking appearance in the third section of the novel; here, we are introduced to Dr. Moshe Mani's obstetrics clinic, where mirrored images multiply, displace, and distort the scene of birth. This spectacular setting underscores both the difficulties of seeing and the confusion of images of the female body. In the mirrored birthing scene that lies at the heart of this section, we find a description of the twelve-year-old Yosef Mani who is "turned to stone" (*me'uban*), as he stands before the open womb of a woman in labor (168/168).[56] Given the nature of the scene, the term *me'uban* here recalls inescapably Freud's comment on the power of the head of Medusa to turn men to stone and his interpretation of that petrifying power in terms of the castration fear that men feel at the sight of the female genitalia. "The terror of Medusa is thus a terror of castration that is linked to the sight of something," writes Freud; "it occurs when a boy, who has hitherto been unwilling to believe the threat of castration, catches sight of the female genitals, probably those of an adult, surrounded by hair, and essentially those of his mother . . . The sight of Medusa's head makes the spectator stiff with terror, turns him to stone."[57]

Freud's brief note on the Medusa's head has received a degree of attention that may be due more to its attribution of horror to the female genitalia and its association of the female body with castration than to any inherent theoretical importance. Nonetheless, reading Freud's text in light of contemporary gender studies should jolt us into awareness of the exclusively masculine perspective from which Freud interprets the Medusa's head. (Hélène Cixous offers an alternative reading in "The Laugh of the Medusa."[58]) From the perspective of male development, one can say that a properly achieved masculinity uses castration fear as one of its components; this is true in the sense that normative masculinity rests, in part, upon the negation of the feminine. Insofar as this scene of *Mr. Mani* brings to mind Freud's brief text, the novel replays a set of very provocative associations. In the mirrored birthing room of *Mr. Mani*, that masculine scenario lends itself to a variation—the birth of the *homo politicus* as a response to the sight of a birthing woman's womb—that remains nevertheless within the purview of Freud's reading of the Medusa's head.

According to the speaker of this section, Yosef Mani regards this moment as his political birth, the birth of the *homo politicus*, (or, as Malka Shaked puts it in her fine article on this subject, from "libidinal" to "political"[59]). With this move of displacement from the female body, the sight of which so traumatized the twelve-year-old boy, Yosef Mani's narrative brings into the foreground the infusion of the sexual into the political, or more precisely, the derivation of the political from infantile sexuality.

If we follow through, as the narrative invites us to do, on the political history of Yosef Mani, we find more than a hint of displacement or perversion in the description of him as a man who is interested not so much in women as in words (163/163). Indeed that detachment or displacement from the feminine is later expressed as a fear of being swallowed up by a womb that is described as the mouth of a predatory animal (*rehem* as *lo'a*) (175/174). Innuendoes concerning his sexuality correspond to his wandering through Palestine as a young man in the early years of the century, roaming among various types of people, collecting languages "as if they were keys to a house with many doors" (172/172).

In fact, the politics of language use and choice comes up in the novel as a further ramification of issues of identity and nationality. Moving backward in time, and forward in our reading of the novel, we find that the clinic of Dr. Mani, the "Sephardi gynecologist" (260/249–50), appears as a polyglot microcosm mingling women of all nationalities, a confusion of boundaries of all sorts that can be linked to the impact of the gaping womb on Yosef, as the son of Dr. Mani.[60] For both Dr. Mani and his son Yosef, the political can be understood as a form of response to the feminine, or more precisely, as the construction of a response to the womb—whether that response expresses itself in the establishment of an obstetrics clinic that serves women of all nationalities or in the political agitation of a self-described *homo politicus*.[61]

Furthermore, Yehoshua makes us aware of the role of language in the construction of national identity: this Hebrew novel mimics not only German, but stages in the development of modern Hebrew, and, through the Manis, plays with the idea of a profusion of tongues that would defeat any identification of language with nationality.[62] Indeed, the last section of the novel maps the travels of Avraham Mani, as he covers the Mediterranean and its Asian and European contiguities before the era of nationstates, while his son/grandson, "little Moses," who is nursed by women of all nationalities, grows up amid a profusion of languages (311/296; 312/299).

At the risk of using an anachronistic term, I find suggestions here of a radical multiculturalism that would resist any consolidation into national groupings. But while the Manis serve as a means of challenging dominant ideologies of whatever sort, they do not themselves offer any viable alternatives. The movement of the novel's five sections, backward in time from 1982 to 1848, has the effect of amplifying the historical record, not by correcting any fact, but by supplying an account of processes that lie underneath or behind the public record.

The counter-direction of the Manis finds its roots deep in the family, in layers of experience and relationship that are prior to the establishment of boundaries and definitions of sexuality and gender. And yet, Yehoshua makes it hard for the reader to find the subject of his narrative, to read the repetition from section to section of "something" that the narrative itself never encapsulates, or decodes. Here, the dialogic serves to conceal, forcing upon the reader labors of reconstruction, reading between the lines, and ultimately, thematizing the repetitions. What gets thematized here are elements of culture that derive from the child's perception of mysteries of sexuality—womb, coitus, and a confusion of objects—whose recurrence does not bring them into greater clarity, but rather reminds us of their inevitable confusion. The novel engages us in a demonstration—a reading—of the confusion, secrecy, and error that enter into constructions of the female body and of sexuality; it prompts our awareness of the function of those confusions and errors in our reading of modern Jewish history.

The novels of Shabtai and Yehoshua engage in demystifications of history and ideology, through their attentiveness to the processes out of which definitions of difference take shape. I have focused on these two writers because their writing exploits indeterminacy in particularly productive ways, but the challenge to ideologies of masculinity that I find in their work can be found in the fiction of other writers as well. Recent novels by Amos Oz try to move in this direction, on a conscious level at least, although my suspicion is that they merely shift their andro- or phallocentrism to another scene. *To Know a Woman* and *Fima* develop protagonists who attempt to reverse social trends and to reject dominant conceptions of masculinity, but the narratives of both novels remain caught up in conventional gender alignments.[63]

In contrast, David Grossman's *The Book of Intimate Grammar* (1991) yields images of the body as grotesque that reflect a conscious move away from the ideologically constructed "body"—the idealized virility— of twentieth-century Zionism.[64] This novel ends with its adolescent protagonist locking himself in a refrigerator on the eve of the Six-Day War. By valorizing the private world of the child's experience of the body and resisting puberty as the point of access to the public stage of masculinity, Grossman's grotesque works to reject the construction of masculinity that brings with it a call to action and an identification with the collective. In different ways, Oz and Grossman use fiction to give expression to discomforts with gender roles, although the world of the fiction remains within those paradigmatic alignments.

Here one might add a word on S. Yizhar's recent autobiographical novels, in particular, *Tzalhavim* (which can be roughly translated as "bright light"), which focuses on a trio of adolescent boys in the period just before the War of Independence.[65] This 1993 novel yields an exposition of states of mind, rendering the boys' doubts, hopes, and moments of loyalty and rebellion, without ever questioning the gender alignments that sustain those assumptions. While the boys are transient figures on an ever-present landscape, that view of the impermanence of human life does not destabilize gender roles that remain anchored in a political context requiring particular modes of behavior. Indeed, in a recent interview, Yizhar, himself a prominent member of the generation that came of age with the State, comments on the loss of "a sense of community that takes precedence over your own needs." Describing his parents' immigrant generation as one which thought of its children "as a kind of agricultural experiment," material out of which "the ideal young Israeli" might be shaped, Yizhar nevertheless acknowledges that the three young protagonists of *Tzalhavim* can be characterized in terms of their "willing acceptance of a yoke that came from belonging to something larger than oneself."[66] The boys may express confusion, but that confusion is the product of the demands of a volatile political situation and corresponding relationships within the family. Each boy must come to terms with his father and a set of male expectations that each may resent, but no one of them ever questions the inevitability of their entry and eventual membership in that male order.

Recent years have seen the emergence of new women writers on the Israeli literary scene. The challenges and difficulties of finding a voice energize the work of these writers. Judith Katzir, Savyon Liebrecht, and Orly Castel-Bloom develop an angle of vision that acknowledges the public arena of history as an incidental dimension of the fictional universe, rather than its primary focus. Moreover, a recent novel by Castel-Bloom goes further as it engages public myths of the State and mixes them up with deeply held conceptions of the mother-child relationship, to produce a brilliant melange of satiric images. Castel-Bloom's *Dolly City* takes on the sacrosanct values of woman as mother and of nationality as rooted in the land and proceeds to subject them to grotesque inflation. The effect is a comic demystification of fictions of corporate identity that sustain ideologies of gender and nation.[67]

Dr. Dolly finds an infant whom she takes on and names *ben* (son). This adoptive mother then finds herself overwhelmed by what the text calls an ungovernable "maternal impulse" (*dahaf 'imahi*) to protect the child from all illnesses and to ward off all dangers to the body. In a series of maternal frenzies, Dolly claims the territory of the child's body: she innoculates him all at once with every possible vaccine and, driven further by her anxiety to verify the health of his internal organs, performs repeated operations on him. This territorializing of the body moves into the domain of the manifestly political, when Dr. Dolly performs a series of incisions, by means of which she inscribes the map of Biblical Israel on the infant's back: "I gazed at the cut up back [*bagav hehatukh*]: it was the map of Eretz Yisrael, there was no mistaking it" (p. 29). Later in the novel, Dolly looks at the 13-year-old boy's back in order to identify him; she finds the same map that she had drawn earlier, but is startled to notice that it has gone back to pre-1967 borders (pp. 88–89). The relationship of mother to child, in which the boundaries between self and other are first worked out, becomes the structure within which political boundaries are established. The child's body, subject to the mother's intrusive actions, offers a microcosmic version of large-scale political conflicts. The effect is to poke fun at boundary-making activities at whatever level they occur.

At another point, the novel takes on A. D. Gordon, a major figure in the development of Jewish nationalism, whose ideology of labor promoted what David Biale describes as a "mystical union of the physical body of the worker with the cosmos."[68] A. D. Gordon puts in a cameo appearance in *Dolly City* as a would-be organic farmer who invites Dolly to inject chlorophyll in her veins to experience what she later refers to as a "chlorophyll trip" (pp. 61–62). In Castel-Bloom's vision, the political rhetoric of fulfillment through the land reaches a startling and yet logical culmination. Her imagination seizes upon and intermingles deeply held conceptions of the mother-child relationship and the notion of "territory" as both body and homeland.[69] With satiric verve, she pushes them to absurd limits that also disclose to us the underlying interdependence of these frames of reference.

To conclude, the political project of the novels I have discussed involves destabilizing fixed conceptions of identity, in part by exposing the roots of their formation and development. In her critique of identity politics, Judith Butler argues for altering the way that we conceptualize identity in terms of coherence, stable boundaries, self-sameness, and I'd like to close with a comment on the relevance of this project to developments in the work of some recent writers of Hebrew fiction. From the perspective that I have been pursuing, modern Jewish history yields a series of shifting positions—identities—occupied by the figure of the Jew, insofar as the Zionist concept of the "new Jew" can be read as a reformulation of the feminized Jewish male who was, in turn, the abjected counterpart to the idealized virility of European nationalisms.

Recent Israeli writers interrogate without dislodging the relation of Zion to Golah, homeland to Diaspora, that has shaped the Jewish imagination for millenia. These writers have not repudiated the conception of Israel as a nation, choosing instead to challenge conceptions of national identity that derive from oppositions between the Land and a geo-graphical space defined as "outside" or "elsewhere." In the fiction of these writers, we can read signs of the working out of a further stage in the politics of Jewish national identity, in ways that are not direct or programmatic, but rather exploratory. Discomforts with existing cate-gories manifest themselves in the fiction in unexpected ways. The effect is a play of possibilities that resists subordination to particular agen-das. These novels open themselves up to exploration of a shared past in which readers might even be able to discern their own implication in history, historical fictions, and fictions of identity that are both indi-vidual and collective.

Notes

1. For a history of constructions of the body and sexual difference, see Wal-ter Laqueur, *Making Sex: Body and Gender from the Greeks to Freud* (Cambridge: Harvard University Press, 1990).

2. See the following books by Sander Gilman: *Difference and Pathology: Stereo-types of Sexuality, Race, and Madness* (Ithaca: Cornell University Press, 1985); *Jewish Self-Hatred: Anti-Semitism and the Hidden Language of the Jews* (Baltimore: The Johns Hopkins University Press, 1986); *The Jew's Body* (New York: Routledge, 1991).

3. Judith Butler, *Gender Trouble: Feminism and the Subversion of Identity* (New York: Routledge, 1990); *Bodies That Matter: On the Discursive Limits of "Sex"* (New York: Routledge, 1993).

4. Butler, *Bodies That Matter*, p. 3.

5. George Mosse, *Toward the Final Solution: A History of European Racism* (New York: Howard Fertig, 1978). See esp. pp. 28, 34, 36, 39, 42–43, and 48.

6. George Mosse, *Nationalism and Sexuality: Respectability and Abnormal Sexu-ality in Modern Europe* (New York: Howard Fertig, 1985).

7. As an update of old stereotypes, the image of the feminized male Jew drew upon medieval myths of the menstruating male Jew.

8. Echoes can be heard here of the cult of manliness that infused German youth groups.

9. Michael Berkowitz, *Zionist Culture and West European Jewry Before the First World War* (Cambridge: Cambridge University Press, 1993), ch. 5, examines the social-material forms through which Zionism shaped Jewish consciousness in Europe.

10. David Biale, *Eros and the Jews: From Biblical Israel to Contemporary America* (New York: Basic Books, 1992), pp. 176–78.

11. On the theme of the *akedah* in modern Hebrew literature, see David Jacobson, *Modern Midrash: The Retelling of Traditional Jewish narratives by Twentieth-Century Hebrew Writers* (Albany: State University of New York Press, 1987); Stanley Nash, "Israeli Fathers and Sons Revisited," *Conservative Judaism* 38, no. 4 (1986): 28–37.

12. Otto Weininger, *Sex and Character*, tr. from sixth German edition (Lon-don: William Heinemann; New York: G. P. Putnam, 1909).

13. According to the logic of classification, they must be allowed to develop to the extent of fulfilling their race and type. Thus, separation and differentiation of the Jews from the nations of Europe will improve the "health" of Jews and Christians alike. Within their assigned borders, each group will be better able to fulfill its type. Max Nordau, *Zionistische Schriften* (Koln: Judischen Verlag, 1909); *Ketavim tsioniyim: Ne'umim vema'amarim*, (Hebrew trans. of Nordau), trans. B. Netanyahu, 4 vols. (Jerusalem: The Jewish Agency, 1954–62).

14. See Berkowitz, *Zionist Culture*, pp. 137–39.

15. See Berkowitz, *Zionist Culture*; Vicki Caron, "The Ambivalent Legacy: The Impact of Enlightenment and Emancipation on Zionism," *Judaism* 38, no. 4 (1989): 502–16; and Anita Shapira, "Reality and Ethos; Attitudes toward Power in Zionism," in *Vision Confronts Reality: Historical Perspectives on the Contemporary Jewish Agenda*, ed. R. Kozodoy, D. Sidorsky, and K. Sultanik (Rutherford, N.J.: Fairleigh Dickinson University Press, 1989).

16. Yaakov Shabtai, *Zikhron devarim* (Tel Aviv: Hakibbutz hameuchad, 1977); *Past Continuous*, trans. Dalya Bilu (New York: Schocken Books, 1985). Subsequent references appear in the text. Page reference is given first for the English translation/then for the Hebrew original.

17. At other points in the novel, the homosexual underpinnings of these relations come to the fore as Israel and Caesar urinate together (26/23), or as Israel, visiting Goldman in his bedroom, recalls their boyhood initiation into sex via mutual masturbation (73–74/57). See also 80–82/62–63.

18. See Luce Irigaray, *Speculum of the Other Woman*, trans. Gillian C. Gill (Ithaca: Cornell University Press, 1985).

19. Sigmund Freud, *The Standard Edition of the Complete Psychological Works*, trans. James Strachey, with Anna Freud, Alix Strachey, and Alan Tyson, 24 vols. (London: The Hogarth Press and the Institute of Psycho-analysis, 1974), vol. 19, *The Ego and the Id* [1923].

20. Sigmund Freud, *Standard Edition*, vol. 7, *Three Essays on the Theory of Sexuality* [1905]. Yael Feldman analyzes the overbearing fathers and neurotic sons that can be found in Israeli fiction of the 1970s. See Feldman, "Back to Vienna: Zionism on the Literary Couch," in *Vision Confronts Reality*, ed. R. Kozodoy, D. Sidorsky, and K. Sultanik.

21. Nissim Calderon takes note of the gap between the reality of the "sons'" existences and the *eqronot* or principles that provide the "fathers" with a standard. Caesar, Israel, and Goldman lack such principles, never manage to complete an action, and fear choice. Nissim Calderon, "Until the Seventeenth of May" (in Hebrew), *Siman qri 'ah* 10 (1980): 431–37.

22. Yisrael Cohen estimates that the novel encompasses forty years and four generations. Yisrael Cohen, "Accents and Punctuation Marks for Literature" (in Hebrew), *Moznayim* 5–6 (1980): 340–47. The time spans themselves are, of course, suggestive. Is Shabtai drawing on this association of nine months with birth when he writes *Sof davar* (*Past Perfect*)? Is the forty-year reach of the novel an ironic reference to the wandering in the desert prior to entry into the promised land?

23. For the full text of the *Somnium*, with notes and commentary interpreting it as an allegory that contains scientific theory, see John Lear, *Kepler's Dream, With the Full Text and Notes of Somnium, Sive Astronomia Lunaris, Joannis Kepleri*, trans. Patricia Frueh Kirkwood (Berkeley: University of California Press, 1965).

24. In light of this reading, I tend to disagree with Yael Feldman's contention

that the overbearing fathers and neurotic sons of Israeli fiction in the 1970s lead to the conclusion that the "Zionist normalcy" sought by the founding fathers has not managed to endure. (See Feldman, "Back to Vienna," pp. 329–30.) That reading limits the fiction to a referentiality that overlooks its value as a medium for exploring intrapsychic, as well as social-cultural conflicts. Zipporah Kagan produces a more optimistic reading of the novel by placing it in the social-historical context of the transition from Eastern Europe to the land of Israel. While she acknowledges the bleak and harsh landscape of the novel, she argues that the language of the novel embodies a flow of memory that is epic in scope and offers an "epic promise," suggesting that novel is simply one chapter in an ongoing historical process. (Zipporah Kagan, "The Tangled Roots of Existence in Yaakov Shabtai's Novel *Past Continuous*" (in Hebrew), 'Alei siyah 9: 71–74.)

25. Yaakov Shabtai, *Sof davar* (Israel: Siman qri'ah, Hakibbutz hameuchad, 1984); *Past Perfect*, trans. Dalya Bilu (New York: Viking Penguin, 1987). Subsequent references appear in the text. Page reference is given first for the English translation/then for the Hebrew original.

26. In *Gender Trouble*, Butler observes that "Gender is the repeated stylization of the body, a set of repeated acts within a highly rigid regulatory frame that congeal over time to produce the appearance of substance, of a natural sort of being" (p. 33).

27. Yaakov Freund observes that the negation of the myth of contemporary Israel comes at the cost of an idealization of the Jewish past. Yaakov Freund, "*Olamam shel ha'erim hu 'ehad: Shabtai umashber hatoda'ah hayisra'elit: 'iyunim besof davar,'*" ("Shabtai and the Crisis of Israeli Consciousness: A Study of *Past Perfect*" [in Hebrew]) *Moznayim* 58 (1985): 51–52.

28. Ephraim Kreitzler observes that the novel is crowded with members of Mapai and traces the decline of the Labor movement. Ephraim Kreitzler, "*He-'arot lasefer 'Sof davar' me'et Yaakov Shabtai*," 'Amudim 484 (1986): 189–92.

29. Sigmund Freud, *The Standard Edition*, vol. 17, *The Uncanny* [1919].

30. Consider the quiz he puts himself through at the end of the first section: Would you give five years of your life to spend one day with mother? Ten years? Fifteen? Giving voice to the infantile components of adult experience, Meir tries to measure the unmeasurable.

31. In Hebrew, the verb *titgalgel* carries a sense of the transmigration of souls.

32. For a study of the figure of Demeter in *To the Lighthouse*, see Anne Golomb Hoffman, "Demeter and Poseidon: Fusion and Distance in *To the Lighthouse*," *Studies in the Novel* 16, ii (Summer 1984): 182–96.

33. See Yaakov Freund (1985), pp. 51–52.

34. In *Three Essays*, Freud paints a theoretical portrait of a blissful infant at the breast as the prototype of sexual pleasure, never to be experienced as intensely again (cf. 209–10H).

35. Nancy Chodorow, *Feminism and Psychoanalytic Theory* (New Haven: Yale University Press, 1989). Hélène Cixous and Catherine Clement, *The Newly Born Woman*, trans. Betsy Wing (Minneapolis: University of Minnesota Press, 1986). Carol Gilligan, *In a Different Voice: Psychological Theory and Women's Development* (Cambridge, Mass.: Harvard University Press, 1982). Luce Irigaray, *This Sex Which Is Not One*, trans. Catherine Porter with Carolyn Burke (Ithaca: Cornell University Press, 1985).

36. A. B. Yehoshua, *Molkho* (Jerusalem: Keter, 1987); *Five Seasons*, trans.

Hillel Halkin (New York: Doubleday, 1989). Reference is made first to the page in the English translation/then to the page in the Hebrew original.

37. In an interview with Avraham Balaban, Yehoshua acknowledged the impact of his father's death, in 1982, in determining his own artistic turn to a more personal past (*Hadoar*, 14 December 1990). Nevertheless, he also notes, in an interview with Yaakov Besser, the ultimate absurdity of the demand that a writer represent his ethnicity. Yaakov Besser, "Mani—Who Am I in the Big Debate?" (in Hebrew) *'Iton 77* 14 (May–June 1990): 28.

38. Halkin works up the metaphor a bit, when he refers to a small room in the West Berlin pension as the "original cell" from which the hotel had grown (336). The Hebrew refers to "haheder harishon haqadmon" (the original ancient room) (321).

39. "It often happens that neurotic men declare that they feel there is something uncanny about the female genital organs. This *unheimlich* place, however, is the entrance to the former *Heim* [home] of all human beings, to the place where each one of us lived once upon a time and in the beginning. There is a joking saying that 'Love is homesickness'; and whenever a man dreams of a place or a country and says to himself, while he is still dreaming: 'this place is familiar to me, I've been here before', we may interpret the place as being his mother's genitals or her body. In this case too, then, the *unheimlich* is what was once *heimisch*, familiar; the prefix '*un*' is the token of repression" (Freud, *Standard Edition*, vol. 17, p. 245).

40. S. Y. Agnon figures as a significant literary predecessor for Yehoshua's exploration of the contradictions that inform the relationship of German Jews to German culture. See S. Y. Agnon, *Shira* (Tel Aviv and Jerusalem: Schocken, 1978); *Shira*, trans. Zeva Shapiro (New York, Schocken, 1989). See also the chapter on Shira and German-Jewish culture in my *Between Exile and Return: S. Y. Agnon and the Drama of Writing* (Albany: State University of New York Press, 1991).

41. A. B. Yehoshua, *Mar Mani* (Ramat Gan: Hakibbutz hameuchad, 1990); *Mr. Mani*, trans. Hillel Halkin (New York: Doubleday, 1992). Subsequent references appear in the text. Reference is made first to the page in the English translation/then to the page in the Hebrew original.

42. Freud comments on the invention of the "heroic myth": "The hero was a man who by himself had slain the father—the father who still appeared in the myth as a totemic monster. Just as the father had been the boy's first ideal, so in the hero who aspires to the father's place the poet now created the first ego ideal." From the narrative of the tyrannical father and the primal horde, Freud goes on to describe the production of a "heroic myth" in which the epic poet tells a tale of the hero's opposition to paternal tyranny that allows his listeners to identify with the position of hero. Freud's speculations suggest some of the narrative activities that support and reinforce the cultural constitution of masculinity. Sigmund Freud, *The Standard Edition*, vol. 18, *Group Psychology and the Analysis of the Ego*, [1921], pp. 136–37.

43. Caught up in this fantasy, it is easy for him to experience the two hills near the labyrinth, the two "Charley's" or breasts in the Australian's phrase, as if he were falling "into the bosom of a beloved woman" (111/115).

44. The ideology of the *Volk* in Germany emphasized an ideal of nature that was located in a specific regional landscape, thus supplying the land in which the *Volk* might feel itself "rooted." Egon shifts the "landscape" to Crete, but his

thinking appears to run parallel to Volkish ideology. See George Mosse, *The Crisis of German Ideology: The Intellectual Origins of the Third Reich* (New York: Grosset & Dunlap, 1964), p. 17. Martin Bernal refers to "the new Romantic concern with ethnicity, current in German and British society in the late 18th century, that brought with it admiration for particular landscapes and the primitive folk who were molded by them." He observes that "space remained important for the Romantics, because of their concern for the local formation of peoples or 'races.' Thus a race was believed to change its form as it passed through different ages, but always to retain an immutable individual essence. Real communication was no longer perceived as taking place through reason, which could reach any rational man. It was now seen as flowing through feeling, which could touch only those tied to each other by kinship or 'blood' and sharing a common heritage." Martin Bernal, *Black Athena: The Afroasiatic Roots of Classical Civilization* (New Brunswick, N.J.: Rutgers University Press, 1987), pp. 28–29.

45. In terms of the psychology of character, Egon's discourse reflects both an Oedipal desire to possess the mother and a more diffuse relationship to the pre-Oedipal mother. Nevertheless, I must observe that the limitations to this sort of analysis become evident as one reads the novel. The extent to which Egon's personal history—as the child of the maid who served as surrogate for the aging woman he calls Grandmother—supplies fertile material for analysis of his theories suggests the degree of self-consciousness with which Yehoshua has constructed this novel. The overabundance of such invitations to analysis produces a virtual parody of the activity of analysis itself.

46. Sigmund Freud, "Female Sexuality" [1931], *Standard Edition*, vol. 21, pp. 225–26.

47. In terms of the contribution of archaeological findings to the construction of an Aryan myth, Martin Bernal writes: "There was a marked difference . . . between reactions to Heinrich Schliemann's discovery of Mycenaean civilization in the 1870s and Arthur Evans' reports of the Cretan one at Knossos in 1900. In the earlier case, several scholars initially suggested that the finds, which were completely unlike those from Classical Greece, could be Phoenician. This was then energetically denied in the following decades. In 1900, by contrast, the culture at Knossos was immediately tagged with the new name 'Minoan' and considered to be 'Pre-Hellenic'; certainly not Semitic, despite the ancient traditions that Crete had been so" (Bernal, *Black Athena*, p. 34).

48. Egon uses a wine cellar (*yekev*: wine cellar or wine press in Talmudical usage) as a means of imprisoning Yosef Mani. Like Kafka's writing machine, the wine press now holds or processes human material (*gelem 'enoshi*) (118/122). In this narrative set on an island in the Mediterranean, Yehoshua acknowledges Kafka's story, with its penal colony on an island remote from the presumably more enlightened homeland. While it is true that Yehoshua's Crete figures as an ancient source of culture and differs as such from Kafka's depiction of a primitive penal colony, there are nevertheless striking resemblances between these two representations of landscapes, each of which yields a depiction of buried (or repressed) strata in the European psyche. Egon's crazy theory of a cure for Germany—"to purify ourselves in the holy womb of our forefathers" (124/120) brings to mind the fanatical fidelity of Kafka's Officer to the order of the Old Commandant. Franz Kafka, "In the Penal Colony," *The Complete Stories*, ed. Nahum Glatzer (New York: Schocken, 1972).

49. Considered from the angle of individual psychology, this is one point where the pre-Oedipal mingles with the Oedipal competition for the mother.

50. See Mosse, *Crisis of German Ideology*, p. 44.

51. Racism, insofar as it involves stereotyping through looks, reflects a "visually centered ideology" (Mosse, *Nationalism and Sexuality*, p. 134). In studying the function of stereotyping in perception, Sander Gilman (*Difference and Pathology*) examines the designation of difference in service of consolidating images of the dominant group.

52. The English translation omits this clause within a sentence.

53. For a recent analysis of the origins of this association of the Jew with carnality, see Daniel Boyarin, "'This We Know To Be the Carnal Israel': Circumcision and the Erotic Life of God and Israel," *Critical Inquiry* 18, iii (Spring 1992): 474–505.

54. Sara Kofman, *The Enigma of Woman: Woman in Freud's Writings*, trans. Catherine Porter (Ithaca: Cornell University Press, 1985), pp. 34–35.

55. "Nationalism," remarks E. J. Hobsbawm, "requires too much belief in what is patently not so." He quotes Ernst Renan's remark that "Getting its history wrong is part of being a nation" (Hobsbawm, *Nations and Nationalism Since 1780: Programme, Myth, Reality*. Cambridge: Cambridge University Press, 1990, p. 12).

56. The English translation refers to the boy as "paralyzed."

57. Sigmund Freud, "Medusa's Head" [1922], *Standard Edition*, vol. 18, p. 273.

58. Hélène Cixous, "The Laugh of the Medusa," trans. Keith Cohen and Paula Cohen, *Signs* 1 (Summer, 1976): 875–99.

59. Malka Shaked sees the displacement from "libdicus" to "politicus" as the key move of the novel. Malka Shaked, "From Libidinal Man to Political Man" (in Hebrew), *'Iton 77* 14, no. 129: 18–20.

60. Malka Shaked comments: "The relation of all the Manis to the secret of the womb and of birth is therefore difficult and complex, and they come to terms with it in different ways . . . Political consciousness can be found here to be something stamped in a man from the moment that he sees the open womb before him" ("From Libidinal Man," p. 20).

61. The novel fuels this analysis with its account of Dr. Mani's attachment to his mother, avoidance of his wife, along with suggestions that Yosef is not the biological son of Dr. Mani.

62. E. J. Hobsbawm observes that "National languages are . . . almost always semi-artificial constructs and occasionally, like modern Hebrew, virtually invented. They are the opposite of what nationalist mythology supposes them to be, namely the primordial foundations of national culture and the matrices of the national mind" (*Nations and Nationalism*, p. 54).

63. Amos Oz, *Lada'at 'Isha* (Jerusalem: Keter, 1989); *To Know a Woman*, trans. Nicholas de Lange (London: Chatto and Windus, 1991); and *Hamatzav hashlishi* (Jerusalem: Keter, 1991); *Fima*, trans. Nicholas de Lange (New York: Harcourt Brace, 1993).

64. David Grossman, *Sefer hadiqduq hapnimi* (Tel Aviv: Hakibbutz hameuchad, Siman qri'ah, 1991); *The Book of Intimate Grammar*, trans. Betsy Rosenberg (New York: Farrar Straus and Giroux, 1994).

65. S. Yizhar, *Tzalhavim* (Tel Aviv: Zmora Bitan, 1993).

66. Hillel Halkin, "Bare Ground and Nothing Above It: An Interview with S. Yizhar," *Modern Hebrew Literature* 12 (Spring/Summer, 1994): 4–6.

67. Orly Castel-Bloom, *Dolly-Siti* (Tel Aviv: Zmora-Bitan, 1992).

68. Biale, *Eros and the Jews*, p. 183.

69. Biale points out that despite a move to install gender equality as part of the Zionist movement, a deeply conservative trend in Zionist thought persisted in viewing women in terms of their procreative roles; furthermore, he notes that many men of the Second and Third Aliyot tended to confuse the role of women as one's mother and as the mother of one's children (*Eros and the Jews*, pp. 188–89).

YAEL S. FELDMAN

From Feminist Romance to an Anatomy of Freedom: Israeli Women Novelists

IF, AS ARGUED by the feminist scholar Nina Baym, the American woman writer "has entered literary history as the enemy,"[1] the Hebrew woman writer has entered *her* literary history as sister, as bride, as comrade in arms. Already in 1897—an early date for a literature that came of age in that very decade—Eliezer Ben Yehuda, the propagator of spoken Hebrew, openly invited women (and particularly his wife, who happened to be a chemist!) to contribute to his journals. The chivalrous reasoning of his invitation is a precious document, reminding us once more that even with insight and good will one may still be unable to escape the snares of gender essentialism. "Only women," Ben Yehuda argued, "are capable of reviving Hebrew, this old, forgotten, dry and hard language, by permeating it with emotion, tenderness, suppleness and subtlety."[2] So the door seemed to have been wide open. Yet women were slow to enter. Perhaps they intuitively sensed that double bind of which recent scholarship has made us aware—the fact that Ben Yehuda's benign encouragement was unwittingly circumscribed by his gender bifocals. For although a number of women graced his journals, none of them left her mark on the history of Hebrew literature. No Hebrew male writer could ever have complained, as did the American Hawthorn, according to Baym, "about the 'damned mob of scribbling women' whose writings . . . were diverting the public from his own" (Baym, p. 63). In contrast to the English or French traditions, Hebrew has not developed a line of women novelists, either within or without the canon. For the first century of its modern phase (or even for its first 150 years, depending on the periodization used) Hebrew prose fiction was primarily the domain of male writers, while women generally found their expression in poetry.[3] Furthermore, the few women who entered the canon as fiction writers wrote short stories and novellas, mainly in the lyrical-impressionistic mode (for example, Devorah Baron, 1887–1956, and the contemporary writer Amalia Kahana-Carmon).

It is only since the early 1980s that prose fiction by women has emerged as a substantially diverse phenomenon, including traditionally hard-core "male" genres such as the historical novel or the fictional autobiography, and even such a popular genre as the mystery novel.[4] Unfortunately, most of this literature is not available in English, nor is it adequately represented in scholarship. Ironically, even a recent volume specifically devoted to *Gender and Text in Modern Hebrew and Yiddish Literature* (1992) preserves the "old" balance: while both Israeli writers whose essays sign off the collection are prose fiction writers who have "graduated" from short stories to novels (Ruth Almog and Amalia Kahana-Carmon, to whom we shall return), the critical articles themselves are neatly divided between women's poetry and men's prose fiction.[5] Clearly, there is a problem of reception or legitimization here, and scholarship is lagging behind a changing reality.

There is no doubt, however, that the new literary map drawn by Israeli women novelists deserves our full attention, as it brings into sharp focus a general point of contention that has been raging among scholars since the 1970s: the relationship between postmodern theories and feminist approaches. Zeroing in on "the death of the [Enlightenment] subject" as the major "loss" announced by postmodern thinkers (other "deaths"—those of philosophy and history—are secondary in this argumentation), feminist theorists have embraced or mourned postmodernisms as either "useful" or "damaging" for their project. Although the demarcation line between these two positions may overlap the French/Anglo-American divide (as suggested, for instance, by Alice Jardine's *Gynesis*), recent reviews yield a more complex picture.[6] While helping feminists question historical and contemporary perceptions of sexual and gender differences, postmodernist critiques of the Enlightenment (pronouncing the "fictiveness" of a "unitary" self and of reason's "truth," among others) seem to threaten and undermine the very foundation of and justification for women's quest for emancipation. For if the self is only a cultural or linguistic inscription to begin with, who is there to be "oppressed" or "liberated" in the first place? Whether or not we go so far as to accept Jane Flax's psychoanalytically based suspicion that this critique is motivated by a *fear* of the "return of the suppressed," by "the [male] need to evade, deny or repress the importance of early childhood experiences, especially mother-child relationships, in the constitution of the self and the culture more generally,"[7] we at least can share her (and other feminists') frustration at the "accidental" coincidence of this position with the very time in which "women have just begun to remember their selves and to claim an agentic subjectivity available always before only to a few privileged white men" (ibid., p. 220). It is clear then that this aspect of contemporary thought is problematic for the so-called "equal-rights" or "liberal individualism" strands of feminist consciousness.[8]

Bearing this problem in mind, we should not be surprised by the low profile of *conscious* postmodernism in the work of the writers analyzed in this essay. In as much as they were selected for precisely their grappling with the representation or construction of female "agentic subjectivities" in a society still inhospitable to such a project, their prose understandably reflects a rather careful selection of issues (rather than poetics) from the postmodernist repertory. (In this they differ from the wholesale absorption of postmodernism evident in works written in the same decade by other [mostly male] authors, such as, Grossman, Shamas, Heffner, Hoffman, Shimoni, Yehoshua, and also the younger female author Orly Castel-Bloom.) In addition to the problem of subjectivity and otherness, so crucial to their writing, their themes include, as we shall see, several questions raised by postmodern criticism: the relationship between gender and genre, feminism and nationalism, ideology and canon formation.[9]

In the first place, the generic divergence evidenced, until recently, by the Hebrew corpus is highly significant for the general debate about essentialistic definitions of gender, an issue that I have explored elsewhere and that has been subsequently addressed in *Gender and Text*.[10] However, no less intriguing is the insight this body of work offers into the problematic relationship between national and feminist ideologies as framed by the postmodernist debate over the canon. One of the most troubling questions this material poses to anyone with even the faintest acquaintance with the ideological roots of the modern revival of Hebrew is the following: Why has the "New Hebrew Woman," ostensibly fostered by early Zionism, disappeared on her way to literary representation?[11]

Modern Hebrew literature, we should remember, was conceived and developed on Russian soil and as such was bound up with nineteenth-century socialism. It had openly propagated—at least in theory—both social and sexual equality for women. However, as recent sociological studies in Israel have shown, not a little was lost in the translation from ideological platform to lived experience. In the view of contemporary scholars, the pre-State Zionist women's movement had not lived up to its own expectations either in the urban settlements or in the kibbutzim.[12] Still, this belated hindsight should not make us lose sight of the ethos (some would say mythos) of equal rights, as it was experienced by both fathers and mothers of the pioneering, founding generation. Nor should it make us belittle the political as well as cultural early "conquests" made by some of these women, Manya Schohat (1880–1959) and Rachel Katznelson (1885–1983), for example, and, of course, the better known writers Devorah Baron and Rachel (1890–1931).[13]

The force of this ethos, at least in some segments of Israeli society, was still felt in the early decades of the State. Paradoxically, it was precisely this force that made "feminism," as it came to be known in the United States in the sixties, seem redundant, as if it were something "we have 'always' known" (albeit under the title of "the woman question"), a latter-day product of a "Western," luxury culture that had finally awakened to some of its social(ist?) blind spots. If this paradoxical position does not make sense to us in the 1990s, we may recall that well into the seventies even Simone de Beauvoir similarly refused to label herself as "feminist"—*The Second Sex* of 1949 notwithstanding—believing that the woman question will be solved by the socialist platform.[14] On the other hand, we should not forget that by the sixties, socialism (or social-Zionism) had already lost its broad popular base in Israeli society. The post-World War II immigration from Europe and the Arab countries had more than doubled the population of the young State and drastically changed the country's demographic and cultural makeup.[15] A large portion of Israeli population has been henceforth unaffiliated with pre-State ideologies. For this community both "old" and "new" feminisms were anathema, a forthright subversion of their traditional (mostly Oriental and/or Orthodox) ways of life. When the pressures of life under constant military siege are added to this complex, it may become clear that, socially speaking, "Western" feminism, as introduced by recent Anglo-American immigrants,[16] could not have had a warm reception in the Israel of the sixties and the seventies, despite a pro-forma adherence to the indigenous, social-Zionist women's movement.

But what about the literary arena? Here we shall do well to remember that until recently most Hebrew writers were allied—either biographically or politically—with the ethos of the pre-State community, with all its ideological trimmings. Neither the Oriental nor the Orthodox sections of Israeli society was significantly represented in the canon of Hebrew literature. (The contemporary picture is significantly different for the former section, but only slightly for the latter.[17]) Yet despite its ideological "baggage," Israeli literary mainstream (some would say "malestream"[18]) seems to be curiously lacking when it comes to fictional representation of women. For the longest time, the "New Hebrew Woman" was destined to remain a rhetorical construct, excluded from works by both male and female authors.

Not surprisingly, her literary debut coincided with the latest wave of prose fiction by women that has swept Israeli literature since the early

1980s. Indeed, it is the belatedness of this debut, its specific literary shape, and its sociocultural implications, that command our attention in the following inquiry.

We will follow this meandering narrative through the mature work of four Israeli fiction writers—Shulamit Lapid, Amalia Kahana-Carmon, Shulamith Hareven, and Ruth Almog; although they all began to publish in the 1960s, it is their more recent novels that hold the key to the belated emergence of their troubled feminisms.

We begin with 1982, the year in which the label "feminist" appeared for the first time on the jacket of an Israeli novel, although not yet in its lexicon. Shulamit Lapid's historical novel *Gei Oni*[19] ("Gei Oni" being the original name of the Galilean settlement Rosh Pinah) told the story of the 1882 early pioneers—so that labelling its protagonist a "feminist" clearly smacked of anachronism.[20] The anachronism seems to have been intended—either by the author herself or by her editor. It made transparent the contemporary relevance of the historical material, directing the reader to see its dramatic unfolding as a displacement of analogous present-day dilemmas. At the heart of the story we find a conflict between Fanya, a Russian-born, fiercely independent young survivor of the Ukrainian pogroms of the 1880s, and the equally fierce Zionist dream that had brought her to the barren hills of the Galilee. It is through this nexus of collective ideology (whether national or socialist or both) and the role of the individual—woman in particular—within it, that the major theme of the novel is introduced and problematized.

Fanya's critique of "her father's dream of rebirth [that] has turned into sacred insanity which is now consuming her youthful years, her life" (p. 102), inadvertently brings to the fore a contradiction that might have been inherent in the Zionist enterprise from its inception, but had been rarely made conscious before the 1970s, and especially before the so-called "post-Zionist" scholarship of the last decade: the potential incommenserability between private salvation and communal redemption.[21] The convoluted manner in which this ideological critique takes on a particularly feminist twist is a complex process, which I have analyzed elsewhere.[22] However, since it is the subversion of this very "twist" that is crucial for my argument, let me reiterate here its final stage in the plot.

Despite its pioneering feminist intentions, *Gei Oni* loses its potentially feminist protest, because its narrative closure reinscribes both the communal and the romantic models that its plot has set out to undermine. As Fanya's husband succumbs to exhaustion and malaria, the reader is ready to embrace Fanya's *Bildung* throughout the novel, which consists primarily of a reversal of gender roles, as a necessary training for her ultimate task—the perpetuation of the Zionist pioneering quest. But in an ironic turn, Fanya, although prepared to undertake this role, perceives it as something alien, not her own script:

> Shall she sell their home? Driving Yehi'el out of his dream? This home and this land were the purpose of his life. Once again fate has decreed that she realized others' dreams. Has she ever had her own dreams? But perhaps everyone is like this? Perhaps everyone realizes someone else's dream? (p. 256)

Is this a "feminist" protest, lamenting the lot of women in general?[23] Or is this a specific charge against an androcentric Zionist dream? And who is the "everyone" of the final questions: Women? All people? The lines seem to blur here, leaving the reader with a sense of unfocused grievance. What is read throughout the novel as a critique of a male-engendered ideology now takes on an existential turn, possibly hiding behind "the human condition."

We may be witnessing here an attempt (prevalent in women's life writing, as demonstrated by Carolyn Heilbrun in her 1988 *Writing A Woman's Life*,[24]) to rationalize away the justified rage against a social system that in the guise of a new ideology has reinscribed traditional double standards toward women. More often than not, Fanya's feelings remain unexpressed. Typically, her frustration and hurt are reported to the reader ("Fanya wanted to scream: And I? And I?, but she kept silent" [p. 176, and cf. 105, 144, 164, 187, 217]), but they always remain confined within the seething turmoil of her narrated inner monologues. When they are actually verbalized, it is only in the framework of private female discourse. Crossing gender boundaries in her occupation and lifestyle, Fanya may have penetrated male praxis, but not its public discourse. The prevailing ideology remains untouched by her feminist critique. In the final analysis, Fanya's "revolutionary" quest for selfhood inscribes itself only as a comment on the margins of an androcentric system.

We should not be surprised, then, that the author does not give her heroine the chance to try to make it on her own. On the last page, the heroine's "euphoric text" prevails, promising a romantic bethrothal beyond the boundaries of the book.[25] Sasha, an old acquaintance, himself a survivor of the Ukrainian pogroms, reappears and asks permission "to help and be helped" (a phrase clearly reminiscent of the Zionist quest "to build and be rebuilt"). With this new beginning, the novel reverts to its two original models: the communal-historical and the romantic. Subjective experience is embedded again in Jewish collectivity, symbolized throughout the story by the legendary Phoenix ("This is what we Jews

act. Starting all over again. Again. And again. And again." [p. 266]),
only to be taken over by an old/new romance closure:

... "I need you, Fanya! Will you allow me to help you?" Fanya looked at him
wondering. Then she thought that if he hugged her, her head would barely
reach his shoulder. And then her eyes filled with tears. (p. 266)

One need not be a devotee of Harlequin romances to recognize the
style. The "New Hebrew Woman," to the extent that she is constructed
in this text, collapses back into a romance figure. As such, this popular novel, Lapid's first (she was born in 1934), may serve as the most
extreme example of what I call "the feminist romance." Through this
hybrid form a "compromise formation" is worked out between feminist
aspirations for masculinist autonomy—the very Enlightenment ideal
pronounced "fictive" by some and labelled "individualist" by others[26]—
and stereotyped feminine patterns of psychological dependency, generally expressed in the form of a romantic attachment. My emphasis here
is on "stereotyped," since these narratives rarely question this received
dichotomy, nor the hierarchical value judgment it implies.[27] There is
nothing new or particularly Israeli about this conflict, of course, except
for the specific novelistic form it takes. Although these narratives are
cast in the genre of the *historical* novel, they can be read as "masked
autobiographies" because they displace and mask the feminist concerns
of their *contemporary* authors.[28] More important, they also share an un-
articulated doubt—usually evidenced only in their plot structures—concerning the limits of the feminist project. Conceived purely in terms of
Enlightenment-style emancipation, this project is generally represented
here as an attempt to synthesize (rather than deconstruct) the two sides
of the coin of gender difference. The heroines of these narratives try
to bridge the two terms of the by now familiar binary opposition—to
be individualist yet relational (Offen), autonomous yet interdependent
(Johnson), separate yet bonded (Flax), or, in Freud's popular definition,
to be able to work as well as to love.[29] The problem, however, is that
in the final analysis they experience this binarism more as a dichotomy
than as an equilibrium.

What I am arguing then is that a close reading of the deep structure of
these narratives may reveal their authors' (perhaps unconscious) distrust
of their heroines' ability to live up to the "work and love" ideal of classical feminism, particularly as it developed here in the 1960s and 1970s.
As we shall see, the treatment of this difficulty differs from novel to novel
in two respects: in the understanding of its "source" (whether it is internal, that is, conceptually or psychologically gender-specific, or external,

that is, sociocultural and circumstantial), and in the degree to which the
conflict is finally perceived as resolvable or at least negotiable. As such,
these narratives address a question that is crucial to the debate over gender identity and sexual difference. The perceptions they offer vary, as
do the limits and boundaries they envision for feminist emancipation.

Shulamit Lapid herself has "resolved" the ambiguity of her first novel
by shifting from the "canonic" historical narrative and the female euphoric text (the romantic bethrothal plot), to a different genre—the
spinster detective story. In a series of popular mystery novels,[30] all set
in a contemporary provincial town, she has constructed a "New *Israeli*
Woman," a lower-middle-class journalist whose first priority is work, and
for whom love is divorced from matrimony. Thirty-some years old and
single, this protagonist, who is proud of her work ethic and her "pro-
fessionalism," is not a descendent of the "New Hebrew Woman" of the
Zionist revolution (Fanya and her like); rather, she is a throwback to the
turn-of-the-century spinster detective of English literature.[31] In Lapid's
version of this genre, masculine autonomy is appropriated without any
equivocation, accompanied by a new (male-modeled) kind of romance
(no strings attached), that makes its appearance—once again—only at
the close of the story.

It is hard to determine whether the simplicity with which sexual difference is overcome in these plots is an indicator of naive conceptual-
ization, or of a projection of a collective fantasy (given the noncanonic
nature of the genre on one hand, and the totally unautobiographic
characterization of the heroine, on the other[32]). Whatever the case, it is
clear that the feminist romance produced here is a mirror image of its
masculinist counterpart. While the sociocultural antagonism it may encounter is given cursory attention, any possible complication by psycho-
sexual difference is blissfully ignored.

The same goes for some of Lapid's later short stories in which romance is replaced by aggression. A straightforward reversal of roles in a
violent rape scene, for example, is the subject of "Neḥitat 'oness" (forced
landing; published in English as "The Bed," but better rendered as
"Forced Entry").[33] The painful experience of what I would call "counter
rape" is focalized through the eyes of the victim—a young man whose
bewildered incomprehension is utterly ignored by his female attacker.
Again, gender difference is here turned upside-down, with the female
grotesquely donning the dark face of masculine subjectivity, aggression.

A more sophisticated treatment of these issues belongs to Amalia
Kahana-Carmon (b. 1926), one of Israel's leading prose fiction writers

and the winner of several prestigious literary prizes. Known for her out-spoken feminist critique of Israeli literature and Jewish culture (which, proclaimed in her lectures and essays, has gained momentum, predict-ably, only since the mid-1980s[34]), her fiction, published since 1956, is nevertheless the most interesting manifestation of the conflicts under-lying the "feminist romance."

To begin with, most of her oeuvre — a collection of stories (1966), two novels (1971, 1992), a monodrama (1976), and two "tryptichs" (three novellas, 1977, 1984) — thematizes women's marginalization in an andro-centric society on a scope and in a style unrivalled in Hebrew literature. This line of writing is precisely what literary theory (particularly on the Anglo-American side) has come to expect of the "first stage" of feminist literature — a subversive exposition of overt and covert biases that lurk in the representation of women in a male-dominated system.[35] Kahana-Carmon's writing, however, is more complex. Her lyrical stories and novels, mostly focalized through the perception of a female protagonist, are generally structured around a moment of a cross-gender epiphany, of a mutual enchantment. Yet the potential romance is always checked, leaving her protagonists with little more than a sense of missed oppor-tunity.[36] Moreover, in most cases they accept their "fallen" reality with a resignation that paradoxically places them too close to traditional gender essentialism. To further complicate matters, a dense network of analogies and figurative connectives (particularly in the longer works) universalize the major themes, thereby undercutting or at least prob-lematizing their female or feminist specificity. (She even goes as far as simply reversing the stereotypes, constructing, in "Sham ḥadar haḥada-shot" (1977), a male protagonist whose dream of work and love is frus-trated by a goal-oriented (American!) young scientist . . .) It is this very ambiguity, I would argue, that has contributed to a certain miscommu-nication between the author and her Israeli readership.

One of Kahana-Carmon's major complaints in her 1980s essays is that the warm reception of her work hinged on its artistic excellence rather than on its "substance." Claiming that this standard is never applied to male writers (in actuality, a claim not easily supported by fact), she has persistently rejected its terms:

This reader will react to the *tools* of the woman writer as if they were objects ("every sentence of hers is a pearl"); he will not respond to the *substance*, con-tained in her words, that created the need for these tools in the first place and then shaped their *form*. Indeed, this *content* is hidden from his eyes . . . much as you and I, unfortunately, cannot enjoy the highly perfected song of the bats in flight . . .

If so, the problem for the woman writer, apparently, inheres in the *subject matter* about which she attempts to speak. In the world of Hebrew fiction, such *material* has low visibility.[37] (Emphasis added)

Ironically, her use of the "classical" distinction between "tools" and "substance" or "content" echoes the Platonic dualism of "form" and "matter" that has been recently shown to be heavily implicated in gender symbolism[38] — except that Kahana-Carmon's complaint involves this symbolism in a gender reversal of which she may not be aware. As the philosophic tradition would have it, "form" is the privileged term, "naturally" associated with maleness, while "debased" matter (or "body") is the realm of the female. The deconstruction of this essentialist dichotomy, by one reversal or another (either associating femaleness with "form" or privileging "matter" and "substance") is of course the dream of any feminist, Anglo-American or French (respectively). But Kahana-Carmon the polemicist is blind — as so often is the case[39] — to options created by Kahana-Carmon the artist. Does her charge that (male) readers "see" only the form of her art because its "matter" — female inwardness — is invisible to them (namely, unrepresentable) reject the terms of "gynesis," the French idealization of female attributes traditionally viewed as negative (otherness, lack, even absence), or does it approve of it?[40] Does her clamoring for cross-gender legitimization of her highly feminine "subjects" (the pun intended) position her on the side of Virginia Woolf's androgyny (otherwise named similarity, universality, equality, or Enlightenment-based liberal feminism), or on the side of [French] "sexual difference" feminism?[41] Does she deplore her heroines' exclusion from male-made history? Does she privilege their otherness? Or perhaps she espouses Kristeva's "third generation" ideology whose task is, among the rest, "the de-dramatization of the 'fight to the death' between rival groups and thus between the sexes"?[42]

As we shall see, this ambivalence is not accidental. On the contrary: it is deeply rooted in the paradoxes animating Kahana-Carmon's fiction. For the fact is that any reader, male or female, initiated into her artistic world — the early fiction in particular — cannot but be struck by the impact of her unconventional, innovative style. Her idiosyncratic use of Hebrew syntax and semantics, of colloquialism and scriptural allusion, and her unique manipulation of narrative and textual expectations — all these are too powerful to be ignored. To treat this aspect of her artistic achievement as just "tools" is obviously a misjudgment, an outdated separation between art and artifice. Yet to consider it an Israeli version of *l'ecriture feminine* has its problems as well. For on the continent, where the concept originated, it has been propagated as a logical conclusion of sexual *difference*, a position much too unambiguous to accommodate the special blend of Kahana-Carmon "feminism."[43] So why doth the lady protest so much?

The answer may lie precisely in the effect her "tools" have on the perception of her "substance." In fact, the artistry she has invested in the evocation of the female condition is so powerful that the line between grievance and glorification tends to blur.[44] It is not always clear, for example, whether woman's private sphere, her inwardness, is her prison or her mansion; whether feminine "passivity" is viewed as a social evil, imposed by patriarchal pressures, or as a deliberate choice, an intentional withdrawal from public action (thereby clearing a path for female creativity); and, finally, whether the penchant of her heroines for the "dysphoric" plot, for dependent, unrequited love attachments, is to be censured as a disruption of their capacity for masculinist work and autonomy, or lauded as a unique, gender-specific endowment, a sort of existential "transcendence."

Kahana-Carmon's "feminist romance" seems then to be torn among several contradictory demands. Her desire to represent an authentic female subjectivity, which she understands exclusively in terms of oppression and passivity, is undercut by two opposing forces: the temptation to idealize or even essentialize sexual difference; and the yearning for universal, cross-gender equality, for an ostensible state of grace before the fall.[45]

It is in the latter, of course, that the "New Hebrew Woman" is to be expected. But she is not readily available in Kahana-Carmon's canon. She inheres in her protagonists' imagination, partly fantasy, partly a memory trace. As an actual reality she is limited to a single time-period—to the 1948 War of Independence or rather the preceding year at the Hebrew University in Jerusalem, as, for example, in her very first story, "The Whirling Sword" (1956), and in her first novel, *And Moon in the Valley of Ayalon* (1971).[46] Like so many women fighters of World War II (such as the British heroine of David Hare's play *Plenty* [1978]), the "morning after" is perceived as a fall from the grace of equality and autonomy experienced in the war years. The post-war protagonist is often conceptualized as an impoverished version of her former self, a frustrated housewife who has lost her capacity for work and even for love.[47] Though she is fully aware of her dependency and depletion, she is unable to act, or, at best, she sublimates the loss by the celebration of female inward subjectivity.

Aware of the danger of essentialism courting this strategy of survival, Kahana-Carmon has finally made an effort to break away from the confines of her own making and construct a female subject liberated from the yoke of passivity and dependent attachment. Predictably,

this experiment coincided with the publication, in 1984, of the first in
a series of programmatic essays, "To Be a Woman Writer," a kind of
an Israeli feminist manifesto.[48] Just as predictably, it took the form of
a quasi-historical novel, ostensibly for "young adults" (that is, another
noncanonic genre). Like Shulamit Lapid in *Gei Oni*, Kahana-Carmon
felt compelled to transpose her protagonist into the past—in her case
all the way back to seventeenth-century Europe—in order to both sub-
jugate her to and emancipate her from the yoke of Jewish/feminine
victimhood. And as if such chronotopical displacement would not suffice, she further distanced both herself and the reader from the issue
at hand by embedding it within a general paradigm of "otherness." In
fact, her novella "The Bridge of the Green Duck"[49] is a typical postmodernist inquiry into essentialism, challenging all major categories of
"difference"—gender, class, and race.

The author herself characterized the book as "a breakthrough . . . a
different direction, a different approach," comparing its role to that of
"The Ladies of Avignon" in Picasso's artistic development. Here, she argued, "my characters try, for the first time, to do something about their
reality;" they try to get out of "their stoic inaction."[50] Whether or not
this is indeed a meaningful turning point is a question to which we shall
return. But first let us explore the broader implications of the captivity
narrative of this story.

As we shall see, "The Bridge of the Green Duck" is not only the story
of a woman's life in exile and captivity within the heavily androcentric society of seventeenth-century Europe; it is also an experiment in
entering the subjectivity of the other. My contention is that the young
protagonist's immature infatuation with her captor-lover should be read
not only as an exercise in popular Freudian psychology (the mechanism
of identification with the aggressor[51]), but also as a literary probing of
the philosophical question of difference, effectively deconstructing the
binary opposition of self and other.[52]

The opening of the novel unexpectedly plunges us into the as yet unnamed narrator's inner monologue, describing the mysterious "they" of
the first sentence: "Not on the road they were galloping." A quick external glance invites the reader to admire their energy, laughter, and
self-confidence; the latter is amplified by the narrator's observation that
"they" have never lost their awareness that they belonged to "a closed,
superior caste, one that 'passes over armed before the camps,' 'people
who dwell alone,' a sect of pioneers who clear the way" (p. 61). In Hebrew, the biblical resonance of *over(et) lifnei hamahaneh* and *am levadad
yishkon* is inescapable. It marshals a host of allusions to the status of a
chosen people and its sense of uniqueness and vocation (see especially

Numbers 22 and 32). When the reader realizes—a few pages into the narrative—that this all too familiar description is attributed here to the "other"; and that the gentile (and of course male) dark horsemen are in fact the enemy, the captors of the (then twelve-year-old) narrator—it is too late. A miracle of sorts has already taken place: By providing a new signified for the biblical signifiers, the text has triggered a process of identification/projection, thereby assisting the reader in imagining the other subjectively. The "preconceived judgment," the image we usually have of the other (particularly of a different gender, nationality, or class, as illustrated in this story[53]) has been partially or temporarily bracketed so that self and other may exchange places, at least for a short while.

Yet this is only the beginning. By the end of the narrative, the same biblical allusion is repeated (pp. 175–76), this time appropriated by the still unnamed narrator, to describe both her own state of mind and that of her recently acquired friend who is (surprise! surprise!) . . . a *black* ex-captive. What has been earlier perceived then as the domain of the elect, the chosen other (the male, European, gentile conqueror) is now triumphantly attributed to a new signified—the self-awareness of the formerly subjugated Jewish female (*Judea Capta?*) and the formerly enslaved black, whose Hebrew name, Eved Hakushi, smacks of heavy allegorism.[54] With this reversal a whole range of boundaries is subverted and crossed over—race, class and gender—so that the marginalized other is allowed the privilege of her or his own subjectivity, expressed in precisely the same figurative language as that of the oppressor. It is this newly achieved self-awareness that enables the narrator to appropriate her first name, the sacrosanct hallmark of the construction of subjectivity. (That this name is accompanied by her patronymic ["Clara, the daughter of Avigdor the merchant," p. 179], is, however, an ironic undermining of this very construction.)

But all this is of course more easily said than done, even in fictional terms. Perhaps predictably, Kahana-Carmon does not accompany her liberated heroine into her new state of being. Although she imagines Clara's psychological growth as wholly determined by object-relations with *male* models (Clara's ambivalence towards her mother, whom she has lost in her childhood, and whom she mostly experiences as remote and cold, is another complex issue to be explored elsewhere[55]), she lets her achieve autonomy—that cherished accomplishment traditionally attributed to masculine identity—only on the last page of the novel. It is only in this last moment of the narrative that Clara finally attempts to shake off her neurotic attachment to the father figures of her life—her own father, Avigdor; Rabbi Zefania (whose name connotes both an enigma and a conscience, *matzpun*); her captor-lover (whose name, Peter, particularly in its Hebrew pronunciation, nicely puns on "patron"[56]); and her friend, the black ex-captive.

From a psychological perspective, Clara's life story is the unfolding of an inner conflict between an all-devouring urge for transference love/dependency and a conscious struggle against it. The obsessive character of her need becomes particularly transparent in the last part of the plot, when, after successfully releasing herself not only from her physical bondage but also from an emotional attachment to her captor (saying "no" to the fleeing Peter who asks her to accompany him as a friend and partner, pp. 140–43), she is all but ready to repeat the same pattern in her relationship with a new authority figure, the liberated slave Eved Hakushi. The encounter between these two "others" (chap. 8), oddly neglected by the scholarship, is a masterfully rendered drama, bristling with metaphoric references to key chapters in the philosophical literature on subjectivity and otherness. To do full justice to its intricacy, a more detailed contextualization is called for (see my *Beyond the Feminist Romance*). What follows is therefore a running commentary briefly tracing the route of this fascinating transformation.

The slave-turned-master (*pace* Hegel), although engaged by Clara as a handyman, teaches her a lesson in existential transcendence. To her horrified observation of his otherness ("The man is black all over. Black and different . . . 'How terrible,' I murmured"), he calmly responds by equating his race subjectivity with her gender subjectivity ("Are you a man in a woman's body? You are not. Is this such a misfortune? Why a misfortune? With you, with me, it is the same thing, more or less" [p. 164]). This lesson allows Clara to engage in a dialogue that surreptitiously "bridges" the differences between them, finally leading them to the symbolic "bridge of the Green Duck" of the novel's title (p. 175), the very location where epiphanic moments in the relationship with her father and Peter took place. But before reaching this stage, a whole comedy of errors is enacted, the core of which is not the issue of race or class difference (this difference seems to have been neutralized with relative ease[57]), but rather that of sexual difference. While the code of the social "communion," typically negotiated via a shared meal, is automatically recognized by both parties ("'Forgive my eating with my hands,' said [Eved], tearing the bread with his teeth. 'Forgive my eating with knife and fork,' said I somberly, tearing the bread with my fingers . . ." [p. 171]), the code of emotional communion is not. Thus the description of the embrace (initiated by Eved) is represented through Clara's consciousness as a veritable web of erotic and incestual allusions ("he opened my father's coat which he was wearing and wrapped me within it, [. . . .] then clasped me to his chest, pushing me against the wall" [p. 171]), only to be interpreted by Eved himself as an act of brotherly love (" 'Why do you hug me?' — 'I am your brother.' — 'My brother?' I said with a jolt. I lifted my face to him *shaken*" [p. 172; emphasis added]). Why is Clara shaken, perhaps even shocked (*nir'eshet*, repeated twice)? Was she wrong? Has she misread the code of intimacy? Or was it Eved's ambivalence that interfered in the production of meaning?

The answer is not immediately forthcoming. For a while, Clara's agitation is replaced by an exploration of the new sense of familial bonding, a process that culminates in the privileged self-consciousness we quoted above (p. 176). Yet this moment of mutual recognition does not last long. In a typical Sartrean fashion, Clara immediately lapses into "othering" her "brother." Asking him to cut off a branch of a prickly bush because "You do not get scratched," she deservedly receives a Shylock-like reproach ("Don't we scratch? Won't we scratch?"), against which she defends herself by explaining, "Not because of your color . . . because of your strength" (p. 176). With this, the terms of the argument have shifted. Admitting to her ostensible weakness, Clara has forfeited her transcendence. Her clinging attachment to the "strong sex" is interpreted by Eved as an absolutely abhoring "search for power" (p. 179). The next stage in their encounter is therefore marked by a Sartrean duel of gazes, precisely like the one that had earlier underlined Clara's entrapment by the predatory arrogance of her captors ("His piercing eye fixed on my piercing eye" [pp. 179, 180; cf., pp. 117, 119, 153]). From here there is but a short step to her full recapitulation. Giving up the opportunity to rejoin the Jewish community from which she was kidnapped as a child, she chooses to follow Eved, her new "br/other." Acknowledging the audacity of her choice ("I have crossed a covert boundary. Now I am clearly beyond the pale . . . like the young Moses I am, who between gold and coals has chosen the coals" [pp. 181–82]), she is nevertheless unaware of the existential meaning of her move. Her inward plea ("Where are you, Eved Hakushi, my heart kept hoping. Woulds't I found you, that I might return home with you" [p. 182]) ironically dramatizes de Beauvoir's analysis of women's complicity in their own subjugation.[58] Yet here is where Kahana-Carmon parts with her philosophical models.

In an unexpected move, the ex-captive refuses to fulfill the role of the master. In contrast to Peter, the young captor-lover who has taken advantage of Clara's dependency (and in the end fell in love with her himself), Eved Hakushi is older and wiser. His recently gained freedom, both social and emotional, is his most cherished possession (but also the source of his ambivalence). It is only through his rejection of Clara's "advances," that his lesson in freedom/autonomy/independence is finally internalized by her (chap. 9). In the last episode Clara "declares" her maturation and self-reliance by demanding (and receiving) the key of a case of merchandise. Although the (Freudian) sexual symbolism is transparent, it does not exhaust the whole drama. For when Eved removes the key from "her father's coat pocket" (p. 191), which he is wearing (and which she had given him), the Lacanian symbolism becomes quite apparent. While Eved's role as substitute father is over, the protagonist herself moves into the paternal position. The case's key is in fact her key to the very trade that Jewish folklore, via the celebrated lullaby, foretells for the (male) baby—commerce in "raisins and almonds" (dried fruit, in the language of the narrative).[59]

"I am staying. To find out. Here, at this place, tomorrow. Concerning trade in dried fruit at our place. Also to buy goods for myself. This is what I came here for," I said, "after all, this was the plan."

Eved Hakushi shrugged his shoulders. But when I turned away he stopped me, laughing:

"How do you plan," he said, "to find a place for the night by yourself, a woman alone, in this city."

"We'll see."

"And how do you plan, tell me, one woman alone, to confront all this city's great dried fruit merchants."

"We'll see."

"You have no idea what you are talking about."

"We'll see."

"And how do you plan to draft a porter tomorrow, tell me."

"We'll see."

"We'll see," he repeated after me, with jeering eyes. (pp. 191–92)

The contrast between this closing dialogue and the closure of Lapid's *Gei Oni* could not be any greater. With her insistent declaration of independence, Clara seems resolved to flee the feminist romance, giving up love for the sake of work. Yet the wry irony underlying this final scene cannot be mistaken. Even her own mentor doubts the viability of her newly acquired autonomy. Once again, we are faced with the ubiquitous double standard—except that this author, unlike her predecessor, ironically acknowledges its subversive power. It would seem that although she has taken this heroine a step further toward masculinist autonomy, Amalia Kahana-Carmon too, like Shulamit Lapid before her, could hardly envision a feasible reality for her "New Hebrew Woman." Framed by the anaphoric repetition "We'll see," this reality is still only a promised land, beckoning the heroine beyond the closure of the text.[60]

What remains unanswered is the question concerning the source of this deferment. Is emancipation just an act of self will, or is it subject to internal and/or external obstacles? Stripped of all former dependent relationships with male figures, would not a typical Kahana-Carmon character find herself at a loss? And would not the dominant social power deny her the "privilege" it had granted to her black friend? More importantly, is it a privilege? Should she/Can she forego love for the sake of work? Questions abound. But satisfactory answers are not readily available. And it was probably this ambiguity, wrapped in a thick layer of allegorism, that perplexed the readers of "The Bridge of the Green Duck." Their waning enthusiasm might have echoed the author's own quandary, contributing to a long hiatus in which programmatic essays took the place of creative writing.

Only in her latest novel, *With Her on Her Way Home*, published almost a decade later (1992), has the fog somewhat dissipated. Foregoing the historic-allegorical displacement, Kahana-Carmon has courageously woven a contemporary story of romance and artistic creativity (a nice substitute for "work"), matrimony, and divorce. Working much closer to home, autobiographically speaking, she boldly paints the ups and downs of two decades in the life and loves of a (fictionally) famous Israeli . . . theater actress. A passing allusion to Kathryn Hepburn, "A Lioness in Winter," conveys both her celebrity status and the pathos of its decline. Me'ira Heller, whose name is in fact a Hebrew rendition of Clara, seems to pick up where Clara has left off. She actually manages to have a successful career, be a mother, and—at the crucial moment of approaching midlife—find the love of her life. Mossik, her lover and the narrator of this love story, is (rather predictably) an Israeli synthesis of Clara's two "loves": The irresistible attraction of his *bon physique*, countlessly reiterated throughout the dialogue, is reminiscent of Peter's predatory hold on Clara.[61] Unlike Peter, however, he is not "white"; he is a "dark Adonis," resembling "a giant from the N.B.A." (pp. 49, 115), whose "silky brown" skin, associated with "perhaps" some "Ethiopian genes" or "negroid blood" (pp. 49, 115), clearly aligns him with Eved Hakushi. Except that here this "racial" otherness is not a cause for alarm but for adoration. In a deconstructionist move, Me'ira mockingly declares herself a "racist" because she cannot see herself with "anyone who is not an 'oriental' Israeli" (*me'edot hamizrah*). This mock-racism says it all: *With Her on Her Way Home* is, on some level, a contemporary "realization" of the allegorical bond between the "others" essayed in "The Bridge of the Green Duck." Two internal Israeli others, a "white" female (Heller) and a *mizrahi* male, a representative of *Isra'el hashnia*, overcome their marginalization by entering into a singular relationship, one that is blithely labelled, once and again, "our infamous bond [*'ahva*, literally brotherhood]" (pp. 36, 48, 73, and passim).[62] Unlike in the earlier story, however, here this "brotherly bond" does not function as a defense, blocking the erotic attraction palpable in Clara and Eved's embrace scene, but rather as an encouragement. Implying cross-gender equality, it is in fact a modern version of the common topos of the lover as a soul-mate or twin, which resonates Aristophanes' androgynites or the biblical *'ezer kenegdo*[63]) In a sense, it is the very condition on which this joyful erotic love is founded. The exquisite portrayal of this unconventional love—spanning twenty years and two lengthy cross-continental break-ups—is one of the most authentic in the author's oeuvre and unprecedented in Hebrew fiction. We could not do justice here to its nuanced stylization, intricate structure, and psychological insights, nor to the rich web of intertextuality that links it to the rest of Kahana-Carmon's work (and to the canon of Hebrew poetry as well).[64] Suffice it to say, for the purposes of our immediate argument, that on the surface, this singular love seems to offer an antidote to the "feminist romance," constructing its own version of "The New Hebrew Woman."

Structured *in opposition* to marital bliss, the dynamics of this plot seemingly explode the captivity narrative of female dependency and gender inequality. Its earlier stages, at least, effect a synthesis between work and love, enhanced by a strong dose of *jouissance*, in the best French tradition (both critical and otherwise). The liberating power of shared intimacy ("the poetics of the body" [p. 43]), both physical and spiritual, is explored here with all its playfulness and humor,[65] but with all its pathos as well. For this idealized brotherly-erotic bond (not to be confused with incestuous love) is undermined by its very catalyst—the human body. And although the "betrayal of the body" is a lament of old standing ("The body is the cause of love," says Yehuda Amichai, "Later, the fortress guarding it,/Later, the prison of love"[66] and cf. Diotima's speech in Plato's *Symposium*), here it has a special poignancy. "Twenty years" is not only the duration of this romance; it is also (roughly) the age difference between the lovers—although not the one we would expect. So that when Mossik has finally outgrown his adolescent fear of co-dependency ("my rebellion without cause against you is over, like measles and whooping cough" [p. 52]); when after seven years of absence he is ready to acknowledge the mutuality of their attachment ("This story of ours, it is only now beginning. We are invincible" [p. 51])—it is precisely then that Me'ira reaches the "eclipse of her light" (in Hebrew the play on her name is quite clear; p. 276), entering a stage of parting, of farewell, of the "body's swan song" (p. 43). "Twenty years later," says Leah Goldberg, in a poem that may be declared the semiotic subtext of this novel, "Emotions are not like old wine:/They do not become more perfect, nor more sublime."[67] Time, "all that has happened in the world," is clearly the culprit in this poem (published in 1955!). Four decades later, Kahana-Carmon is able to cut closer to the bone: It is not (or at least not only) what happened in the world, she seems to be saying, but what happened with us, in our bodies (and souls), that makes the river of Time so menacing.

Yet in this particular case, it is not only the truism of the transitory nature of love (and life) and the decline of the body that is at stake. What Me'ira is concerned about is the violation of the equilibrium (*'anahnu kevar lo' kohot shavim*, p. 276) which their relationship had enjoyed earlier. With the realization that this condition is gone, reached late in the story and in the narration, Me'ira is struggling with her own verdict to give up the relationship despite her continued attraction to Mossik's *bon physique* (p. 295). At the close of the novel Me'ira paradoxically finds herself at a crossroad not that different from Clara's, *mutatis mutandis*: She has to choose between the unhappiness of dependent love and the unhappiness of lonely aging. In fact, it is the obsessive evocation of her coming to terms with the latter that renders this narrative both powerful and exasperating. For this is a grim prospect for a relationship that had been earlier experienced by both parties as the rarified flight of the Condor over the Andes (pp. 51–52) or the discovery of Africa, the uncharted continent (pp. 49, 74, and passim[68]). Yet, although the question of "what went wrong?" is always at the heart of Me'ira's reflections, she never questions the nature of her glorious past, the ostensible equilibrium now lost. It is left to the attentive reader to ask: What's wrong with this picture?

We can begin by reconsidering the nature of the "infamous equilibrium." The fact is that despite the idealization, the two parties were never on an equal footing. At the time of their fateful meeting—which occupies the middle section, the longest of three that make up the narrative (pp. 79–219)—Me'ira Heller was at the peak of her career, while Mossik was young and socially uninitiated, a kind of an Israeli Rastigniac (see Balsac's *Père Goriot*), groping his way in the metropolis. But it was precisely this reverse hierarchy that enabled Me'ira to feel equal in some way to Mossik. Theirs was the bond of the weak, producing a false sense of egalitarianism. As long as his low social status compensated for her basic "feminine weakness" (the need for dependency and the worshipping of masculine "strength," which are the same for the immature and disadvantaged Clara and the celebrity of the Tel Aviv stage), the illusion of equilibrium could hold forth. But this illusion eventually gives way to "sexual difference": While social realities change, psychological structures do not. Even in this best of all possible relationships, Kahana-Carmon is unable (or unwilling?) to imagine a truly non-hierarchical male-female interaction. In the final analysis, the change of scenery has not affected the fundamental dynamics of her "feminist romance."

When all is said and done, her latest protagonist is the victim of gender essentialism just like her predecessors, despite the clamoring for cross-gender equality. Once again, Kahana-Carmon has carved out the most touching, insightful, and compelling dramatization—not of "The New Hebrew Woman" (namely, feminist liberation), but of sexual difference and female otherness.

We have to look elsewhere then for more accomplished attempts by Israeli novelists to go beyond the feminist romance. The first is para-doxically Shulamith Hareven (b. 1930), who already in her first novel, *A City of Many Days*[69] (published in 1972 after several collections of poetry [1962, 1969] and short stories [1966, 1970]), problematized the essentialistic approaches inherent in Israeli culture. Inspired by Virginia Woolf's much debated "androgyny," Hareven astutely deconstructs re-ceived dichotomies of gender roles.[70] In a way, she turns the idealistic options of cross-gender position choices recommended by the French "non-feminist" Julia Kristeva[71] into a realistic literary convention; and like the latter, she declares herself a non- or "selective" feminist. More-over, Hareven is notorious for her (extratextual) rejection of the cate-gory of women writers altogether, and for her belief in the separation of art and life. It should come as no surprise, then, that her "New Hebrew Woman" is refreshingly different from childhood on, carrying this dif-ference through her romantic, marital, and maternal relationships. In her "feminist romance," work, love, and even motherhood (as implied by the protagonist's name, Sarah) seem to mingle peacefully.

This is no Cinderella story, however. In a typical Israeli fashion, war intervenes; or, as Hareven puts it, the power of history, embodied in the City, Jerusalem, circumscribes human action, subsuming both anguish and pleasure under its impersonal workings: "The city abides no one's decision about who they are. She decides for them, she makes them, with the pressure of stones and infinite time" (p. 121/129). It is against this setting that the myth of androgyny collapses. The pressure of World War II, of the historical contingencies, creates, Hareven tells us, the group self, the notorious "first person plural" of Israeli society. Subjec-tivity, female or otherwise, is suspended when the cannons are roaring. Consequently, the romance, feminist or not, is not even an option for this protagonist. In fact, it is precisely the rekindled romance of her youth that has to give way under the pressure of the war. Thus in her last interior monologue the protagonist positions herself as a mother, one whom others recognize (*makirim 'oti*) as "having three sons and very little time."

Unwittingly, Hareven offers here a Lacanian insight: Reflected in the gaze of others, the subject of necessity perceives herself as an object ("me," *le moi*).[72] But does this mean that the subject is *in principle* alienated from her/his own selfhood, as Lacan would have it? Not quite. For unlike Lacan (and unlike the Judaic postbiblical tradition, one may add[73]) Hareven optimistically harbors a circumstantial rather than ontological "explanation" of the structure she has created. The celebration of the self, any self, is temporarily compromised under the historical circumstances dramatized in this novel. The sociopolitical conditions that have given rise to the ideology of "we," the "stupid plural" as one of her characters calls it (p. 182/197), have also dictated the suppression of the feminist quest. In this, Hareven had novelistically anticipated what political scientists have later concluded ("Gender Equality? Not in a War Zone!" is the succinct title of a 1989 essay by Naomi Chazan[74]). Yet the acceptance of this inevitability does not undermine her belief that the objectivization of the subject is historically, not universally or essentially, determined. And if the female subject of her narrative cannot be privileged with full subjectivity, she is allowed the empowerment of existential transcendence: Stretching from Genesis to eternity, it is the big *female* "other," Jerusalem, that offers a moment of ecstasy, of metonymic submersion:

Now this is me, she told herself, now this is me . . . with this feeling of great peace [reconciliation] . . . Now this is me in this moment of hers . . . A place to touch the sky: now it is close. To breathe in mountain-and-light. Now. (p. 189)

The uniqueness (among Israeli writers) of Hareven's position on gender essentialism, is paralleled by the splendid isolation of her heroine among Israeli female protagonists. In no other novel had the gap between lofty ideals (both authorial and Zionist, both intratextual and contextual) and the limitations of reality been so sensitively (but also ambivalently) dramatized. In some sense, this novel was ahead of its time. In the early seventies the horizon of expectations was not yet ripe for a literary discussion of the tension between nationalism and feminism, even in this moderate, selective form. Female victimization was convincingly evoked by the early work of Kahana-Carmon, but it would take her, as we have seen, more than a decade to get to a stage of protest and action; and even then she would stop, as I have argued above, on the brink of masculinist autonomy. In poetry, one could hear some revolutionary tones in Yona Wallach's verse, but not too many were willing to listen. No wonder, then, that *A City of Many Days* was received as another nostalgic tale about Jerusalem, "lacking," in the words of a leading Israeli scholar, "highly significant themes and conceptual contents."[75] That the issues of female subjectivity and cross-gender equality, as well as their conflict with the historical constraints, are central to the novel—this passed totally unnoticed. It goes without saying that the potential critique of Zionist ideology implied by this material was not even surmised.

A whole decade had passed before the next attempts materialized, and this not without the impact of the Yom Kippur War (1973) and its aftermath: the protest movements, in which women were taking an active role; Knesset member Shulamit Aloni's treatise on women's deplorable status within the legal system (*Women as Human Beings*, 1973); British-Israeli psychologist Lesley Hazelton's demythologizing of "The Realities behind the Myth" (*Israeli Women*, 1977); and the first report of a Knesset commission on the status of women (1978).[76] The same years also saw the republication of Sara Azaryahu's 1947 *Chapters in the History of the Suffragist Movement in Palestine, 1900–1947*, prefaced by Marsha Friedman, the American lawyer whose unsuccessful attempt to import American feminism into Israel (and into the Knesset) would come to fruition only by the late eighties.

By the mid-1980s, the missing "New Hebrew Woman" began to show small signs of coming back to life. *Nogah*, the first feminist Israeli journal, was established in 1980. In 1982 sociologist Dafna Izraeli published *The Double Bind*, her analysis of the catch-22 of Israeli women. Israel Women's Network (IWN), spearheaded by Professor Alice Shalvi (another Anglo-American import) was organized in 1984, "combating a climate of opinion in which feminism was considered irrelevant because Israel was perceived as having already achieved equality between the sexes"![77]

This paradoxical "climate" can be detected in the literary arena too: on the one hand, the older generation's struggle against the "feminist romance" as we have seen in the novels by Lapid, Kahana-Carmon, and (earlier) Hareven;[78] and on the other, prose fiction by an unprecedented number of younger women—particularly towards the end of the decade—who mostly follow the lead of the early Kahana-Carmon, rather than the novels of the eighties.[79] Hareven's anti-essentialistic androgyny has been all but forgotten until the nineties,[80] and for a good reason: Just like her early heroine (1972), Hareven herself let the historical momentum take over her creative production. Throughout the eighties, her short stories (1980), masterful essays (1981), and allegorical novellas (1984, 1988) were mostly preoccupied with the examination of the political and social fabric of Jewish/Israeli culture, generally from the perspective of an outsider. Women, to the extent that they figure in these works, function as the outsider too, indistinguishable from most of their male counterparts. Hareven seems to have made good, then, of her principled objection to "gender specific" thematics and style; in her later work (except for a few stories in the collection *Loneliness*, 1980) the woman question is subsumed—in a typical Israeli fashion—by the concerns of the collective.[81]

Against this background, we should be able to appreciate the publication, in 1987, of Ruth Almog's ambitious novel *Shorshei avir* (Dangling roots), which constitutes the boldest departure from the feminist romance in Israeli literature.[82] A prolific writer of short stories (1969, 1975, 1986, 1993) and novels (1971, 1980, 1982),[83] Almog (b. 1936) justifiably won the hearts of both critics and readers with this complex, prize-winning narrative. Structured in two dissimilar parts, ranging from turn-of-the-century Palestine to 1960s Europe, this novel offers a critique not only of her predecessors' optimistic androgyny or masculinist liberation, but perhaps also of some of the master narratives of Enlightenment-based liberal feminism in general.

Interestingly, this critique is implicit rather than explicit. For on the surface, *Dangling Roots* is a typically "masculine (virile), political novel" as the author herself suggested in an interview: "I was trying to engage large, important themes . . . I was inspired by a woman who impressed me with her courage—a feisty woman, diametrically opposed to the passive women I have treated so far."[84] This "transition" rings a familiar tone—a few years earlier Kahana-Carmon declared a similar turning away from passive characters to active ones. Following in her footsteps, Almog was determined to counteract what she saw as the Israeli marginalization of women's experience ("In Israel, if you do not write about national issues and you do not have a sociopolitical message—you [f.] do not exist!" [ibid.]). But here the resemblance ends. For unlike her predecessors, Almog has woven together two novelistic modalities hitherto employed mostly by *male* Israeli writers: the fictional autobiography and the historical novel.[85] Book I of the novel, "Madness Is the Wisdom of the Individuum" (pp. 7–160), is a dialogic narrative, in which the two modalities alternate antiphonally chapter by chapter. In one, Mira Gutman, a conventionally autobiographic narrator, recounts her atypical life story in a typical *moshava* in the early years of the State. (Notice the here and now of this strand of the story line.) In the other, she attempts to piece together, somewhat frantically and chaotically, the life story of her maternal great grandfather, Lavdovi (or perhaps Levadovi, "Mr. Alonely"?), an eccentric Zionist of the First Aliyah. Her involvement with this father-figure is not historical in the strict sense of the word. It is psychological and ideological, displacing contemporary concerns that reached their peak in the wake of the 1982 Lebanon War

(Jewish-Arab relations and general attitudes towards power) to the historical events. Yet it is this strand of the narrative that contains the seeds of the "political masculine" novel that would come to fruition in Book II of the novel, "Anatomy of Freedom" (pp. 161–359).

Almog allowed her heroine, then, both the closed intimacy of stereotypic female *Bildung* and the ostensibly open horizons of the male hero's quest. Furthermore, more than any Israeli woman writer before her, she fully developed both the psychological and the sociopolitical matrices of her protagonist, making her the first Israeli heroine to narrate a complete life-span—from childhood in a small town (modelled on Zichron Ya'akov), through urban adolescence in Jerusalem, to an allegedly autonomous adulthood abroad. Thematically and generically, *Dangling Roots* comes as close as possible to the "malestream" of the Hebrew literary canon; a fact that has no doubt contributed to the warm reception it received from the literary establishment and the reading audience alike.

At the same time, however, the novel sports some highly "feminine" features. Most significantly, Mira is the first Israeli female protagonist to be endowed with a mother who cuts an impressive figure, crucial to the shaping of her daughter's life. In this she is indeed fundamentally different from Almog's earlier (and later!) heroines who as a rule suffer from a "father fixation," without the benefit of a viable maternal role model (most notoriously, the collection *Nashim* [Women], which appeared shortly before the novel, in 1986). This shift to mother-daughter relations deserves our attention not only because of its novelty (it has subsequently been discovered by younger Israeli writers[86]), but because it makes Almog's take on feminism so complex and, in the final analysis, also subversive. If we recall that it was precisely this psychological nexus that has been unearthed from Freudian unknowability by feminists on both sides of the Atlantic (to different ends, to be sure), the significance of its belated entry into the discourse of Hebrew feminism may surface.[87] Curiously, however, none of the reviews of *Dangling Roots* even mention this feminist connection.[88] Apparently, Almog succeeded in her ploy: Her novel was perused for all the "serious," namely, politically relevant issues it explored, as well as for the psychological implications of the symbiotic co-dependency of its two heroines, but not, as far as I know, for the potential questioning of feminism it harbors. In what follows, we will reverse this procedure: Relegating to another occasion the rich stylistic and ideational tapestry that comprises the novel,[89] we are about to claim *Dangling Roots* as the last Israeli variation on the theme of the "feminist romance."

To begin with, Mira's mother, Ruhama,[90] is portrayed as a stereotypically feminine charmer, covering almost every cliché in the book: She is attractive, sensuous, artistic, imaginative, in tune with nature (and with her own sexuality), communicative when she feels like it and enigmatically distant when she does not, and, most importantly, an expert inventor of stories. At the same time, however, she is a woman alone, an outsider living on the outskirts of the small town. Independent by default (she was left by her estranged husband to run the estate by herself), she is hopelessly self-centered and capricious, hysterical, and suicidal (as her name unobtrusively implies). Living in a fantasy world and always on the brink of emotional breakdown, she is heavily dependent on Mira, who, in a reversal of roles, loyally "mothers" her with all the ambivalence that such family dynamics of necessity entails. This unhappy woman, in short, could have readily been another "madwoman in the attic,"[91] had this not been a 1980s novel whose first part carries the enigmatic title "Madness is *the Wisdom* of the Individuum" (emphasis added).

That the "exoneration" of madness is at least one of the psychological questions with which this book grapples, is no doubt clear. The title of Book I, as well as several of its major themes, clearly smack of R. D. Laing's idealization of schizophrenic "madness," from *The Divided Self* (1960) through *The Politics of Experience* (1967). We may recall that these theories enjoyed quite a vogue among left-wing ideologues of the 1960s—precisely the time frame of Book II of our novel and the ostensible "moment of writing" of its autobiographic narrator. If we add to this Almog's general fascination (both textual and extratextual) with the "thin line" between sanity and insanity, and particularly her equivocation over the question of whether or not an escape into madness is a matter of free choice, a conscious rebellion against the social order,[92] the deep structure of the novel would begin to emerge. The legacy of madness, woven together by the two narrative strands of Book I (both Mira's mother and her great-grandfather), may have been inspired by Laing and Esterson's *Families of Schizophrenics.*[93] Although not schizophrenic in the clinical sense, Mira's family bears some features typical of Laing's case histories: the centrality of the mother-daughter relations (accompanied by an "absent father"), as well as "the feminine predicament" of "leaving home and letting go."[94] Yet Almog's treatment of this paradigm takes another route. While Book I both foregrounds and problematizes a Laingian idealization of individual madness (namely, the "wisdom" of this ostensible personal freedom), Book II offers a merciless analysis of the other side of the coin—the use and (aggressive) misuse, both personal and political, of the philosophies of freedom and of existential choice.

Bearing in mind this nexus of madness and freedom under question, we may better understand the significance of Lavdovi's act of self-mutilation or Ruhama's symbolic castration of her daughter (her furious cutting of Mira's beautiful long hair). On another level, it may explain Mira's tolerance of her mother's other deviances, the playful as well as the grievous (her attempted suicides). Still, one is hard put to accept Mira's total acceptance of her mother's rationalization for her symptomatic flights into fantasy:

> Mom told me once, and I have never forgotten it: "What did God give humans imagination for, if not to invent things. I am telling you, to invent stories is the most marvelous thing there is. Fantasy knows no limit. One can even invent a life for oneself."
> . . . And when Dr. Shapira would reprimand her for fibbing, she would say: "This is no fib. It is fanciful and amusing. After all, life is so gray. Nothing interesting ever happens here. Ever. So I tell stories and make life more exciting. And you know what? Sometimes such a story even becomes true." (p. 75)

"Nothing interesting ever happens here"—could this description be out of an Israeli novel? Is this a valid assessment of life in a country as volatile as Israel? Wouldn't it require a greater measure of the suspension of disbelief normally expected of the reader? I suspect it would, particularly if the reader is preconditioned by the androcentric canon of Hebrew literature, notorious for its preoccupation with the always urgent issues of the public arena. But this is, of course, precisely Almog's point. In order to have her younger protagonist experience both the pleasure and the pain of the "real" world, she must make her break away from the "private sphere"—the prison-house of female experience—in which, presumably, "life is so gray."[95] For although her mother's strategy of self-invention, the age-old Scheherazade foible of spinning stories, is approved by the protagonist as an act of personal freedom ("I did not care. Like Mom, I believed that anyone had the privilege to invent his or her life any way they wished"), it will not serve as her role model. Mira is not going to stay home and amuse the neighbors with potentially self-fulfilling stories; she will actively make one of these stories come true.

That the model she chooses is typically androcentric should come as no surprise: This may be one more link in a tradition we have been unearthing in recent Israeli literature—the Enlightenment masculine-modeled feminist strategy of self-invention. What is less predictable is Mira's attitude to this model. For although Mira—like Clara, Kahana-Carmon's seventeenth-century heroine—fashions her life in the image of several father figures (Lavdovi, her half-imagined great-grandfather; Alexandroni [her mother's lifelong admirer][96], her own father, and, later, also her lover/husband Jacques Berliavsky), she does not do this out of blind admiration. If her penetrating critique of her own father is any measure, she is fully cognizant of the true dimensions of his [masculinist] world. Indeed, it is this insight that makes Mira's evolution so psychologically interesting. On the face of it, Almog seems to offer a "feminist" corrective to the Laingian predicament, reinscribing the absent father into Mira's life. This psychoanalytic "missing third term"[97] is supposed to help her over the hurdle of the claustrophobic (if not schizophrenic) feminine symbiosis with her mother, and move her into the world of political action and masculinist freedom. And so it does. But at what price?

[Mira] told herself that her father was a man who looked into a small mirror all his life, but there was nothing one could do about this, because he was unable to be any different, he was simply not capable of looking into a bigger mirror, because such a mirror did not exist for him, at least not in his reality. There, in his world, only two options existed: either a tiny mirror, or a magnified picture, namely: national concerns. [. . . .] But this was not all . . . Not only was his mirror small, it was also always positioned in the same right angle and it would never dawn on him that it was possible, really possible, and sometimes even greatly needed, to position the mirror diagonally, for example, perhaps in a 45 degree angle, or 135 degree or even 180 . . . True, the portrait reflected in the mirror might be slightly cut off, at the chin or the forehead, but instead some other views might be reflected in the free areas along it. Yes, yes, Mira told herself, Mira's Dad is an onlooker, merely an onlooker, not an insightful observer. This is how his eyes are built, that's all. This is why, Mira thought, his opinions are so predetermined and unequivocal, and this is why he is preoccupied only with issues external to him. (pp. 133–34)

The apologetic tone of this inner monologue is unmistakable. Mira is clearly caught between an Oedipal idealization of her father and a ruthless adolescent observation of his dogmatism and self-centeredness.[98] She therefore uses the mirror metaphor defensively, protecting herself from fully comprehending the brunt of her own accusation. Moreover, this is the first time that the "autobiographic" narrative voice splits itself into first and third persons, being itself conscious of the defensive function of this specific technique:[99]

Yes, with all this turbulence of fear, rage, and insult, also came elucidation. And I told myself that at times I stopped being me and that Mira particularly stopped being me when she was thinking about her father, that father of Mira . . . Mira wanted to protect him for me, she wanted to protect him from me, because it was important to keep him away, safe from my harsh disappointment, from my hurt. It was important to keep him for herself in some way, because she did not want to lose him completely and she was afraid of me, because I exposed and befouled him. (p. 133)

Fettered by one of the oldest psychological taboos, Mira is unable to integrate her father's betrayal—his refusal to help her get rid of an unwanted pregnancy. Her solution to the conflict is ingenious: Instead of splitting off the "bad" father, she externalizes her own forgiving, ratio-nalizing self, while "internally regressing into her 'deviant' thinking," which she uses as "a dam against the rage he would arouse in me" (p. 134). It is here, in this crucial event, that the protagonist of *Dangling Roots* emerges as a postmodernist (Lacanian) split subject. Yet this split is doubly motivated, as it bears the unmistakable stamp of the modern *female* condition. For Mira, an integrated self is unrealizable not only because of the universally endemic gulf between one's authentic per-ceptions and those approved by the "Symbolic Order," but also because of her very personal impossible choice between the Scylla of Mom's rich but totally vicarious fantasy life and the Charybdis of Dad's active but narrow-minded public life.

Indeed, it is this tragic conflict that is dramatized by the break in the hitherto smooth flow of Mira's first-person retrospection: From now until the end of the Book I, her strand of the narration shuttles between first and third persons, indecisively moving from the ostensibly authen-tic but private "I" to the "other," more public "Mira" who is perhaps better socialized but also more repressed and alienated from her "true" self. That this splitting originates in the mock mirror-stage scene attrib-uted to the father is of course part of an inescapable irony—trying to escape one kind of vicarious life, Mira unwittingly undertakes another. And although the last word is given to the narrating "I," its actual ac-tions speak louder than its discourse: "I then crossed the street. There, on the other side, Dad was already waiting for me. Together we entered the port and boarded the ship" (p. 160). The choice is made; the Rubi-con crossed. The protagonist has left behind mother, home, hometown, and homeland. Now she is on her way to join the sound and fury of her father's world, that other world of which she used to be so critical. Un-like her mother, she is going to invent a life, not a story of a life. But will she escape the typical female lot, shared by her mother as well, of living vicariously? Will she emerge as the first "New Hebrew Woman" to sidestep the trap of the feminist romance? Will she, in short, live up to the "work and love" agenda of feminist expectations?

Ruth Almog's answer seems ambiguous. Yes, she allows her protago-nist the freedom of choice (Book II is entitled "Anatomy of Freedom") and sends her off to Italy to study medicine. True, she releases her from the prison-house of the female private sphere, where "nothing interest-ing ever happens," and plunges her into the "colorful" world of inter-national journalism and left-wing politics (this is Europe of the 1960s, the student revolts, and the Russian invasion of Prague). At the same time, she immerses her in the discourse on freedom, both personal and political, of that generation (behaviorism vs. existentialism, Freudianism vs. Marxism, Marcuse vs. Fromm, possessiveness vs. ego boundaries, authenticity vs. power relations), only to find out their blind alleys (pp. 176, 182, 190–96ff., 237ff.). She also involves her in one of the most intriguing love affairs of Hebrew literature, enabling her to conduct a dialogic discourse on love and female desire, while testing first-hand the practical in/validity of the rhetorics of freedom. The eccentric, unpredictable, and finally also unreliable Professor Jacques Berliavsky is one of the most exasperating, finely drawn character portraits in Israeli fiction. Yet one should not miss the irony implied by the title of Part A of Book II, "Freedom According to Jacques," pp. 163–266.[100]

This version of the "New Hebrew Woman" has definitely got a fair share of work and love. But they do not dwell happily together. Nor do the protagonists. In a twist that might be unexpected in the heroine's "euphoric text" but is quite predictable for the sober realism of this novel, Mira's "total, absolute love" (p. 189ff.) founders on the rocks of marriage (p. 218ff.). And although the reason for its foundering is overdetermined (her dependency, the vacuousness of his "freedom"), it clearly takes Mira one step further in the deconstruction—which began with her critique of her father—of the masculine ideal. The hard lesson of her exercise in "freedom according to Jacques" is that "love and work" elude not only aspiring young females, they are rare in the male world as well. Other differences notwithstanding, Jacques' "balance sheet" turns out to be just as warped as her father's. From this perspective, it is not Mira who has failed the test of the "masculine, political" plot, rather, it is the ideal that has failed her.

Nevertheless, she is denied a continuous voice, an uninterrupted line of discourse. Although Mira remains the central consciousness through which Book II is focalized, she loses her own voice. As we meet her again in Book II, she is presented to us mostly through third person narration, with several exceptions: her brief homecomings (for her wedding and for her mother's funeral; pp. 207–222, 298–317), her traumatic fantasy, evoking the "primary neurosis" of her childhood—her jealousy of her beautiful mother (pp. 258–59), and her final long letter to her father (p. 333ff.).

It is on the pages of the latter that the autobiographic quest for self-knowledge finally materializes. And it is here that the protagonist discovers the paradoxical truth about the "otherness" of her self. For although successfully disengaged from her mother's vicarious life, Mira has not really come into her own. To her surprise and perhaps horror she learns that in all her love ("object") choices she has unconsciously recapitulated the structure of her relationship with her father, thereby "ensuring" their failure. Furthermore, her ideological positions are constantly referred to as "borrowed," "recited," "cheap recipe," and so on. In the final analysis, it was not her own life that Mira has invented. Although in a different fashion, her self turns out to be no less vicarious than her mother's; and her "freedom"—both political and psychological—seems nothing more than spurious. The road to freedom, Mira finds out, leads through a history of male violence and aggression, terror and rape (which she experiences first-hand). Fraternity is taken over by fratricide, equality by oppression. It is therefore not surprising that the charming autobiographic "I" of Book I has almost no place in the harsh world of Book II. By the inner logic of this novel, autobiographic introspection and political or other "malestream" activism are mutually exclusive.

Dangling Roots both continues and transcends two novelistic trends recently developed by Israeli women: the "feminist romance" and the "masked autobiography." Without these antecedents, the specific features of this novel in their particular combination would have been unthinkable. At the same time, however, Almog deserves credit for the steps she took to transform these models both structurally and thematically. Unlike her predecessors, she is far from idealizing the masculinist construction of the female self; neither does she trust compromises of either Virginia Woolf's androgyny or Julia Kristeva's "third generation" women, to which some of her peers subscribe; nor does she find consolation in the apotheosis of sexual difference argued by Irigaray and Cixous and ambivalently practiced by Kahana-Carmon.

Hers is the sober observation of the specific, intensely personal, psychological matrix of a female subject (filtered in this novel through the prism of various psychoanalytic models), and the no less intense and painful political contingencies imposed upon it. Her protagonist stands alone in Israeli fiction in her endeavor to actually carry out, here and now, "classical" feminist expectations. But at the same time, the outcome of Mira's "education" undoes or deconstructs the very ideal it has set out to achieve. Almog's venture, the inscription of a female protagonist into "a masculine, political novel" (her own wording) has turned out to be its own best refutation. That this endeavor takes place in exile, outside of the borders of Israel, is of course part of the critique implied in the structure of this novel. Yet the critique is double-pronged, for this "portrait of the feminist as a young woman" crashes against the unyielding realities of both the protagonist's internal (psychological) and external (sociopolitical) worlds. In the final analysis, the source of discontent in this novel is not easily determined (or perhaps it is overdetermined?):

Is the inhospitality of Israeli culture to blame for the exile, if not disappearance of the "New Hebrew Woman," as repeatedly argued—extratextually—by Ruth Almog herself[101] (as by Kahana-Carmon before her)? Or is Western feminism itself under scrutiny here, exposing the naiveté and risky optimism of some of its basic propositions?

Almog's answer to these questions is imbedded in her narrative, of course, by means of plot, discourse, and closure. Although at the end of her sad story, Mira is still in exile, smarting from her psychological and ideological wounds, her final actions harbor a glimpse of hope: Lifting the lid of repression off her childhood traumas, she is finally ready to embrace the "madness" of her maternal heritage which she has attempted to suppress throughout Book II (p. 335ff.). Replacing her mother's oral storytelling with the autobiographer's pen, she is about to find her authenticity in (creative?) writing, not in political action. Given the limitations of our condition, Almog seems to be saying, creativity is the only true freedom, one that transcends gender, class, and national divisions. "Artistic imagination fashions the unconscious memory of failed emancipation, of a betrayed promise," Mira finds in one of Jacques' books, followed by a quote from Adorno, that "Messiah" so "often quoted by her German friends: 'In the absence of freedom art can preserve the spirit of freedom only by negating non-freedom' . . . Mira grimaces and closes the book. The words sound hollow. She, at least, does not understand them" (ibid.).

Mira may not understand; but her imagination does. "Jacques hates disorder, she thinks, for him everything has to be in place. Only within order he feels free . . . only within order . . . only within order . . . How? How?" (p. 356). Needless to say, she does not find out how. Rather than decoding the secret of the obsessional scientist's "Symbolic Order," she gives in to the rhythms, sounds, and fragrances of her near and distant memories. In a tapestry of free associations her imagination shuttles back and forth between past and present, the real and the imaginary, finally replicating the very language that was earlier used to represent her mother's unique bond with nature. With this, Ruhama's madness is not only internalized, it is also redeemed. The Freudian (Greek) connotation of her name (*rehem*, womb, *hystera*) gives way to its biblical (Hebrew) meaning (*rahamim*, compassion, love). Exhibiting the cadences of Freudian primary processes, of Lacanian pre-Oedipal Imaginary, or of Kristeva's maternal Semiotic, these final pages hold the promise for artistic sublimation. We are not sure whether Mira will return from her exile ("I do not want to walk in the footsteps of my maternal great-grandfather . . . and be called a madwoman" [p. 358]), or whether she will fare better in her future love choices, but we feel confident that she may be able to "befriend" her legacy of madness and contain it within the "chaos" of artistic creativity.[102]

A few years ago, in an article discussing some of the predecessors of *Dangling Roots*, I asked why none of the Israeli women writers of the seventies and eighties could imagine a protagonist with the same artistic freedom they themselves enjoyed, why none of the "masked autobiographies" I analyzed were in fact a "portrait of the artist as a young woman."[103] Ruth Almog's novel finally does precisely that. And just like her male peers,[104] she does not shy from baring some very personal wounds that have engendered (pun intended) her artistic mending. She thus brings our search for literary constructions of the "New Hebrew Woman" to an appropriate close. From the perspective of the post-Zionist 1990s, this is one more *grand recit* whose time is over. Younger (and not so young) women writers who emerged towards the end of the last decade either bypass this model of feminist narrative or parody it altogether (as in, Castel-Bloom's *Dolly City*, 1992). In recent publications devoted to women (the journal *Politika* of July 1989; *Feminine Presence*, a catalogue of an exhibit of Israeli Women Artists at Tel Aviv Museum, 1990; *Zeman Hanashim* [Women's Time], an issue of the historical quarterly *Zemanim* [Winter 1993]), the Enlightenment metanarrative is often eclipsed by postmodernist or Continental models. Although Israel is still far from being a haven for feminism, there is a new androgynous consciousness and even a few male feminists (see *'Ani feminist*, by Kobi Niv, 1990). Veteran male writers have announced their fascination with the literary construction of women, but could not avoid killing off their female protagonists while so doing (Oz in *Lada'at 'ishah* [*To Know a Woman*], 1989; Yehoshua in *Molkho* [*Five Seasons*], 1987). Even so, the Oedipal masterplot is put under scrutiny, giving way to other narratives, the maternal in particular (*'Ima yesh rak 'aheret* by Devorah Repled-Zilberstein, 1994). Other plots explore female desire (Katzir) or construct fractured, postmodernist, or postcolonial subjectivities (Dolan; Matalon). As this essay goes to print, postmodernist-feminist criticism has marked its presence by a heated exchange (pulling no punches in a manner that should disclaim any argument for sexual difference) carried out on the pages of *Teoria uvikoret* (Theory and Criticism: An Israeli Forum).[105] Apparently, a kaleidoscopic portrait of new Israeli women—artists, critics, political activists—is slowly emerging, no doubt fashioning new modalities of feminist consciousness for the coming century.

Notes

1. Nina Baym, "Melodramas of Beset Manhood: How Theories of American Fiction Exclude Women Authors," in *The New Feminist Criticism*, ed. Elaine Showalter (New York: Pantheon, 1985), p. 68.

2. Quoted by Yaffa Berlovitz, "The Literature of the Early Pioneer Women" (in Hebrew), *Proza* 66–67, (July 1983): 31–33.

3. Even as poets, women entered the mainstream only in the 1920s. On the problematics of this late entry, see Dan Miron, *Imahot meyasdot, ahayot horgot* (Founding mothers, stepsisters) (Tel Aviv, 1989, 1990); for a partial English rendition, see his "Why Was There No Women's Poetry in Hebrew Before 1920?" in *Gender and Text in Modern Hebrew and Yiddish Literature*, ed. Naomi B. Sokoloff, Anne Lapidus Lerner, and Anita Norich (New York: JTS, 1992), pp. 65–94. For a rejoinder see Michael Gluzman, "The Exclusion of Women from Hebrew Literary History," *Prooftexts* 11:3 (1991): 259–278.

4. See my articles "Historical Novels or Masked Autobiographies?" *Siman Kri'ah* 19 (1985): 208–213; "Gender In/Difference in Contemporary Hebrew Fictional Autobiography," *Biography: An Interdisciplinary Quarterly* 11, no. 3 (1988): 189–209; and "Ideology and Self-Representation of Women in Israeli Literature," in *Redefining Autobiography in Twentieth Century Women's Fiction*, ed. Colette Hall and Janice Morgan (New York: Garland, 1991) pp. 281–301.

The new territory covered by women writers is represented in English by Batya Gur's (b. 1947) mystery novels, published since the early 1990s, e.g., *Murder on Saturday Morning*, trans. Dalya Bilu (New York: HarperCollins, 1994).

5. The only exception is Hamutal Bar Yosef's article on Bialik's poetry; see *Gender and Text*, pp. 145–170. Similarly, Esther Fuchs' pioneering study, *Israeli Mythogynies*, treats only one woman writer despite the generalized claim of its subtitle, *Women in Contemporary Hebrew Fiction* (New York: SUNY Press, 1987).

Nor is the situation much different in Hebrew. As this article goes to press, *Hakol ha'aher* (The Other Voice), the first ever volume of prose fiction by Israeli women, has made its appearance (Tel Aviv: Hakibbutz Hame'uchad/Siman Kri'ah 1994, ed. Lily Rattok). The significance of this collection notwithstanding, once more it foregrounds women's short stories while relegating their long fiction to comments in the accompanying editorial essay (pp. 261–349). While this choice is of course technically unavoidable, it adds to the particular slant of this selection—the focus on the difference underlining the female experience, particularly as it is highlighted by the biological life cycle and the traditional gender roles. I would argue, however, that this wholesale acceptance of the politics of sexual difference eclipses some of the more interesting rewritings of Western feminism produced by Israeli novelists in the last two decades, an aspect rarely touched in this volume.

An English version of this collection, *Ribcage: A Hadassah Anthology* (ed. Carol Diament and Lily Rattok, 1994), includes a different selection, probably dictated by the availability of translations, plus a partial rendition of Rattok's introduction (pp. xvi–xxxiv). Both volumes, however, conspicuously ignore feminist and gender-oriented criticism of Israeli prose fiction written on this side of the Atlantic for the last decade.

6. "Gynesis" was first presented in *Diacritics* (Summer, 1982): 54–65, and

later published as *Gynesis: Configurations of Woman and Modernity* (Ithaca, N.Y.: Cornell University Press, 1985).

For a fuller history of "feminism" as a historically changing concept and movement, see Karen Offen, "Defining Feminism: A Comparative Historical Approach," *Signs* 14, no. 1 (Autumn 1988): 119–157; this review is particularly helpful in understanding the earlier roots of European and French feminism as isomorphic with earlier Zionist "feminism."

The debate over the feminism/postmodernism nexus within the American camp is evident in the exchange between Daryl McGowan Tress and Jane Flax in the same issue of *Signs*, pp. 196–203. Although criticized for siding with postmodern deconstruction of subjectivity, Flax's later wide-ranging probing of this issue, *Thinking Fragments: Psychoanalysis, Feminism and Postmodernism in the Contemporary West* (Berkeley: University of California Press, 1990), clearly spells out the "*un*usefulness" of this practice for "feminist emancipation" (see esp. her "No Conclusion," pp. 225, 230, and passim. For a different perspective on this question, see Judith Butler, *Gender Trouble: Feminism and the Subversion of Identity* (New York: Routledge, 1990).

More generally on this problem, see *Feminism/Postmodernism*, ed. Linda J. Nicholson (New York: Routledge, 1985), and *Feminism and Postmodernism*, ed. Margaret Ferguson and Jennifer Wicke (Durham, N.C.: Duke University Press, 1994).

7. *Thinking Fragments*, p. 232. In fact, Flax translates Luce Irigaray's Continental (that is, philosophical and metaphorical) indictment into the Anglo-American language of Object Relations theory, and extends it to the texts of contemporary writers (Irigaray stops with Freud). See also her distinction between the notion of the "unitary" self and a "core" self, p. 210ff.

The difficulty of giving up the notion of a "core" self is not unique to feminist theories. See most recently Gabriele Schwab, "The Insistence of the Subject," in *Subjects without Selves* (Cambridge: Harvard University Press, 1994), pp. 1–22.

8. Julia Kristeva seems to accept this death sentence with impunity, suggesting different strategies of action for "women" (not "feminists") of the "third generation," a generation for whom "identity" is relegated to metaphysics . . . But, of course, she is criticized for abandoning feminism altogether. See her "Women's Time" (1979), in *The Kristeva Reader*, ed. Toril Moi (New York: Columbia University Press, 1985), pp. 187–213.

9. Scholarship has not paid attention to this phenomenon yet; the only work of which I am aware is David Gurevitch's "Feminism and Postmodernism", *Alpayim* 7, 1992, pp. 27–58 (in Hebrew), whose heroines are Grace Paley, Cindy Sherman, and the late Israeli poet Yona Wallach. In his "Postmodernism in Israeli Literature" (*MHL* 15, Fall/Winter 1995, pp. 10–13), he treats, on the other hand, also the young Orly Castel-Bloom, without so much as mentioning her gender-specific themes. Conversely, the radio-symposium on this theme, conducted by Avraham Balaban and published in the same issue (pp. 3–5), sorely misses central foci of recent postmodernist discourse, some of which are explored in the present study. Similarly, his recent book on postmodernism in Israeli fiction (*Hagal ha'aher*, Jerusalem, 1996) treats male writers only.

10. See my "Gender In/Difference" (1988) and "Ideology and Self-Representation" (1991). Cf. *Gender and Text*, Anita Norich's Introduction. A further discussion of gender essentialism in the Jewish tradition is developed in my

"'And Rebecca Loved Jacob,' But Freud Did Not," in *Freud and Forbidden Knowledge*, ed. Peter Rudnytsky and Ellen Handler Spitz (New York: NYU Press 1994), pp. 7–35. Cf. Daniel Boyarin, *Carnal Israel* (Berkeley: University of California Press, 1993) and Elliot Wolfson, *Through a Speculum that Shines* (Princeton, N.J.: Princeton University Press, 1994).

For the general question of gender essentialism, see Flax, *Thinking Fragments*; Diana Fuss, *Essentially Speaking* (New York: Routledge 1992); Butler, *Gender Trouble*.

11. "The New Hebrew Woman" is my own genderized version of "The New Hebrew Man" of Zionist ideology. The latter has been recently introduced and interpreted for the English reader in Benjamin Harshav's *Language in Time of Revolution* (Berkeley: University of California Press, 1993).

12. Findings on this issue have been published in Hebrew since the early 1980s. For an overview in English, see Deborah S. Bernstein, ed., *Pioneers and Homemakers: Jewish Women in Pre-State Israel* (New York: SUNY Press, 1992). Of special interest to our topic are the essays by Yaffa Berlovitz, Dafna Izraeli, and the editor. Cf. Barbara Swirski and Marilyn P. Safir, eds., *Calling the Equality Bluff: Women in Israel* (New York: Teachers College Press, 1993).

13. Manya Schohat's biography, *Before Golda*, told by Rachel Yanait Ben-Zvi, is available in English, translated by Sandra Shurin (New York: Biblio Press, 1988). See also Shulamit Reinharz, in Bernstein, *Pioneers and Homemakers*, pp. 95–118. On Rachel Katznelson, see Miron, *Imahot meyasdot, ahayot horgot*, pp. 249–272, and Harshav, *Language in Time of Revolution*, pp. 183–194.

14. See Toril Moi, *Sexual/Textual Politics: Feminist Literary Theory* (London and New York: Routledge, 1985), p. 91. Cf. Andrea Nye, *Feminist Theory and the Philosophies of Man* (New York, Routledge, 1988), ch. 4, esp. p. 82 ff. See also Moi in *Feminism and Postmodernism*, pp. 86–102. According to Offen ("Defining Feminism," p. 149), "Beauvoir's arguments were received with greater enthusiasm in English-speaking countries than in her own," apparently because of the socional legacy of French feminism. Her anchoring of this legacy in "France's seemingly perilous demographic position" from the early twentieth century on (p. 147) brings home the analogy to the Israeli context.

15. See Yonatan Shapiro, *'Elit lelo mamshichim* (An elite without successors), (Tel Aviv: Sifriyat Po'alim 1984).

16. E.g., Marsha Friedman, who finally gave up and returned to the United States. Lesley Hazleton's *Israeli Women: The Reality Behind the Myth* (New York: Simon & Schuster, 1977) is a good illustration of the gulf between the Israeli (female) self-image and the way it was perceived by Western (feminist) eyes.

17. See my "The 'Other Within' in Israeli Fiction," *Middle East Review* 22, no. 1 (Fall 1991): 47–53.

18. See Mary O'Brien, *The Politics of Reproduction* (New York: Routledge, 1980), p. 235 and passim.

19. Shulamit Lapid, *Gei Oni* (Jerusalem: Keter, 1982). Like most of the novels discussed in this essay, this novel is not available in English. Translations are mine.

20. Although Offen traces the term to late nineteenth century Europe, she does not find it in Russian—the background of this novel—before 1898.

21. I explore this issue in my essays, "Zionism—Neurosis or Cure? The 'Historical' drama of Y. Sobol," *Prooftexts* 7, no. 2 (May 1987): 145–62, and "Back

to Vienna: Zionism on the Literary Couch," in *Vision Confronts Reality*, ed. R. Kozodoy, D. Sidorsky, and K. Sultanik (Rutherford, N.J.: Fairleigh Dickinson University Press, 1989), pp. 310–325.

22. See "Feminism Under Siege," *Prooftexts* 10, no. 3 (September 1990): 493–514.

23. The language clearly echoes de Beauvoir's charge that women "still dream through the dreams of men" (*The Second Sex* [New York: Penguin, 1974], p. 161).

24. Carolyn G. Heilbrun, *Writing a Woman's Life* (New York: Norton, 1988).

25. See Nancy Miller, *The Heroine's Text* (New York: Columbia University Press, 1980).

26. See Offen, "Defining Feminism," p. 134ff.

27. A helpful "corrective" of the received binarism of male independence and female dependence has been recently suggested by Miriam M. Johnson in her *Strong Mothers, Weak Wives* (Berkeley: University of California Press, 1994). Distinguishing between "dependency" and "interdependence" or between "dependent" and "relational" (or "expressive"), she argues that, "Whereas a woman's relational needs get defined as her 'dependency,' men may disguise their dependency needs because they are being met everyday by women . . . women are financially dependent on men, but this dependence must not be confused with psychological dependency" (p. 46).

The literature on the psychology of gender difference is too vast to be enumerated here. The debate over the complicity of philosophy and psychoanalysis in the valorization of gender stereotypes, opened by Luce Irigaray's *Speculum of the Other Woman*, trans. G. Gill (Ithaca, N.Y.: Cornell University Press, 1985) is still raging. Cf. Genevieve Lloyd, *The Man of Reason: "Male" and "Female" in Western Philosophy* (Minneapolis: University of Minnesota Press, 1984). Later writings emphasize the politics of gender identity, as in the works of Flax and Butler. Cf. Daniel Boyarin, *A Radical Jew: Paul and the Politics of Identity* (Berkeley: University of California Press, 1994).

28. For a detailed analysis of this displacement, see my essays "Feminism Under Siege," *Prooftexts*, 1990, and "Ideology and Self-Representation."

29. "The communal life of human beings had, therefore, a two-fold foundation: the compulsion to work, which was created by external necessity, and the power of love," Sigmund Freud, *Civilization and Its Discontents* (New York: W. W. Norton and Company, 1962) p. 48. Despite the inclusive language ("human beings") Freud's gender essentialism reasserts itself as the sentence continues, positing two different love objects for the two sexes: "[the power of love] made the man unwilling to be deprived of his sexual object—the woman—and made the woman unwilling to be deprived of that part of herself which had been separated off from her—her child."

Viewed from this perspective, it could be claimed that one of the aims of the feminist revolution (at least in its "Enlightenment" phase) was an erasure of a "double" sexual difference. Happiness was to be achieved by a "Freudian" equilibrium between work and (erotic rather than maternal) love.

30. *Mekomon* (Local paper), 1989; *Pitayon* (The bait), 1991; *Hatachshit* (The jewel), 1992.

31. On the English tradition of spinster detectives, see Susan Katz, "Singleness of Heart: Spinsterhood in Victorian Culture" (Ph.D. diss., Columbia University, 1988), ch. 5: "The Intriguing Heroism of the Spinster-Sleuth." On the inter-

section between this genre and feminist scholarship, see the life work of Carolyn Heilbrun, alias Amanda Cross, author of amateur sleuth Kate Fansler, Ph.D.

32. Shulamit Lapid herself is a happily married mother and the former Chair of the Israeli Writers Association.

33. In the collection *Happy Spiders* (*Akavishim semehim*), 1990; an English translation appeared in *Lilith* (Summer 1989). It should be noted that Lapid's earlier stories (1969, 1974, 1979) rarely touch on feminist protest.

34. For an annotated bibliography and a sample essay in English, see *Gender and Text*. On her earlier work, see Gershon Shaked, *Gal hadash basifrut ha'ivrit* (A new wave in Hebrew literature) (Tel Aviv: Sifriyat Po'alim 1971), pp. 168–179; Avraham Balaban, *Hakadosh vehadrakon* (The saint and the dragon) (Tel Aviv: Hakibbutz Hameuchad 1979); Lily Rattok, *Amalia Kahana-Carmon: Monograph* (Tel Aviv: Sifriyat Po'alim 1986); Esther Fuchs, *Israeli Mythogynies* and her essays in *Signs* and *Prooftexts* (1988).

35. See Jonathan Culler, "Reading as a Woman," *On Deconstruction* (Ithaca, N.Y.: Cornell University Press, 1983), pp. 43–64, and Showalter, *The New French Criticism*, 1985.

36. See on this point Shaked, *Gal hadash*; Balaban, *Hakadosh vehadrakon*; and Rattok, *Amalia Kahana-Carmon*.

37. "The Song of the Bats in Flight," originally published in *Moznaim* (Nov.–Dec. 1989): 3–7. I quote from Naomi Sokoloff's translation in *Gender and Text*, p. 236 and passim. It should be noted that all the different synonyms used in the translation in opposition to "tools" or "form" represent a single Hebrew term, *tochen* (or *techanim*).

38. See Irigaray; Lloyd; Fuss; Butler; Boyarin, *A Radical Jew*.

39. Most notoriously, the disparity between A. B. Yehoshua's political polemics and his much more sophisticated novelistic representations of these issues. See on this point my "Back to Vienna," and "Back to Genesis: Towards the Repressed and Beyond," in *Bakivun hanegdi: Critical Essays on "Mr. Mani,"* ed. Nitza Ben-Dov (Tel Aviv: Hakibbutz Hame'uchad 1995; in Hebrew).

40. See Jardine; Moi; Flax.

41. See Johnson's succint summary in *Strong Mothers, Weak Wives*, p. 16ff. The overlapping of the tactical dichotomy (equal rights vs. sexual difference) with the geographical one (Anglo-American vs. French) is commonplace. Even constructions of *The Female Body in Western Culture* (ed. Susan Rubin Suleiman [Cambridge: Harvard University Press, 1985]) are neatly organized around this principle as evident in the "prooftexts" used by the editor in her opening essay, "(Re)Writing the Body: The Politics and Poetics of Female Eroticism" (pp. 7–29).

42. Julia Kristeva, "Women's Time" (1979), in *The Kristeva Reader*, p. 209 and passim.

43. The pro and con arguments concerning "feminine writing" have been raised and summarized by Moi. See also Jardine and Ann Rosalind Jones, "Writing the Body," *Feminist Studies* 7, no. 2 (Summer 1981): 247–63.

Whether or not this concept, and especially the feminist ideology it implies, is applicable to Kahana-Carmon is an issue that requires further discussion (see my forthcoming *Beyond the Feminist Romance*). Suffice it to say that while Kahana-Carmon's style has been often cited as "feminine," it has also been recognized as the heir of the impressionism of U. N. Gnessin (1879–1913) and S. Yizhar (b. 1915), two major male writers of Hebrew prose. The question then is: Is there anything inherently (that is, essentially) feminine about this style, or is it identified as such because a woman happened to fashion it? Another option is to adopt Julia Kristeva's notion of a supra-gender "feminine" (which she ironically applies mostly to male writers), which indeed would include all three writers; a position that seems to me no less "essentialistic," despite (or perhaps because of) its "metaphysical" position.

44. Aptly analyzed by Fuchs, *Israeli Mythogynies*, p. 101 and passim, and in her "Amalia Kahana-Carmon's *And Moon in the Valley of Ajalon*: A Feminist Reading," *Prooftexts* 8 (1988): 129–141.

As can be expected, stylistic analyses of Kahana-Carmon abound, not always, however, with an eye to its feminist function.

45. For her simultaneous denial and affirmation of the role of gender (as well as other existential parameters—origin, class, income, political conviction) in the novelist's art, see *Veyare'ach be'emek 'ayalon* (And moon in the valley of ayalon), (Tel Aviv: Hakibbutz Hame'uchad, 1971), p. 199.

46. See *Veyare'ach be'emek 'ayalon*, ch. 3–4. Cf. "The House with the Blue-Painted Stairs," in *Bikhfifa 'ahat* (Under one roof, stories) (Tel Aviv: Hakibbutz Hame'uchad, 1966), pp. 83–91.

47. Cf. Balaban, *Hakadosh vehadrakon*, p. 54 and passim.

48. "Lihyot 'Ishah Soferet," *Yediot aharonot* (13 April 1984): 20–21. Other programmatic essays followed in 1985, 1989. As we shall see, 1984 was a good year for feminist activities in Israel.

49. In *Up on Montifer* (Lema'la bemonifer) (Tel Aviv: Hakibbutz Hame'uchad 1984), pp. 59–192. The "triptych" includes two additional stories that construct more contemporary (yet less explicit) "correctives" of Kahana-Carmon's earlier characters. All translations are mine.

50. "Hasisma hanechona" (The correct slogan), an interview with Orly Lubin, *Ha'aretz* (9 March 1984). As is her wont, the author accompanied the publication of the book with a detailed commentary, also published that year, "Hineh hasefer," *Moznaim* 68, nos. 5–6 (1984): 12–18. Although this essay contains fascinating clues to some structural problems in the narrative, it will take us too far afield to deal with it here. The same goes for the novel's rich allusive language and its intertextual ties with the Hebrew canon (i.e., Bialik, Agnon, Alterman, Rahel, Dalia Rabikowitz).

51. See Rattok, *Amalia Kahana-Carmon*.

52. I place this probing in a wider socioliterary context in my "The 'Other Within' in Israeli Fiction."

53. See especially p. 116: "Gentiles and Jews, they are like men and women, my father always said . . . Only because of preconceived judgments. Of each side: about oneself; about the other, too . . . Each side has its own picture . . . its image of the other. Therefore, when addressing someone from the other side, to the image and not to the person one would speak."

54. The allusion is to Jeremiah (38:7–12 and 39:16), where *eved-melech hakushi* saves the prophet from the pit (38) and then is rewarded by God (39). It is the only biblical reference in which a *kushi* ("Ethiopian" in the Bible, but used in modern Hebrew to signify "a black") is identified as a royal servant or slave (*'eved*). By omitting the "king" (*melech*) from the title and using it as a proper name, the author not only invokes modern black slavery but also points to its allegorical function.

55. See my forthcoming *Beyond the Feminist Romance*.

56. After her last, liberating encounter with Peter, Clara states twice: *'Ish 'eino patron li 'od* (No one is my patron anymore), pp. 154, 158.

57. See the move from Eved Hakushi's friendly kiss on Clara's cheek (p. 165) to her observation, "Eved Hakushi does not obey my orders. He is just intent on stepping behind me as a walking-tower" (p. 167), on to the reversal in which he leads the way through the dangerous streets ("where a woman cannot walk alone," p. 170) and Clara "silently admits: now it is I who step behind him" (p. 171).

58. *The Second Sex*, pp. xxiv–xxv. See Lloyd's analysis in *The Man of Reason*, ch. 6.

59. See Avrum Goldfaden's version of "Rozinkes un mandlen" in his play *Shulamith*. This "matrix" is acknowledged earlier on in the narrative: "With commerce in raisins it began. And in time, to the commerce in figs and all kinds of dried fruit it evolved" (p. 111).

60. Like the repetition of so many shorter motifs and figurative coins, this verbal duel is a stylized intensification of an earlier one, the parting duel between Clara and Peter (pp. 143–44).

61. Amalia Kahana-Carmon, *Liviti otah baderech leveita* (With her on her way home) (Tel Aviv: Hakibbutz Hame'uchad, 1992), pp. 71, 276, and passim. This novel comes closer than any of the author's earlier works to "writing the body," French style.

62. Again, a biblical subtext is instrumental in creating this concept: *Ha'ahva hayedu'a leshimtza* is a contemporary transformation of Abraham's peace offering to Lot in Genesis 13:8, *Halo' 'anashim 'ahim 'anahnu* ("for we be brethren" [King James], or "for we are close kinsmen" [New English Bible], which is cited early on in the narrative (p. 36) as the basis of the relationship. The frequent use of the allusion tends to obliterate two ironic moves that operate in the transformation of the subtext: First, for Abraham and Lot this statement of fact introduces the proposal of a peaceful solution for a sibling rivalry (parting or separate coexistence rather than cooperation)—perhaps an ironic foreshadowing of the denouement of our plot. Secondly, it assumes two *male* siblings, which is precisely what the "translation" into the contemporary idiom *'ahva* seems to undo. Generally translated as "brotherhood," this nongenderized abstract noun carries a strong connotation of egalitarian friendship (as in the slogan of the French Revolution), for which English does not offer any satisfactory equivalent. My translation, "brotherly bond," is meant to preserve the root of the noun, both grammatically (*'.h.h.*) and intertextually (the "brethren" of the Genesis allusion), as well as its modern, nongenderized connotation; it fails, however to capture the homophonic pun on the word *'ahava*, "love" proper.

63. Literally, "counter help"; the complementarity implied by Genesis 2:18 is better rendered by "counterpart" than by "helpmeet." I elaborate on this point in my essay " 'And Rebecca Loved Jacob.' "

64. Bialik, Rahel, and Leah Goldberg are just a few that come to mind; they are joined by "citations" of works of art, music, and other literary traditions, thereby bringing this novel into the orbit of postmodernist poetics.

65. For the effect of marital "playfulness" and sibling (rather than Oedipal) dynamics on the construction of gender that is at the heart of biblical "patriarchy," see my essay " 'And Rebecca Loved Jacob.' "

66. *Yehuda Amichai: A Life of Poetry 1948–1994*, trans. Benjamin and Barbara Harshav (New York: HarperCollins, 1994), p. 371.

67. "'Aharei 'Esrim Shana," *Mukdam u'meuhar: Shirim* (Collected Poems), (Tel Aviv: Sifriyat Po'alim, no date), p. 184. Translation mine.

68. Although both the novel and Kahana-Carmon's commentary ("How

Does the Elephant Imagine Itself?" *Massa' [Davar]*, 23 April 1992) insist on the vitalizing element of discovery in the metaphoric use of "Africa" ("the utopist yearning to dig into yourself as if into another country, a country of mystery; a mystery of power, of magic, that is inside you . . . but about which you somehow were not aware"), one cannot avoid the association—very appropriate here, in my mind—with Freud's "dark continent," the female psyche. It would seem that Kahana-Carmon transforms Freud's negative "unknowability" of the female in the same way as Julia Kristeva has transformed Lacan's (and Derrida's) woman's "otherness" and absence into the semiotic locus of creativity; see *Revolution in Poetic Language*, trans. A. Waller (New York: Columbia University Press, 1984). I develop this analogy in my forthcoming *Beyond the Feminist Romance*.

69. Shulamith Hareven, *'Ir yamim rabim* (A city of many days) (Tel Aviv: Am Oved, 1972). The English translation, by Hillel Halkin, has been recently reissued by Mercury House (San Francisco), 1993. References are to the Hebrew and English editions, respectively. In contrast to other Israeli women writers, most of Hareven's fiction is available in English. *Twilight and Other Stories* was published by the same house in 1992.

70. I have demonstrated this process in detail in my 1990 essay, "Feminism under Siege." For Virginia Woolf's traces in Israeli feminism, see my chapter "A Woolf of Her Own" in my forthcoming *Beyond the Feminist Romance*. In Hebrew, see my forthcoming "Androgeniut bematzor," *Siman Kri'ah* 23.

71. See Moi, *Sexual/Textual*, and p. 164 passim; Paul Smith, "Julia Kristeva et al.; or, Take Three or More," *Feminism and Psychoanalysis*, ed. Richard Feldstein and Judith Roof (Ithaca, N.Y.: Cornell University Press, 1989), pp. 84–104.

72. Jacques Lacan, *Ecrits* (1936), trans. Alan Sheridan (London: Tavistock, 1977), pp. 1–7.

73. See Boyarin, *Carnal Knowledge*, and my " 'And Rebecca Loved Jacob.' "

74. In *Israeli Democracy* (Summer 1989): 3–7.

75. Gershon Shaked, *Gal 'ahar gal* (Wave after wave in Hebrew narrative fiction) (Jerusalem: Keter, 1985), p. 23.

76. See Dafna Sharfman, "The Status of Women in Israel—Facts and Myths," *Israeli Democracy* (Summer 1989): 12–14.

77. Alice Shalvi, in *Networking for Women* 8, no. 1 (January 1995), p. 6.

78. A glaring exception to this rule was the publication, also in 1984, of *Hako'ah ha'aher* (The other power), by veteran writer Yehudit Hendel. After a long hiatus (her early books appeared in 1955 and 1969), she reclaimed her writing career with this paean to her deceased husband, the artist Zvi Meirovitz. Interestingly, her next collection, *Kesef katan* (Small change) (1988), shows a selective treatment of feminist issues. In her later books she explores other explosive issues such as national bereavement and mourning (1991) and post-Holocaust Poland (1987).

79. One such "disciple" who does stand out as having carved her own voice is Savyon Liebrecht (b. 1948), especially in her latest collection of short stories, *Sinit 'ani medaberet 'eleicha* (1992; earlier collections 1986, 1988).

Among the younger group that made its appearance in that decade the most audacious and innovative by far is Orly Castel-Bloom (b. 1960) who has already left her mark on Israeli prose fiction (1987, 1989, 1990, 1992, 1993). Less prolific but nevertheless deserving attention are Dorit Peleg, Judith Katzir (b. 1963), Leah Eini (b. 1962), and Ronit Matalon (b. 1960). Only Katzir's *Closing the Sea* (New York: Harcourt Brace Jovanovich 1992) is available in English. Trans. Barbara Harshav.

80. Androgyny is explored, interestingly enough, by several veteran writers, both male and female, whose earlier concerns lay elsewhere: children's storyteller Nurit Zarhi, mystery writer Batya Gur, scriptwriter and postmodern novelist Avraham Heffner.

81. A third allegorical novella, *After Childhood* (Tel Aviv: Devir, 1994) a sequel to the two "biblical" stories, "The Miracle Hater" (in English, 1983) and "Prophet" (in English, 1990), features a heroine who is in conflict with the "patriarchal" establishment—a resurgence of the conflict underlying *A City of Many Days*.

82. Jerusalem: Keter, 1987. All translations are mine. Portions of the following analysis were presented in a number of lectures between March 1991 (at Yale) and May 1993 (at Brandeis).

83. Her only novel to be published in English, *Death in the Rain* (1982; 1993), is analyzed by Risa Domb, *Home Thoughts from Abroad: Distant Visions of Israel in Contemporary Hebrew Fiction* (London: Vallentine Mitchell, 1995), pp. 62–78. Almog's preoccupation with European culture, central to this novel as well as to her earlier *Don't Hurry the Journey* (1971), is crucial for *Dangling Roots* as well. Also available in English is her feminist critique of Israeli culture; see "On Being a Writer," *Gender and Text*, pp. 227–234.

84. Leah Fuchs, "An Interview with Ruth Almog," *Hadoar* (13 January 1989), pp. 14–15. In other interviews, Almog revealed the identity of her model: the late Livia Rokah, the daughter of the mayor of Tel Aviv, who in the sixties was a left-wing activist in Italy, married there, and stayed in exile until her premature death by her own hand.

85. On the fictional autobiography in Israel, see my "Gender In/Difference."

86. Most notoriously, Gur's recent *Afterbirth* (1994); but see also Dorit Zilberman's *Woman inside Woman* (1991), Ilana Bernstein's *Provision* (1991), Yehudit Katzir's *Matiss Has the Sun in His Belly* (1994) and Repled-Zilberstein's *Mrs. Reader is Not the Mother* (1994) and some short stories by Savion Liebrecht, Hana Bat-Shahar, Shulamit Gilboa, and Ofra Ofer.

87. The general shift from the Oedipal to the pre-Oedipal in psychoanalytic theory, typical of the Object Relations school, foregrounds the role of mothering in general and "corrects" Freud's untested theories about female psychology in particular. The psychosociological implications of this shift were argued by Nancy Chodorow, *The Reproduction of Mothering: Psychoanalysis and the Sociology of Gender* (Berkeley: University of California Press, 1979), who claims that the symbiotic identification of a daughter with her [same-sex] mother is one of the reasons for the female's capacity for empathy and hence for the *difference* of the female ego–its less firm boundaries and its more relational attitude to the external world. Similarly, Hélène Cixous and Luce Irigaray attribute the fluidity of the female psyche to the fact that the girl retains much of her initial bonding with the mother. Unlike Chodorow, however, they use this "sexual difference" for a deconstruction of the heterosexual paradigm, much like Adrienne Rich on this side of the Atlantic, who moved from an emphasis on motherhood and daughtering (in *Of Woman Born* [New York: Norton, 1976]) to a "lesbian continuum" in "Compulsory Heterosexuality and Lesbian Existence," *Signs* 5 (1980): 631–60.

For scholarship on the literary representation of this paradigm see *The Lost Tradition: Mothers and Daughters in Literature*, ed. Cathy N. Davidson and E. M. Broner (New York: Ungar, 1980), and Marianne Hirsch, *The Mother/Daughter Plot: Narrative, Psychoanalysis, Feminism* (Bloomington: Indiana University Press, 1989). Recent reevaluations include Johnson, *Strong Mothers*, and *Daughtering and Mothering: Female Subjectivity Reanalysed*, ed. Janneke van Mens-Verhulst et al. (New York: Routledge, 1993).

88. The literature on Almog consists mainly of short book reviews and interviews, but no extensive study has yet been written about her work.

89. See my forthcoming *Beyond the Feminist Romance*, ch. 7.

90. Translated as "the loved one" (but literally, 'the object of compassion/mercy'), the name derives from Hosea, where *Lo'-ruhama* (i.e., 'the unloved one'), the allegorical daughter of the prophet's wanton wife (1:6) is promised redemption by being renamed *Ruhama* (2:2). The etymology of the name, however, is *r.h.m*, from which Hebrew derives also *rehem*, womb, the Greek *hystera . . .* The semantic field of this name thus brings together several themes developed in the personality of the mother: female sexuality and hysteria, compassion and "redemption."

91. The reference, of course, is to Gilbert and Gubar, *The Madwoman in the Attic* (1979), which deals with nineteenth century "mad" heroines. Feminist scholarship on this heavily loaded issue of women and madness ranges from Phyllis Chesler's book (Doubleday, 1972) through Shoshana Felman's 1975 essay by this name, in *Diacritics* (Winter 1975): 2–10, to Marilyn Yalon's *Maternity, Mortality and the Literature of Madness* (University Park: Penn State University Press, 1993). Within this general theme, hysteria holds a special position ever since its "discovery" by the nineteenth century medical establishment. Its Freudian career and its post-Freudian reevaluation by Foucault, Lacan, and French feminism (esp. Cixous in her *Portrait of Dora*, 1975) is well known and need not be documented here. A most useful summary is *Hysteria Beyond Freud* by Sander Gilman et al. (Berkeley: University of California Press, 1993). See esp. Elaine Showalter's "Hysteria, Feminism, and Gender" (pp. 268–344) for a different position on this issue (pp. 327, 333, 334). However, the theory of madness most relevant to our text is, as we shall see, R. D. Laing's. Romantically interpreting madness as existential freedom, this approach, developed in the stormy 1960s, was absorbed into the revolutionary discourse of that period.

92. Plato's praise of madness, "the gift of God" (Phaedrus), is used as the epigraph of her book *The Stranger and the Enemy* (1980). To the question if one can choose insanity, Almog answers: "I don't know. I once thought it was possible, but today I do not know. I once even thought one can consciously choose insanity. But new scientific findings undermine this supposition." See an interview with Ora Zarnitzky, "Shehikah" (Erosion), *Devar hashavu'a* (4 December 1987).

93. London: Tavistock, 1964.

94. For an exposition of the evolution of Laing's theories and a critique of their implication for female psychology and feminist ideology, see Juliet Mitchell, *Psychoanalysis and Feminism* (New York: Vintage, 1974), pp. 227–73.

95. Almog herself reacted in a similar vein to the question "Why don't you write about your daily experience?" in an interview conducted after the publication of her earlier novel, *Death in the Rain*, 1982: "To write about this? Never. This is what I want to escape from. My real life takes place elsewhere . . . when I begin to travel, in my imagination." (Interview with Avraham Balaban, *Yediot aharonot*, 1982, no date).

96. Mira's later attempt to consummate Alexandroni's attachment to her mother through his devotion to her resonates with shades of Agnon's *Bidmi yameiha* (At the prime of her life). In both cases the older lover is the bearer of knowledge, of the symbolic order (signified here by his name, evoking Alexan-

dria, the ancient site of wisdom). Berliavsky also belongs to her parents' generation, an incestual choice that exacerbates her jealousy of her mother.

97. Mitchell, *Psychoanalysis and Feminism*, p. 285ff.

98. Seriously motivated as this passage may be, one cannot avoid its tragicomic effect on a reader versed in contemporary psychoanalytic discourse: This paternal figure seems to be stuck forever in an unfinished infantile mirror-stage, a travesty of Lacan's great symbol of the birth of the human 'split' ego.

99. The self-consciousness of the protagonists, here and elsewhere in the novel, is in fact one of the weaknesses of this novel. Whether in dialogues or inner monologues, the characters are often (particularly in Book II) too transparent to themselves and to the reader, as if the author had very little trust in her readers' ability to infer and generalize.

100. In addition to reverberations of John Irving's *The World According to Garp*, 1976, "Jacques" invokes the name of Jean Jacques Rousseau, the father of the romantic philosophies of freedom, the source of "liberté, égalité," etc. *Mutatis mutandis*, it also brings to mind the other two 'Jacques' of the 1960s, Lacan and Derrida.

101. In English, see her essay in *Gender and Text*.

102. It is hard to determine whether Almog sides with Juliet Mitchell who claims (*pace* Cixous) that "the woman novelist must be an hysteric, for hysteria is simultaneously what a woman can do to be feminine and refuse femininity, within practical discourses" (*Woman: The Longest Revolution* [London: Virago 1984], p. 288ff.), or with Elaine Showalter's counter-argument that "female hysteria seemed to be on the wane, as feminism was on the rise" and that "the despised hysterics of yesteryear have been replaced by the feminist radicals of today" (Hysteria, Feminism, and Gender," pp. 327, 334). Significantly, Almog's latest book is entitled *Tikun omanuti* (Invisible [lit. Artistic] mending), 1993. In it she artistically "mends" the life stories of a variety of characters who are socially marginal without necessarily being mad and/or female.

103. See my "Feminism under Siege."

104. Oz, Bartov, and Shahar. And see my "Gender In/Difference."

105. In vol. 5 (1994), under the title *Viku'ah: sifrut nashim* (Women's literature: A debate), pp. 165–182, Lily Rattok, Orly Lubin, and Rivka Feldhai acrimoniously argue over Kristevan and other subversive readings of Kahana-Carmon's early stories, while each of them forcefully holds onto a hegemonic position within the critical discourse.

NANCY E. BERG

Sephardi Writing: From the Margins to the Mainstream

In this area literature has something to say. And something to do. It can raise up forgotten cultures, and create characters whose actions and behavior are the main point although they naturally also have something to say. It can help us to get to know—our neighbors, our forefathers, our forefather's forefathers, ourselves. To know and maybe to value. Until one knows one cannot value.[1]
—Amnon Shamosh

There is a measure of absurdity to this whole Sephardi question: no one expects a young man whose parents came from Hungary to be loyal to his Hungarian heritage, yet where people whose background is oriental are concerned such demands are made of them. It is as though coming from a place that is regarded by some as "low" you must display loyalty to the weaker class. The implied demand is "you came from them, therefore you must remain with them."
—A. B. Yehoshua

OVER THE PAST two decades Israeli literature has seen a flourishing of works giving voice to those previously relegated to the margins. As evidenced by the other articles in this volume, this has been a very heady time for readers of Hebrew. Perhaps the most provocative among them is the category of Sephardi writing—that is, writing by and about Sephardim. The explosion in fiction finds its complement in poetry and other artistic genres.[2]

This chapter sets out to complicate the mapping of Israeli literature, adding to our understanding of a complex phenomenon usually ignored or viewed simplistically. Until recently, Sephardim—as writers and as characters—have been marginalized by Israeli literature and all but dismissed by the standard literary histories. In the last generation, Sephardim have been proclaiming their presence, moving toward the center, and pushing others to the background if not off the page. Sephardi writers are redrawing the literary map, whether claiming their rightful place in the existing canon, or contributing to a new canon.[3]

First a few words about terms and categories. The category of Sephardi itself is questionable, owing to the fact that it is marginalized by the mainstream—that is, defined by Ashkenazim (Euro/Sabra) as "other." We use it inclusively to refer to Jews who trace their lineage back to the Spanish/Iberian population (*sephardim tehorim*), those from Arab and Islamic lands (*mizrahim*),[4] and members of the Old Yishuv (the community of Jews living in Palestine before the rise of modern Zionism). There is of course overlap among these categories. But the term is used with the awareness that it is imprecise. It is also problematic to group these writers together when EuroSabra writers are not similarly grouped. The issues raised here are not unlike those encountered in the discussion of women writers and their respective "ghettoization." The assumption is that they have more in common with each other than do Ashkenazim, as if they are more different from Ashkenazim than from each other. Not only is each writer an individual, but as a group they also come from dissimilar backgrounds. In the end, their only real commonality is the way the mainstream readership/establishment responds to them as Sephardim. This is at times inaccurate, misleading, and almost always a misreading.

Be that as it may, the reality of the situation is that these writers are seen, read, and discussed as "ethnic" writers (using the term here in the uniquely Israeli sense where nothing Ashkenazi is ethnic), and this does bind the writers in one discussion. There is still some value in considering these writers together and in exploring how the designation of "Sephardi writers" illuminates or obstructs our understanding of their works. As these writers have matured, their writing has broken out of the "ethnic" category. So too, the mainstream's recent embrace of its margins has led to a greater openness toward more generous and more accurate readings. As these writers from Arab lands and Sephardi heritage enter the mainstream, the ethnic label is less of a definitive marker.

To understand the category, I have chosen to focus on novels that most overtly explore Sephardi identity. In these works by Sami Michael, Amnon Shamosh, A. B. Yehoshua, Shimon Ballas, and Dan-Benaya Seri, we can best observe the move from the margin to the center, the shift from the mainstream to Sephardi, and alternatively, the decision to remain on the outside. Overall, these writers' works present a challenge to the master Zionist narrative—that is, literature written by the EuroSabra heterosexual Jewish male—whether by knocking at the door looking for a way in or by threatening total subversion.

Not all of these works are necessarily selected by a purely literary set of criteria; rather, they are chosen because of their place in the discussion about ethnic writing. The following discussion is based on a selection of works in which the writer's Sephardi identity seems to have some bearing on the text, and those works which have had an impact on the development of Israeli literature.

The earliest of these works is Sami Michael's debut novel, *Shavim veshavim yoter* (*Equal and More Equal*, 1974).[5] It is not Michael's best book, but it has had a great impact. In some ways, as his first (and weakest) novel, its importance has worked against him, allowing some critics to dismiss him. Yet this book gave literary expression to the ethnic question and introduced the DDT motif, which will be explained shortly, into the literary lexicon.

Sami Michael is one of the most significant contemporary writers from an Arab background. Michael was born in Baghdad in 1926, and began his literary activity there. Because of his involvement with the Iraqi Communist party he was sentenced to death in 1948. He fled to Teheran and eventually arrived in Israel "by accident" a year later.[6] In his first years in Israel he continued to be active in the Communist party, worked at the paper (*al-Ittihād*), and lived in a mostly Arab neighborhood in Haifa. After his obligatory army service, he worked for the hydrology service until retiring in 1981 to write full time. The transition from Arabic to Hebrew (and from short story to the novel) took many years, and he began publishing fiction in Hebrew relatively late. His first book garnered an unusual amount of attention from readers and critics because of its subject matter.

Michael's novel, which centers on the experience of a Sephardi immigrant, arrived on the scene of Israeli literature shortly after the Yom Kippur War, the downfall of the Labor Party, and the end of consensus (or the myth thereof). It introduced a relatively unknown writer and a hitherto little explored experience to Israeli literature. This is not to say that there were no Sephardi characters in books (such as Haim Hazaz's Yemenites)[7] and films (*Sallaḥ!*), nor Sephardi writers (Mordechai Tabib and Yehuda Burla, early A. B. Yehoshua) before, but here we have the beginnings of a continuing literature written in authentic voice. The characters are not created to entertain and delight the mainstream and elite; rather, they lay claim to a new position and legitimacy in the Israeli cultural scene.

Equal and More Equal tells the story of David Asher, a young immigrant who arrives in Israel with his family from Iraq. Ostensibly a novel of protest, it is ultimately affirming of Zionism and the dream of ingathering. The novel alternates between two narrative levels, the earlier one detailing the Asher family's arrival, their initial shock, the hardships of life in the *ma'abarah* (transit camp), and the difficulties of assimilation.[8] The later narrative describes David's experiences in the Six-Day War. The narratives shift position as the story progresses with the war narrative emerging from secondary to primary importance. The two finally mesh in the last chapters. The merging narratives signify David's integration as a whole person.[9] This tale of transition is a kind of *Bildungsroman* as well, including issues of individuation, sexual initiation, success and failure.

The protagonist becomes an angry young man in the transit camp narrative. He amasses a list of insults and offenses. The first is the greeting upon arrival at the Israeli airport that falls far short of their dreams and expectations.

A grey group of grey clerks came toward us. Father hesitated a moment at the top of the ramp—and then began to descend slowly, with great dignity . . . We all knew that he was hiding his bitter disappointment because of the importance of the moment. It was an impressive effort, but without hope. Within five short minutes the new homeland succeeded in turning my father from an energetic man standing at the height of his powers into an old humiliated broken human being. While still on his way down the ramp, when we were all burning with excitement to feel the enchantments of Israel of which we had dreamed—from out of the grey group that came toward us sallied forth one who was holding a large sprayer in his hand. Before we could understand what was happening—a cloud of DDT surrounded us. It whitened Abu-Shaul, formerly a respected citizen and leader of the Baghdad community. (p. 15)

This scene is burnt into David's memory, much as it enters the Israeli literary vocabulary as a metonym.[10] In the novel it signals the beginning of the father's disintegration.

The Iraqi family, as represented by the Ashers, is shown in all of its warmth and closeness, with the father the traditional head of the household. But the conditions in Israel pull them apart and upset the conventional familial pattern: the oldest daughter is married off to a cousin of dubious value, and the youngest son is sent to a kibbutz to ease the pressure on the family. The parents and the youngest child are killed in a tragic fire, leaving David and his older brother bereft and orphaned. Thus the destruction begun by the DDT is continued by substandard housing and bureaucratic neglect.

The central plot becomes a variation of the Romeo and Juliet story, in which David falls in love with Margalit, the only daughter of the only Ashkenazi present in the transit camp.[11] The mother, Tzipporah, is not only opposed to this budding romance, but engineers the destruction of their marriage, David's professional downfall, and Margalit's remarriage. Ironically, Margalit takes as her second husband a Mr. Zhidovitz, who turns out to be the same man who turned down David's job application and then hired Margalit. Such a development further emasculates the young man, who comes from the traditional society where the woman stays at home. Never a fully drawn character, Mr. Zhidovitz is the embodiment of the enemy Ashkenazi.[12]

David succeeds not in the male equivalent of the marriage plot but through a plot of adventure.[13] It is the onset of the war that saves David. Though initially angry and unsoldierly, David risks his life to rescue his comrades and is thus redeemed by his heroism.

The novel was written after the influx of immigrants from the Soviet Union. The Russian immigrants received government financial aid (those from the United States were exempted from many tariffs), while many of those from the mass immigration of 1948–52—and disproportionately the Sephardim among them—still struggled to meet their basic needs.

The characters are almost stereotypes, crudely drawn and easily categorizable. The Ashkenazim/Yiddish-speakers are the oppressors; the Sephardim are the oppressed. The women characters do not fare better; they either fit into the madonna/whore dichotomy or are less than fully drawn. The novel's lone Arab, David's companion on the beach, listens to David's tale of woe, and he serves to mitigate David's feelings of alienation by representing someone even further outside of Israeli society. Presaging the upset of Labor in the 1977 elections, the politicians are skewered, both those who use the Asher family tragedy for their political gain, and Reuven, the Iraqi, who succeeds by allowing himself to be the token ethnic.

The plot is also simplistic, a combination of formulas: tragic romance and the redemption through (military) heroism. Although the bilevel narrative strategy adds some interest, its potential is never fully realized. Michael does not make full use of possible connections between both levels; each narrative could have been separated out until they merge at the end. Furthermore, the writing is not subtle; the issues, like the characters, are drawn in black and white. While the style mimics the mood of the narrative, it is still not too delicate. The writer himself has since spoken critically of the editor, whom he blames for eliminating the subtleties; afterward Michael shifted to another publishing house and another editor.

The novel has been generally read as publicizing the trauma suffered by the immigrants from Arab lands. Playing off the *bourekas* films of the sixties,[14] and the earlier *Shesh kanafaim l'ehad* (Everyone has six wings),[15] the birth of a child is not automatically seen as a sign of hope for the future and the intermingling of cultures. The character of Shai, the child

of David and Margalit, does not initially bring cheer. Even his grandmother is ashamed of his dark skin; the father abandons him easily with
the divorce. Not until the father proves himself through his heroism
can he bequeath to his child "full Israeli citizenship." The book calls for
modifying the message of Zionism to include Sephardim and their suffering, to add the Second Israel to the Zionist narrative. Rather than
being a novel of protest as it has been read by many critics, then, *Equal
and More Equal* in fact reaffirms Zionism and basic Israeli institutions like
the army.

Nevertheless, the angry tone and the crude lines of conflict shocked
many readers. Michael's debut novel is one of the first books to challenge the Zionist master narrative from the outside. It does not ask the
question of the alienated New Wave protagonist: "What do we do now,
we privileged and disaffected sons of the founding fathers?" but rather
"Where can we fit in, we unwelcomed immigrants?" We will return to
Michael and his most recent novel below; first, in order to begin to
understand the question asked, we need to know from where these immigrants have come.

For this we turn to other books written by immigrants to Israel from
Arab lands, which explore the glorious past and the ending of this glory.
These tales of disillusionment constitute a complementary or competi-
tive narrative to the story of the Holocaust that was just then beginning
to unfold. The silence of the postwar era was broken after the acceptance of war reparations from Germany and the Eichmann trial, when
survivors began to get the chance to tell their stories. The Sephardim
suffered in their own way, and wanted others to know of their experience. While some authors closer to the mainstream were rewriting the
Zionist narrative to include the story of the Holocaust—that out of the
great tragedy, the State of Israel was born—the Sephardim were offering alternative "rewrites," which described the Diaspora as home and
Israel as not-home.

Questions of genre, voice, and authority frame these narratives. The
Iraqi-born writer Itshak Bar-Moshe offers his memoirs written in Arabic as "a novel if you wish and a collection of short stories if you wish,
and autobiography if you wish too."[16] In Yizhak Gormezano-Goren's first
book about growing up in Egypt, he asks: "Should I tell it in first or third
person? Should I call people by their names, or perhaps just give them
fictitious ones and write that 'Any resemblance, etc. is purely coincidental'"[17] and has his present day narrator return home from a distance
of twenty years to look up the ten-year-old protagonist. The Arab writer
Samīr Naqqāsh, a compatriot of Bar-Moshe and Michael's, further blurs
the illusion of reality. In his novella "Laylat 'Urābā" (The night of Ho-

shana Raba, 1980) he undermines his narrator's authority, concluding a moving episode with the words, "But this never happened."[18]

The traditional family closeness of the Sephardim is well portrayed in these books. In the earliest volume (chronologically) of Bar-Moshe's memoirs, *Bayt fī Baghdād* (House in Baghdad, 1983), the family moves from their large house, and different branches move out on their own, but they stay very close. The men continue to consult one another in business, the women visit each other, and the children play together. Samīr Naqqāsh uses the minor holiday of Hoshana Raba to describe the family gathering, where all of the relatives and close friends are "like beads on a necklace," in a time when "people used to get together just to get together,"[19] and just one person missing left a horrible gap. In *Kayiẓ Alexandroni* (Alexandrian summer, 1978), Gormezano-Goren introduces the Hebrew reader to his family's institution of the "Kudjukum" (could-you-come), the gathering of the immediate family in the parents' bedroom after the daily siesta. Amnon Shamosh (b. 1929 in Aleppo, Syria) writes a family saga discussed below in which succeeding generations set off for the far flung corners of the earth, yet they continue to name their offspring after the grand patriarch and his wife, to run the business of Michel Ezra and sons, and to honor the family.

They write these stories for different purposes, to preserve and memorialize, as well as to educate the Israeli reader. Naqqāsh and Bar-Moshe both write in Arabic. They are mostly unread except through limited translation. While they are almost exact opposites in their use of language—Bar-Moshe writes in a journalist's basic Fuṣḥa (literary Arabic); Naqqāsh writes in arabesques of literary Arabic and spoken dialects—they are similar in their deliberate position of writing in a minority language. Few Israelis actually read their works in the original.[20] Whether written in Arabic or in Hebrew these works attempt to recover a lost paradise. Sometimes the nostalgia is even acknowledged, as in this excerpt from an essay by Amnon Shamosh, a founding member of Kibbutz Ma'ayan Barukh near the Lebanese border:

It is clear that from the heights of the kibbutz silo and past the eucalpytus forest, Aleppo seems prettier, all of her dimensions and all the depth of her unique culture—from the top of the tower the look is more sober, more encompassing and more piercing. From Ma'ayan Barukh, Aleppo seems not only nicer, but also becomes prettier, not just prettier than reality but also prettier than what her sons, the builders of Zion and Jerusalem, thought about her. They placed her lower than every city and town perfumed from afar with the fragrance and spirit of Warsaw and Vilna and Odessa, but it was not justified. Before the first Jew arrived in their cities there was a magnificent Jewish community in Aleppo who established sages and *paytanim* and kabbalists and lovers of Torah and lovers of Zion and . . . *mashallah* lovers of money, who spread their businesses on the face of the great earth.[21]

Amnon Shamosh is perhaps the most conscious of the potential of the Sephardi communities and most deliberate in his purpose to educate the Israeli reader. Aware that most Israeli Ashkenazim and Sabras do not know the Sephardim, the author describes his implied reader:

He saw their clothing in an album and on holiday and at a museum and tasted their foods with gusto, but didn't succeed in peering into their internal world, to understand their way of thinking and their reaction.[22]

Shamosh's *Michel Ezra Safra uvanav* (Michel Ezra Safra and his sons, 1978) is significant because of its place in the tapestry of Israeli popular culture. Widely read, the book was also adapted for the first Israeli television miniseries.[23] The story establishes and reinforces paradigms of Sephardi wealth and good fortune, family closeness and legendary business success. In contrast to *Equal and More Equal*, Shamosh's work does not make direct criticisms of Israeli society and absorption. The didactic tone of the work plainly answers the questions of the intended audience.

From the first page, Arabic phrases, formalities, and customs are described, glossed, and explained throughout the story. The narrator is clearly interpreting for the Israeli reader, and he occasionally interjects editorial asides to offer this mediation.[24]

Michel Ezra Safra was among the prominent of our city. A wealthy businessman, a wise and educated Jew, and with equals—a friend of pleasing conduct. The Jews of Aleppo called him Hakham Ezra, despite his not being a rabbi and that in our area the title *hakham* was only given to rabbis. Non-Jews differed: Muslims said Khawaja Safra, the word Safra (or Zafra) is Arabic and means yellow; and Christians, Arab Christians, called him Monsieur Michel. Whoever considered himself an intimate, whether a member of the covenant or not, called him Michel Effendi out of respect and friendship, and flatterers (or those needing to flatter him) added Pasha or Basha to his name. (p. 7)

Shamosh recreates a community of Jews through the character Michel Ezra Safra, who is both representative of the Jewish community of Aleppo and an individual of greater wealth and higher status than most. The character Michel Ezra is almost larger than life. Family and business are the two most important aspects of his life, and nearly interchangeable. One of the most important tenets of his business practice is "don't rely on strangers," and he "employs" his wife to conduct all of the French language correspondence. Even among family members, information is given only on a need-to-know basis. He nearly disowns his son Albert, because he seems not to be interested in the business.[25]

The family is close—like the families portrayed in Bar-Moshe's *House in Baghdad*, Naqqāsh's "The Night of Hoshana Raba," and Gormezano-Goren's *Alexandrian Summer*—and stays so even when the members disperse to Argentina, London and Jerusalem. Their concern for family extends to most of the Aleppo community. Linda, Michel Ezra's wife, exerts great efforts in her informal but productive matchmaking services among the families of Aleppo.

The book does not idealize the main character. Michel Ezra's desire for profit makes him follow a questionable morality. For example, he differentiates between what is kosher in food and in business—the latter is anything that shows a profit (although he is lax in regard to *kashrut* when traveling abroad). He justifies dubious business practices with outsiders because it is acceptable to steal from thieves. And despite the international nature of his company, he avoids paying for toll calls by encrypting buying and selling instructions in carefully coded requests for person-to-person calls.

Michel hobnobs with the important personages of Aleppo. This theme, of relationships between people of different religions, is a common ingredient in most of these works reconstructing the lost world.[26] Kamal Pasha is a "close friend" whom we first meet when he asks Michel to consider running for the Jewish seat of Parliament. This character introduces an ironic foreshadowing that becomes more meaningful later in the narrative—"Pray to your God a lot, ya effendi," Kamal says to his Jewish friend, "that in the parliament of the Jewish state to be they'll worry about representing the Jews of Syria." Kamal is also the one to tell Michel that Damascus is emptying of Jews, to forecast the creation of the Jewish state, and to provide protection for Michel and family during the 1946 riots.

Even before the riots, there is a sense of the beginning of the end. The happier, earlier times are referred to as "the days before the flood." Michel Ezra is warned by his business partner of troubles to come. Linda's dream warns Michel from accepting Kamal Pasha's political offer, and in fact the man who runs for the Parliamentary seat representing the Jewish community is later attacked by an unruly mob. The horrors are less detailed here than is the *Farhud*[27] in Bar-Moshe's memoirs or in Sami Michael's novella for young adults *Sufah bein hadekalim* (Storm among the palms).[28] But the beginning of the end is a familiar trope in the writings of Jews from Arab lands: the smoke in Naqqash's "The Night of Hoshana Raba," the sense of security that begins to unravel in Bar-Moshe's *House in Baghdad*, the atmosphere of fear and persecution in Shimon Ballas's short stories.[29] The narrator tells of those who sniffed the approaching independence and began by damaging the Jews' honor and property. "Aleppo was good to the Jews as long as foreigners ruled" (chap. 8) He tells of the Jews who respond by selling their businesses and homes and leaving, and of Michel who secretly liquidates most of his assets and transfers his funds to Geneva.

The description of the Syrian pogrom lets the Israeli reader know that it was not only in Europe that Jews suffered. While not necessarily competing with the narrative of the Holocaust, and mitigated by the picture of pluralism and earlier tolerance, it does awaken the Hebrew-reading audience to the trials of the Sephardim, offering an alternative view to the miracle of the creation of the Israeli state. "We paid for Zionism," states one of the Safra daughters. "Not anyone else. And got nothing for it. We paid the highest price and got less than everyone" (p. 87). When asked, she defines "we" as "the Jews from Arab lands. We left everything there," she explains, "And what did we get?" (p. 88).

The rift between the Ashkenazim and Sephardim is not as dominant in Shamosh's novel as in *Equal and More Equal*, but it is clearly stated. The Ashkenazim, who are referred to as "our brothers" from the comfortable distance of Aleppo, are resented once the Aleppan Jews live beside them in Israel. The Syrians have no opportunities for success, because the Ashkenazim do business only with each other. The story is told of the Aleppan who gets nowhere in business until he changes one letter in his last name to the very European-sounding Schreiber. His business doubles overnight. These inequalities are played out in the linguistic arena as well. "We spoke Hebrew and they arranged everything in Yiddish. Among themselves" (p. 88). Or, responding to the question of why there are no Sephardim in top positions, one replies, "Ask why—you'll be a clerk. Ask *warum* and they'll answer *warum nicht* and appoint you to management." [30] The primacy of Yiddish is also noted in other novels. While an earlier novel by Shimon Ballas, *Hama'abarah* (The transit camp, 1964), introduces the Hebrew reader to the label "Yiddish" for the Ashkenazim because of their language, Eli Amir's *Tarnegol kapparot* (Fowl of atonement, 1983) deals with the primacy of the Ashkenazim through their language in a humorous way. Nuri remembers his father's admonition to "Learn Yiddish, my boy" when he falls in love with a recent immigrant from Eastern Europe. [31]

In a discussion among Michel Ezra's family during the Yom Kippur War, an earlier conversation is recalled: "You promised us that all problems would be solved in a generation. 'It's a matter of twenty to thirty years' you said. Twenty-five years have passed; what's solved? What's moved? Musa Sharim is Moshe Shamir, but what else is changed?" (chap. 37) [32]

The words echo the author's own thoughts. In an essay, Shamosh discusses the two groups comprising Syrian Jewry: the "Arabicized" (those who absorbed Arab and Middle Eastern culture and contributed to it) and the "Franks" (waves of emigrants from the Spanish exile until the eighteenth century). "After one generation of confrontation the two tribes merged—different in culture and in interests—and became one community. Not easily and not without dissension but with impressive success. I wish it would be so in this country, here and now."[33]

While Shamosh's viewpoints are expressed by various characters, Michel Ezra's son Avrum (né Albert) is the closest to the author's alter ego. He is the son who does not join the family business, but instead ends up on a kibbutz. His father brings him to the kibbutz the first time, underscoring the gap between the Aleppan businessman's way of thinking, and the Sabra principles of the kibbutz. The father cannot believe that they do not get paid and asks, "By the way, Albert, did you see a synagogue there?"

The secularism, communalism, and socialism of the kibbutz is foreign to the Syrian Jews, as well as to those Iraqis and to the token Moroccan in *Fowl of Atonement*.[34] The dominant paradigm of Zionism is alienating to these newcomers. But the novel ends on a sense of hope, for through knowing them, it is asserted, one can come to value them. And it is up to the writer to present and interpret them for the Hebrew reader. In a lecture given on the occasion of the publication of *Michel Ezra Safra and His Sons*, the author noted the importance of perspective:

Looking back it is clear to me today that I wouldn't have been able to write "Michel" if I hadn't been born and grew up in the East, and I couldn't've written it this way—if not for having left it. I left and didn't leave.

If I hadn't absorbed in my childhood the ways of life and the way of thought and the ladder of values of the Sephardi-Mizrahi Jew (as far away from me today as the east from the west) and if I didn't respect them in my heart—I wouldn't be able to present in the face of the reader the spiritual and internal world of Michel and Linda and their sons and daughters as I presented them. And if I hadn't distanced from them and left for a different culture that is Israel and kibbutz and a socialist-humanist world view—I wouldn't have been able to write on them as I wrote, out of the same ironic distance that endears them to the reader. (p. 15)

The very myths reinforced in Amnon Shamosh's novel and in others are those held up for closer scrutiny or even deconstructed in more recent works. One of the most explicit examples of myth-breaking is Michael's latest novel *Victoria*.[35] It appeared twenty years and several novels and plays after the appearance of *Equal and More Equal*. *Victoria* surprised the critics, the readers, and the writer himself with its popularity. In many ways it is not typical of Sephardi writing, telling neither about the difficulties of transition to a new country, nor the glory that was home. It lays bare myths about the Sephardi that the earlier works helped construct: narratives of wealth, culture, privilege, and images of idealized family closeness.

Victoria is the story of a young girl growing up in a poor courtyard in

Baghdad at the turn of century. The narrative is structured similarly to Michael's first novel in two intertwined narrative lines. Here the structuring, like the writing, is more complex and sophisticated. The novel breaks the myth of the close, warm Sephardi family, the mystique of the *sephardi tahor* (literally, pure Sephardi), and the grandeur of the culture. The rich heritage of Babylonian Jewry was forgotten as if it never was.

In Baghdad I was completely ignorant about the heritage of Babylonian Jewry. Like Victoria, they robbed me of historical memory. I got Iraqi Jewry at the beginning of its awakening and knew nothing of its past. There I never even heard about the Babylonian Talmud or about the glorious yeshivot.[36]

Victoria is not at all about the glories of the past. The narrative describes a crowded courtyard whose inhabitants suffer abject poverty.

The house, which had been built decades before, was home to countless hidden occupants: ants, fleas, worms, ticks, scorpions, beetles, mice and snakes. What with the want, the deadly seasonal diseases and the cyclical epidemics, the human occupants humbly recognized their transience. Consequently they invested a minimum of effort in the upkeep of the building. Months went by before a broken window pane was replaced. Sometimes it was replaced by wooden boards or cardboard. The cesspits were emptied only when they overflowed. Broken floor tiles were left to disintegrate. The present occupants were in no hurry to wield hammers and picks. The line between the natural and the supernatural was thin and fragile, and few dared to touch it or cross it. Young and old, the members of the household believed that under the floor the earth was alive and kicking with demons and harmful spirits. It was better to ignore a cracked tile than risk startling the vengeful forces of the underworld from their slumbers. (pp. 52–53)

The levels of education, hygiene, and civility are almost uniformly very low. Women are treated as chattel, nearly sequestered in their homes to cook, to clean, and to bear children (preferably sons). The family members bear no responsibility for each other. One branch of the family is left to starve, and they survive only by stealing from their relatives. Relationships are based on rivalry rather than cooperation. The friendship of the cousins (and perhaps sisters) Miriam and Victoria is therefore even more startling against such a background.

As for the "purity" of the family, the quality of virtue is rare. Relationships are made murky by questions of adultery. Episodes of incest, pedophilia, and rape follow on each other's heels. Murder is almost added to the list when a newborn, mistakenly thought to be another girl, is left to die on the rooftop. This newborn, another Albert, is the writer's alter ego in this case as well.[37]

The life of the title character, Victoria, is surprisingly not all bleak. Despite the trials and tribulations of living in poverty and in conditions that can best be described as primitive, there are moments of light.

Where the reader sees a life of hardship and toil, Victoria has memories of joy. Her greatest rival is also her closest friend; their friendship weathers all sorts of adversity and challenges. Victoria's marriage to a man who cannot stay home and cannot stay faithful, who seems to arise from his sickbed only to return to it, is the source of her strength and happiness. Her love for him is the only permanence in her life. The multiple hardships do not make the book a catalogue of drudgery; instead, her strong character shines through.

The Iraq portrayed in Sami Michael's novel comes from an earlier point of time, a less modern society; it involves a much less affluent family than the ones described in the works that precede it.[38] Zionism plays a much smaller role here than it does in the aforementioned stories. The action in *Victoria* covers a much larger period, and the treatment of time is more complex, less clearly linear than in the narratives that recreate lost worlds with warmth, regret and some nostalgia. Michael's realism is bleaker (although not despairing), and verges on naturalism.

Victoria skirts the period of transition from the Arab world to Israel, leaping from the World War I era nearly to the present day. Because of the time period and the protagonist, the issues involving choices of Zionism, Communism, or nationalism, are barely relevant.[39] For Michael, although Israel becomes a refuge for Iraqi Jewry, Zionism itself is not the sole solution to their problems.[40] Instead, the Iraq described in Michael's latest novel is similar to the setting in the works of other Iraqi-Israeli writers that take place in a time before politics, before the twilight of the community.[41] But this is the other side of the courtyard: poverty rather than wealth, infidelity rather than faithfulness, rivalry and bitterness rather than family closeness and love. The *jinn* (mischievous spirits) in this story come up from the cellar and take human form—incest, rape, birth defects, abandonment, death from starvation. The move to Israel liberates the Baghdadi Jews from these demons.

While unraveling many of the myths established or reinforced by works such as *Michel Ezra Safra and His Sons, Victoria* creates a replacement myth: look how far we have come. It still belongs to the category of works presenting a challenge to the Zionist narrative from the "East." Without glorifying the past, the novel speaks to the pride of a people and adds another dimension to the mostly Ashkenazi, mostly Sabra canon of modern Hebrew literature.[42]

A more unrelenting deconstruction of some of these myths is found in the writing of Dan-Benaya Seri (b. 1935 in Jerusalem). The narratives of richly textured language, mixing simple constructions and archaisms, create an atmosphere of sin and superstition. Laconic dialogues express repression and isolation. The pervasive ignorance of sexual and social intercourse would be comical if it did not lead inexorably to tragedy.

Seri's first book, *Ugiyot hamelah shel Savta Sultana* (Grandma Sultana's salted biscuits, 1980), introduces us to the character of Eliahu. He fails to become a *shohet* (kosher butcher) because his hands tremble. He fails to consummate his marriage with the young Clara because neither of them knows what is expected of them. Impatiently awaiting signs that her daughter-in-law is pregnant, Eliahu's mother Zohara asks him:

"How is Clara in the bedroom?"
"She's sleeping."
"Not now, when she goes to sleep."
"She prays."
"And after she prays, does she do nice things?"
"What things?"
"Heh, heh, you know."
"I don't know."
"How is it you don't know?" (p. 46)[43]

For her part, Clara does not understand her mother-in-law's interest in her flat stomach. Dutiful, she fulfills her mother-in-law's directions as well as the instructions her mother gave her before her wedding night:

If he wants to touch her dress she should let him. It is a nice thing between any woman and her husband, even more so between Eliahu and her. It seemed extreme to her. What did Eliahu need with her dress? But if her mother told her so explicitly she would let him do what he wanted. In the nights following their wedding she put her dress on the back of her chair and pretended to sleep. She wanted to know what Eliahu would do with it. More than that [she hoped that] he should not dirty it, heaven forfend, with his black fingernails. The nights passed like this until she got tired. In the morning she would find the dress the way she left it, clean and unwrinkled on the chair. She was happy inside, and more than she liked him for what her mother told her, she liked him for not ruining her dress.

In the days after, when she'd go with him to her mother's, she could not restrain herself and talked in the kitchen so her husband could not hear. "Every night I do what he wants." Her mother covered her neck in kisses. "So it should be," she said, and the same week she [the mother] told her [Clara] that she had begun knitting a brown sweater for the baby. (pp. 79–80)

Such miscommunication and ignorance cannot lead to happiness. The tragic end is foreshadowed. Grandma Sultana protests at Zohara's dowry of copper: "Now the whole house is full of the smell of Arabs!" (p. 28). Zohara recalls a neighbor who went to work for the Ashkenazim and came back with child. Hassan comes to sell his copper the same

week Zohara despairs of Eliahu and Clara's consummating their marriage.

A few weeks later, Zohara rejoices at the first signs of her daughter-
in-law's pregnancy. Her joy quickly turns to anger when she realizes that
Clara has conceived a child with Hassan, the Arab copper merchant.
"Sultana," she cries to her own mother-in-law, "Clara's baby is a child of
Ishmael" (p. 120). Her reference to the child's Muslim father as Ishmael,
and her justification of poisoning the newborn "Sultana, did you want
them to name the child after Yitzhak?" (p. 136) reverberates with biblical echoes. Similar motifs recur in Dan-Benaya Seri's *Elef neshotav shel
Siman-Tov* (Siman-Tov's thousand wives, 1987). In this novella, the twice-
widowed groom masturbates rather than consummate his marriage.
After the young bride is seduced by the cloth seller, the groom hastens
her end (and keeps his secret) by serving her tea laced with rat poison.

The connection between Jerusalem, the Sephardim, and sexual perversity in Seri's stories has echoes in A. B. Yehoshua's masterpiece *Mar
Mani* (Mr. Mani, 1991), one of the most important Hebrew novels.[44]

While Avraham B. Yehoshua (b. 1936) has been a major contribu-
tor to this canon, readers have rarely noticed the subversive elements.
Mr. Mani has been read as the author's great coming-out novel as if he
had earlier denied his Sephardi roots. But his background had never
been a secret.

Although A. B. Yehoshua was at first reluctant to be identified as a
Sephardi writer (and understandably so, when we see how the ethnic
label has been used to limit the reading and reception of others), there
is no evidence that he ever tried to conceal or deny that aspect of his
personal identity. His cultural background differs greatly, however, from
that of Michael and others who imbibed Arab culture from infancy.

Yehoshua traces back his family five generations in Jerusalem on his
father's side; his mother came from a Moroccan background. Neither
was closed off from the dominant Ashkenazi culture; his mother grew
up speaking French, his father associated with the Ashkenazi intellectuals. A. B. Yehoshua himself studied at the Hebrew Gymnasia in Rehavia,
an elitist German institution, and was as steeped in the mainstream culture as he was in the family heritage.

Unlike most mainstream authors, he has consistently included Sephardi characters in his novels. For Yehoshua, Sephardi means *sephardi
tahor* in both direct and ironic ways. His Sephardim are, like him, of
Spanish descent. (The rare Mizrahi characters such as Levana in *Gerushim meukharim* [Late divorce, 1982] and Dr. Naqqash in *Shiva mehodu*

[Return from India, 1994] are the exceptions.) Yet these Sephardi characters are usually associated with mental and/or physical illness.

Less so in his short stories (published prior to the works under consideration), but certainly in his novels, Yehoshua directs a cast of characters whose Sephardi credentials are uncontested. Likewise, when the Sephardi characters are at the center of the stories, their Sephardism also becomes more central to them and the narrative. This gallery of characters challenges the Zionist narrative that Yehoshua himself helped to construct. The cumulative effect of this ongoing project, climaxing in *Mr. Mani*, offers an alternative to the EuroSabra version of the Israeli experience.

Before elaborating on *Mr. Mani*, let us look briefly at Yehoshua's earlier novels in order to appreciate this cumulative effect. His first novel, *Hameahev* (The lover, 1977), is set during the Yom Kippur War. The story questions the values of Israeli society in the wake of the disaster suffered by Israelis in the conflict.[45] Each character functions as an allegory, no one more so than Veducha Ermozo, who descends from a well-known Sephardi family. Her history resonates with the history of Israel. The woman was born, significantly, in 1881 (the date of the Russian pogroms that led to the birth of modern Zionism). Just as significantly, she is in a coma at the beginning of the war. She awakens from her coma, and is taken care of by an Arab youth named Naim. She has a deeper and more affectionate connection to him than any of the other characters have to her. This includes her grandson, Gabriel Arditi.

Gabriel shows up in Israel to await her death and claim his meager inheritance, which includes a blue 1947 (the year of the partition plan) Morris. Not only does he have a history of mental illness, but he is also a *yored*[46]-turned-deserter and imposter hiding out in a community of ultra-Orthodox: the antithesis of the Israeli patriot (as well as the antithesis of a committed family person and religious Jew). He is no longer a part of Israeli society or even of any alternative to it. While the book ends on a note of hope, it is not for the Sephardim; the grandmother dies, and the grandson disappears from the story.

The parade of Sephardi characters continues with Rafael Calderon in *Late Divorce*, Yehoshua's second novel.[47] Rafael is peripheral to the family at the core of this novel. A banker who has only recently discovered his homosexuality, Calderon is the aging lover of one of the sons of the family, Zvi. Though drawn sympathetically, he is not a positive character; lovesick and obsessed with Zvi, he reacts in extreme ways, forces himself on the family, and gives his lover insider financial information. He is especially delighted to discover that Zvi is part Sephardi. The Sephardi connection, it should be noted, is on the side of the mother, who has been committed to an asylum for attempting to kill the father. Granted, none of the characters in this book or almost any others by Yehoshua are truly admirable, but it is clear that Rafael's pride in his Sephardism is misplaced.

With Yehoshua's third novel, *Molkho* (1991; the English translation is *Five Seasons*), the Sephardi character is the center of attention. The name of the book and the protagonist is of Saloniki origin, recalling that vibrant Jewish community. "Molkho is one of those old time Sephardis, one of the veterans, one of those who are not connected to what is known as the 'oriental' communities in the classic sense of the term."[48]

The novel begins with the death from cancer of Molkho's German-born wife and with his obsession with selling the leftover medicine. Molkho is a slightly pathetic character who has not developed his Sephardi ethnic identity; the novel is a book of self discovery. As a Sephardi he is aware of his lower status and looks up to his wife's heritage: "I can become a Christian, or a Moslem, but there's no way I can become a German Jew" (p. 53).

After his wife's death, Molkho develops his high culture side. His thirst for classical music and opera leads him to attend the symphony early during his period of mourning and to go as far as to Berlin for opera. However, these highbrow tastes are somewhat misleading. He attends the symphony because he hates to waste the already-purchased ticket. The opera trip is more of a case of going to extreme lengths for a date, rather than any genuine hunger for Wagner. By natural inclination, Molkho is not very discriminating. He prefers plenty of trumpets and drums (p. 57) and has limited knowledge of classical music, never even having heard Vivaldi's overworn *Four Seasons*.

The narrative follows the widower from indulging in his wife's cultured tastes to dissociating from them; first he acknowledges that he enjoys the company of central Europeans that his wife would not have approved of (p. 70); later, he decides that he has had enough culture for the time being (p. 123), and opens himself to enjoying nature (p. 154), something his wife, "like many intellectuals," could not. In the end he even spurns the opera, preferring to return to East Berlin on his second trip to Germany.

The novel is less open to a reading that summons up Zionist ideology and Israel as allegory than Yehoshua's earlier works. It is a love story or an anti-love story in which the protagonist seems to accomplish nothing in the year following his wife's death beyond realizing the need to fall in love. This is, however, a great achievement in itself. Moreover, the character also extricates himself from the desire to be Ashkenazi, from a reverence bordering on worship for German Jews (as expressed by his bizarre attraction to his mother-in-law's German Jewish nursing home). While it is not obvious that he has embraced his Sephardism, the novel ends with hope expressed for its protagonist similar to the conclusions of *The Lover* and the later *Return from India.*

In *Molkho* Yehoshua clearly plays with the notion of self-portrait. His descriptions of Molkho as "a stoutish man with curly gray hair and dark Levantine eyes," (p. 53),[49] and also as a fifth-generation Jerusalemite (p. 72) with relatives from an aristocratic old Sephardi family (p. 63) are equally applicable to the author. In earlier works, the author is present in a cameo role—a man who types late into the evening (and fascinates Dafna) in *The Lover*; the writer whom Dina visits in *Late Divorce* and works in an apartment suspiciously similar to that described as Yehoshua's work place. In these earlier novels as well as in the more obvious case of *Molkho*, it is not the autobiographical Yehoshua that he is representing; rather he is playing with the notion of self-representation in his fiction. Interestingly enough, however, the writer's alter ego becomes more central in these books as the Sephardism becomes more of an issue.

Yehoshua interrupted writing *Mr. Mani*, his Sephardi tour de force, in order to create *Molkho.* On the occasion of the publication of *Molkho*, the writer declared:

Today I take a far greater interest in my own Sephardi past. You remember the chapter from my unfinished novel "Mr. Manny" [*sic*] . . . in which I went back to the beginning of the century. I have not continued to write this novel because I did not feel attraction to earlier generations of my family. But I am not talking of a nostalgic search for roots. What interests me is the components of the Israeli identity, to which I have a certain commitment.[50]

The scholars duly note Yehoshua's introduction to his father's book about the Sephardi community of Jerusalem, "Recherche du temps Sephardi perdu."[51] His father had begun publishing only after the son had already made a name for himself. *Mr. Mani* is dedicated to Yehoshua's father, paralleling Yehoshua's father's dedicating *his* book to *his* father.

Mr. Mani is a strange book to dedicate to one's father. The book is a collection of five monodialogues (only one speaker's half of an extended conversation is recorded) arranged in reverse chronology. A combination of the parallel fields of archeology and psychology, the narrative digs into the past of a Sephardi family from Jerusalem. Like Michael's *Victoria*, it is a variation on the family saga, in which the family values exhibited are of dubious quality. Furthermore, as does Victoria, Mr. Mani shows heroism through the not so simple act(s) of survival.

It is, in fact, the opposite of the novel of generations, and not just with regard to the narration of time. The family at the center is rarely given voice, the fortunes of the family do not flourish, and most important, the family connections are dubious. Blood ties are at best questionable, thereby mocking a central tenet of the family saga. The Mani "dynasty" is established in the story's last chapter through an act of incest.

This fifth conversation gives us the only speaker who is a Mani. In one of many reversals, Avraham Mani comes to his teacher, Rabbi Shabbetai Hananiah, as the rabbi is dying, to give confession.

And so I too roundaboutly, along an arc bridging the two ends of Asia Minor, entered your bed, señor, a bed I had never dared climb into even as a lonely boy running down your long hallway in my *blouson*, scared to death of the cannons firing over the Bosporus. Now in Jerusalem, I slipped between your sheets and lay with your Doña Flora, thirty years younger, in her native city, in her childhood home, in her parents' bed, smelling your strong tobacco in the distance, giving and getting love that sweetened a great commandment carried out by a great transgression. At dawn, when old Carso knocked on the door to take me to the Middle Synagogue for the morning service and the mourner's prayer, he scarcely could have imagined that the bereaved father he had left the night before was now a sinful grandfather. (p. 355)

Clearly not an ode to Sephardi identity, the dominant theme here is the obsession with Sephardi identity. There is a play on the concept of *sephardi tahor*. In each generation of Yehoshua's fictional Mani dynasty, in each chapter, there is mystery, perversity, and more than a touch of madness. The narratives all lead back to Jerusalem, the source of the Jerusalem syndrome, "the city [that] is forever greater than its inhabitants."[52] In this narrative the sense of place is as strong if not stronger than the sense of place in the aforementioned works: Aleppo in *Michel Ezra Safra and His Sons*, Alexandria in Gormezano-Goren's *Alexandrian Summer*, Baghdad in *Victoria*.

While literature often criticizes the mainstream or challenges the status quo, it normally does so within certain bounds or from the outside. Here Yehoshua is using his insider status (much as Eli Amir can use his insider status to articulate harsher critiques in *Fowl of Atonement* than did Michael in *Equal and More Equal*) to call for a radical rewriting of the Zionist narrative. Neither sparing nor idealizing the Sephardim, he posits an alternate narrative. Sephardim participate in the traditional Zionist story and create their own version. By placing Dr. Mani with Herzl at the Zionist Congress meeting in 1899, Yehoshua effectively includes Sephardim in this European enterprise. European Zionism is embodied by the figure of Herzl, shown to be weak and ailing, on the verge of total collapse; by contrast the Sephardi counterpart is robust. The Mani (read: Sephardi) attachment to the land of Israel is not political, ideological, or interchangeable; rather it is organic. Like Veducha of *The Lover*, the Manis are the link to the land, and also the bridge to the Arabs, the true indigenous people.[53]

Sephardim in the novel personify survival and cultural syncretism. Yehoshua records such a cacophony of tongues that Hebrew is virtually wrenched from any link to the land or to national identity. The nation-state is undermined as the major achievement of the Zionist movement. With all of the attention paid to dates in this reversed history, the absence of 1948 is an omission fraught with significance. European Zionism is weak and fails; the Lebanese War of 1982, background to the first conversation (and the Intifada, briefly mentioned in the postscript to that conversation), shows the State at its worst. It may be that those who have a strong and even mysterious link to the land lay claim to the true history and future of Zionism. Yet Ashkenazim are not completely off the page. It is the ironically named Hagar, the EuroSabra kibbutz daughter, who gives birth to Roni, thereby assuring the survival of the Mani family for another generation.

The cross-culturalism of the Sephardim, and the idea of the Sephardim as the link between Jews and Arabs, are further developed in the works of Shimon Ballas. Ballas's background is similar to Michael's, at least superficially. Born in 1930 in Baghdad, Ballas was educated in the Jewish schools and in the Communist movement. He continued his activity in the movement for a number of years after his arrival in Israel in 1951. A writer of short stories and novels, he is currently a professor of Arabic literature at the University of Haifa.

Throughout his Hebrew literary career, Ballas has written about the experiences of outsiders.

The problem of the exile, the problem of the stranger, the problem of the man different from his environment—occupies me in all of my work, in novels as well as in short stories. Here is a projection of my situation. I also see myself as a product of Arab culture. I wrote in Arabic and things happened so that I write in Hebrew . . .

After beginning with a description of the immigrant experience in *Hama'abarah* (The transit camp, 1964), and a collection of short stories, *Mul haḥomah* (Facing the wall, 1969), Ballas wrote a second novel, *Hitbaharut* (Clarification, 1972), about an immigrant from Iraq who is left out of the 1973 war. *Ḥeder na'ul* (A locked room, 1980) follows an Arab Israeli who returns to Israel from self-imposed exile in France to work on his autobiography and to confront himself and his identity. *Ḥoref aharon*

(The last winter, 1984) is a *roman à clef* based on the last year in the life of Henri Curiel, an Egyptian Jewish Communist in exile in France. Most ambitious of all in structural technique, *Hayoresh* (The heir, 1987) layers intertwining stories to construct a mystery centering on the quest for identity. The protagonists are caught between opposing constructions of identity, and belong to neither.[54]

Vehu aher (The other one, 1991)[55] examines Iraq after the mass exodus of the Jews. The novel explores alternatives for Jews who chose not to leave Iraq. Each of these strategies—to continue a literary career in Baghdad as a Jew, to struggle against the regime, or to convert to Islam— is realized by a character in the story.

The novel begins with an occasion celebrating the publication of the narrator-protagonist's book about the history of the Jews of Iraq. The upcoming celebration gives the fictional author—our narrator—an opportunity to reminisce about his life. This fictional autobiography is a modified *roman à clef* (similar to *Horef aharon*). The protagonist, Harun Sawsan, is based on Ahmed (Nissim) Sawsan, a writer who converted to Islam in the thirties, and had several books published in Iraq; he died only a few years ago.[56]

His close friend Asad Nissim chooses literature as the expression of his Iraqi nationalism. He is a fictional representation of the famous Iraqi Jewish poet Anwar Shaul, who stayed in Iraq after most of the Jewish community left.[57] As late as 1969, Shaul wrote a poem expressing his loyalty to Iraq.[58]

The third friend, Kassem Abd al-Baky, is most probably a composite sketch of several people rather than a portrait of a specific person. Kassem is a Marxist revolutionary who dies as an exile in Europe (reminiscent of *Horef aharon*'s protagonist, Andre Sorel), betrayed by the revolution.

As narrated in the novel, Sawsan's life story is fraught with ambivalences and dualities. From the beginning, his relationship with the Jewish community is problematic. His first break from the community is triggered by the article he writes promoting army service for all. (Jews had previously been exempted from the draft by paying a tax; the new government policy cancelled the exemption.) He marries a Christian woman. Most dramatic of all, he converts to Islam.

The seventh of November 1936 is the date of my conversion to Islam according to the law, and from that day my name is Ahmed Haroun Sawsan. I decided to keep my family name and private name so as to deflect the slander that I deny my origins, to the contrary. In my book *My Path to Islam* I wrote that I am a Jew to whom God has shown the way to the true faith; it is my obligation to turn to the Jews first and foremost and implore them to free themselves from their isolationism and to join the Islamic nation in which they live. (pp. 79–80)

He travels to Egypt to convert—as if the distance will provide a buffer between him and the Jewish community in Iraq. His ambivalence is further expressed when he tells Kassem but not Assad about his conversion. His naiveté is shown both in his motivation and in his admiration for the Egyptian law requiring the convert to get permission from the appropriate church or Jewish authorities. (Ironically, the otherwise politically astute Sawsan does not consider the expediency of such a requirement.) Despite his authorship of *My Path to Islam,* his conversion seems less than spiritual. He claims that had his older brother Reuben reacted differently to his intermarriage, he might not have converted. He also credits his conversion with sparing him the suffering that comes from maintaining the duality of Iraqi Jewish nationalism, as in the case of Asad. In point of fact, his conversion further estranges him from his family and community; during the *Farhud* (the 1941 pogrom) he is completely alone.

The idea of history frames the narrative and recurs in the book as a central motif. The celebration opening the story honors the fictional Sawsan's book about the history of the Jews in Iraq. The occasion causes Sawsan to recall his personal history. This fictional autobiography traces the character's search to find his identity in the past. Sawsan's dissertation analyzing British policy in the Middle East after the construction of the Suez Canal enables him to reconsider his personal history in light of national and world events. External events and personal history mesh; Sawsan himself suffers from an alienating and unrelenting ambiguity. His life is a complex of dualities: two families, two identities, two religions. He is a Jew in Iraq, and a Muslim from a Jewish background, an engineer and a historian. As an engineer he destroys Jewish homes; as a historian, he writes a study of Jews in Iraq, recreating these homes for perpetuity. In going so far as to convert in order to belong, he instead alienates himself from any real community; his adopted community abandons him. Others recognize his statelessness. When studying at Johns Hopkins University, his professor asks, "Why don't you go to Palestine?" (p. 21)[59]

The novels of Ballas challenge the Zionist narrative differently from the novels discussed above. His works strain to be part of world literature, not Israeli; his narrative is equally at home in Paris, Baghdad, or Tel Aviv. These are the respective settings for the three novellas in *Otot stav* (Signs of autumn, 1992).[60] The very different settings, very different protagonists, very different plots, are united in their sense of estrangement in the autumn of each protagonist's life. "Iyah" replays the exodus of the Jews from a vantage point previously ignored. It centers on Zakiyah ("Iyah" in the mouths of the children), the loyal servant of a Jewish family, as they prepare to depart for Israel. Despite her many years of loyal service, despite the strong ties of affection developed over the years, despite her estrangement from the husband of her youth, Iyah is left behind. As a parting gift, she receives a copy of the Koran, a gift moving in its simplicity and its symbolism.

The 'otherness' in Ballas's stories is not easily transversed. Rather than cancelling each other out, the layers of estrangement accumulate relentlessly. Unlike *Victoria*, in which the character's female identity serves her in good stead during periods of transition and adversity, for Iyah it is an additional dimension of marginality. While the author is equally at home setting his stories in Iraq, Israel, or France, the characters are not at home. The loyalty of characters as different as Sawsan and Iyah goes unrewarded and their alienation remains unrelieved. Ballas's works remain outside of the Zionist narrative offering yet another counternarrative. Mohammad Siddiq reminds us that:

It is important to bear in mind that the counter-narrative is oppositional only to the extent that it aims to fragment, decenter and deconstruct, but not to supplant, the hegemonic master-narrative.[61]

Israeli literature has been characterized as a literature of fathers and sons. The story of the *akedah* (the binding of Isaac), the son sacrificed by the father, has served as a crucial paradigm for understanding the literature (and the society) until now. The Sephardi literature does not abandon this paradigm; it is still a literature of fathers and sons. (With the exception of essayist Jacqueline Kahanoff, poets Amira Hess, Shelley Elkayam, and a few others, it is still a literature written by sons.) Yet it recasts the motif in new ways.

Equal and More Equal portrays a father emasculated and destroyed by the Zionist enterprise. In a reversal of the *akedah* he is sacrificed on the altar of the new state. The ending is hopeful when the main character accepts his role as a father to his sabra son. The father and founder of the Safra clan rules the family and dominates the story of *Michel Ezra Safra and His Sons*. This is true even after his death midway through the saga. His death in Argentina saves him from the difficulties of acclimation to a new home ("From the moment that Michel left his city he lost his peace," p. 108). Like David Asher's father in Sami Michael's first novel, Michel turns to gluttony. Like the biblical Moses, he sends his children off to Israel but does not himself enter the promised land. His death also saves him from the guilt he feels when his grandson falls in the battle for Jerusalem (sending sons off to war is a more common variation on the *akedah* theme).

Even *Victoria*, a portrait of the author's mother, was initially based on his father (the character Rafael),[62] with whom Michael admittedly had a complex relationship. Although the privileged position of sons in the world described is mitigated somewhat by Victoria's special relationship with her father, by the strong presence of the grand matriarch Michal, and by the insignificant achievements of many of the sons, the pattern of fathers and sons is not supplanted. It is, in fact, emphasized by primary and secondary characters. Their neighbor Ma'atuk Nunu is banished by his father and exacts his revenge after the father's death. Victoria's father holds a central position in the courtyard until Rafael usurps it. Rafael himself has three "fathers"—biological, spiritual, and rival—who draft the outlines of his life's story. From his birth father he inherits his wanderlust, from one uncle a weak constitution, and from the other uncle a lusty appetite. Rafael's own son Albert brings him back to the family fold, calling an end to his wanderings, and later memorializes him through the narration. This father-son relationship is not explicitly analyzed in the story itself, yet the real-life relationship between the father and son (Michael) on whom these characters are based is explored through the very writing of the story.

The relationship between the father Yitzhak and son Eliahu is underdeveloped in *Grandma Sultana's Salted Biscuits*. The mother, Zohara, is dominant; the father, Yitzhak, dies early in the narrative. Yet the theme of the *akedah* is prominent in the story of the murder of the baby.

Mr. Mani, an inverted novel of generations, offers us a entire series of fathers and sons, from the kibbutznik's boyfriend and his suicidal father to the first Manis. Siddiq and others have noted the variation on the *akedah*, the Oedipal reversal at the core of the novel.[63] Abraham, the father, establishes the lineage through an incestuous liaison with his daughter-in-law after "killing" his son—first through impotence and then suicide. The fathers are not the builders of Zionism and the sons are not the fighters or the newly disillusioned, but they are indeed reworking the same *akedah* story in Sephardi variations.

In conclusion, the "Sephardi" novels are as varied in style, content, tone, and quality as any random collection of Israeli novels. When we persist in reading them as ethnic, we deny them full voice, miss much of their texture, and may, on occasion, invert their meaning. In confronting the earlier cultural hegemony, the Sephardi writers, those from Arab and Islamic lands in particular, have made great contributions to contemporary Israeli literature. They are among the first and foremost to write immigrant literature, to develop the political novel, and to restore the reconstruction of the past to the literary scene. As such, they are no longer the "other" but an integral part of the development of Israeli literature.

Notes

1. The Hebrew words "to know" and "to value" are homonyms.
2. This is also true of writing by Israelis from non-Arab Islamic lands, such as Shlomo Avayou from Turkey and Shmueliyan from Iran.
3. See for example: Ammiel Alcalay, *After Arabs and Jews* (Minneapolis: University of Minnesota Press, 1993) and Yerash Gover, *Zionism* (Minneapolis: University of Minnesota Press, 1994).
4. The term "Sephardi" technically refers to Jews of Spanish/Portugese descent who can trace their heritage back to the exile of 1492, in opposition to Ashkenazi, and more casually to Jews who come from Arab and Islamic lands as well. The technical Sephardi thus becomes the Sephardi tahor (lit. "pure Sephardi"; see below), and the term "Sephardi" is used to cover Mizrahi Jews as well. The latter term, lit. Eastern or Oriental, also fails the test of strict standards of accuracy as it does not account for the fact that North African Jews originate at a point geographically west of Eastern and Central European Jews (who are, unequivocally, Ashkenazim). Greater detail will lead to greater confusion. In the novel under discussion below, the word "Sephardi" is used to describe the Jews from Iraq who trace their roots to a community that predates the Sephardi presence in Iberia.
5. Tel Aviv: Boostan, 1974.
6. He had planned to deplane on a scheduled stopover in Paris, not knowing the flight plan announced was fictitious.
7. E.g. *Hayoshevet baganim*, 1938.
8. In the early days of the State, newcomers were given "temporary" housing in transit camps where they were also supplied with food, clothing, sanitary facilities, and some job opportunities. These camps were often overcrowded, the housing inferior, and the sanitation inadequate. Because of the postwar economy and general ill-preparedness for the large numbers of immigrants who came in the late forties and early fifties, many ended up staying in the cloth tents and tin shacks in these transit camps for much longer than originally intended. For more of a description, see Shlomo Hillel, *Operation Babylon*, trans. Ina Friedman (London: Collins, 1988), p. 287.
9. Nancy E. Berg, *Exile From Exile* (Albany: State University of New York Press, 1996).
10. See also Rahamim Rejwan, *'Al gehalim* (On coals) (Tel Aviv: Sifriyat Tarmil, 1985); and Eli Amir, *Tarnegol kapparot* (Fowl of atonement) (Tel Aviv: Am Oved, 1983), trans. Dalya Bilu, *Scapegoat* (London: Weidenfeld and Nicolson 1988).
11. It is never explained why this family is there, especially because it comes out later that Tzipporah's brother lives in Israel. (They are, however, the first to move to their own apartment.) This may have something to do with the myth of family unity, showing the Ashkenazim as having less a sense of mutual responsibility.
12. "Zhid" is itself pejorative; an English equivalent might be "Jewstein" or worse.
13. Compare to Nilly in *Fowl of Atonement*.
14. A film genre popular in the sixties, named after a food typical of Mizrahim. These movies are characterized by broad comedy, Mizrahi stereotypes, and happily-ever-after endings (often resulting from the union of an Ashkenazi and a Mizrahi in a "mixed" marriage).

15. By Hanoch Bartov, Tel Aviv: Sifriyat Po'alim, 1954. It is the story of a successful immigrant absorption; one of the last scenes describes a young immigrant couple naming their Sabra child after the lone native Israeli character.

16. Itshak Bar-Moshe, *Bayt fī Baghdād* (House in Baghdad) (Jerusalem: Association of Jewish Academics from Iraq, 1983) preface, p. 20. In Arabic.

17. Yizhak Gormezano-Goren, *Kayiz alexandroni* (Alexandrian summer) (Tel Aviv: Am Oved, 1978), pp. 8–9.

18. Samīr Naqqāsh, "Laylat urābā" (The night of Hoshana Raba), *Yawm habalat wa-ajhadat al-dunya* (in Arabic) (The day the world was conceived and miscarried) (Jerusalem: Al-Sharq Al-Arabiyya, 1980) p. 214. This preceded Anton Shammas's *Arabesques* (1986), which used the same technique to similarly strong effect.

19. Ibid., p. 176.

20. Naqqāsh has mostly academic readers. See, for example, his responses in his interview with Ammiel Alcalay in "Keys to the Garden: Israeli Writing in the Middle East," *The Literary Review* 37, no. 1 (1994): 195–205.

21. Amnon Shamosh, *Min hama'ayan* (From the source) (Jerusalem: Karta, 1988), p. 15.

22. Ibid., p. 17.

23. Amnon Shamosh, *Michel Ezra Safra uvanav* (Michel Ezra Safra and his sons) (Tel Aviv: Massada, 1978). Walter P. Zenner, "Aleppo and the Kibbutz in the Fiction of Amnon Shamosh," *Shofar* 6, no. 3, pp. 25–35.

24. Compare also to the narrator's self-deprecating comments: "Surely among the readers there are those who'll understand these things better than I. I give you leave to laugh at my ignorance and smile at my naiveté." (*Michel Ezra*, p. 15).

25. Albert ironically becomes his kibbutz treasurer in Israel, managing a seven-figure budget, and running the factory well on the profit side.

26. Compare to the beginning of Jacqueline Kahanoff's memoirs about her childhood in Egypt: "When I was little it seemed natural to me that people understood each other even when they spoke different languages and were labelled differently, such as, 'Greek, Muslim, Syrian, Jew, Christian, Arab, Italian, Tunisian, Armenian.' Even so they were like each other." *Memizrah shemesh* (Essays) (Tel Aviv: Hadar/Yariv, 1978), p. 11.

27. The *Farhud* is the name of the May 31–June 2, 1941, pogrom that took place in the Jewish Quarter in Baghdad. Factors including the defeat and demoralization of the Iraqi army, the delay of the British entry to the city (thereby creating a power vacuum), and the Jews' celebrating the holiday of Sukkot led to two days of pillaging and chaos that left approximately 180 Jews dead and many others wounded. The pogrom surprisingly did not spread to other neighborhoods or towns. A British inquiry into the matter placed the blame on several discredited Iraqi politicians and led to payment of reparations.

28. Yizhak Bar-Moshe, *Yawmein fi Khazeiran* (Two days in June [in Arabic]); Michael, *Sufah bein hadekalim* (Storm among the palms) (Tel Aviv: Am Oved, 1975).

29. Samīr Naqqāsh, *Yawm habalat wa-ajhadat al-dunyā* (The day the world was conceived and miscarried); Shimon Ballas, *Mul hahomah* (In front of the wall) (Ramat Gan: Masada, 1969).

30. *Warum* means "why" in Yiddish; *warum nicht*, "why not."

31. Shimon Ballas, *Hama'abarah* (The transit camp) (Tel Aviv: Am Oved,

1964); Eli Amir, *Tarnegol kapparot* (Fowl of atonement) (Tel Aviv: Am Oved, 1983), p. 171.

32. "I made money, true. I made it in the big world, true. But Sephardi I am and Sephardi I remain. A member of the Oriental ethnics."

"What did you want?"

"To be an Israeli."

"So what prevents you from feeling like an Israeli?"

"My accent. My name."

"You can change your name."

"No, my friend, not before Ashkenazi-ness disappears from the land."

"I don't know what you call Ashkenazi-ness."

"The key to success and preference." (p. 231)

33. *Min hama'ayan* (From the source), p. 16.

34. See *Fowl of Atonement*, p. 41: "What? Jews without a synagogue?"

35. Sami Michael, *Victoria* (Tel Aviv: Am Oved, 1993), trans. Dalya Bilu (London: Macmillan, 1995).

36. Sami Michael, personal communication, 29 December 1995.

37. Michael makes no secret of the nonfictional basis of the book, or that the character Victoria is based on his mother. In fact, the writer told the story of his birth and rescue in an interview that predates the novel by several years.

38. Including both Michael's own *Hofen shel arafel* (Handful of fog) and *Ahavah bein hadekalim* (Love among the palms), works by Naqqāsh, Bar-Moshe, and Ballas as well as the contemporaneous *Mafriah hayonim* (The pigeon keeper) by Eli Amir (Tel Aviv: Am Oved, 1992. The English title on the inside cover is *Farewell, Baghdad*). Because both *Victoria* and *The Pigeon Keeper* were best-sellers in the same season; written by Iraqi-born writers and set in Iraq, they inevitably invite comparison. But their similarities are mostly superficial: both stories begin in Iraq and end in Israel; both consider some of the same issues—the status of women, the effects of modernization—in a similar physical and social environment (marital infidelity, prostitutes, etc.), in each case invoking a world forever gone. Yet the approaches to this lost world, and the worlds themselves, are very different.

It is even in the similarities that the differences are revealed. In both cases the birth of a male child gives life and hope to his parents. Victoria's pregnancy initially fills her with suicidal despair—she thinks it will be another daughter—but the birth of her son Albert gives her reason to look forward to the future. His birth corresponds loosely to his father Rafael's rebirth (his cure from a fatal illness). It also signifies the regeneration of the once glorious family into future glory.

In *The Pigeon Keeper* the father insists that his next male child be born in Israel. Upon their arrival to this dreamed-of land, his disappointment is palpable. He sinks into the mud (physically and, of course, symbolically), and is brought back to the *ma'abarah* to hear the news of the birth of his son. As in *Shesh kenafaim lehad* (Each one has six wings) and even Amir's own *Fowl of Atonement*, the birth of a Sabra son signifies hope and the promise of a new beginning in a new home. (See Dan Laor, "Ha'aliyah hahamonit ke'tokhen venose' basifrut ha'ivrit bish'not hamedinah harishonot" (Mass immigration as content and subject in Hebrew literature of the first years of the state) *Haziyonut* 14 (1989): 161–175.)

39. The focus on the period leading up to and immediately following the

uprooting of the Iraqi Jewish community is detailed in *The Pigeon Keeper* and Michael's works before *Victoria* (see previous footnote). The individual authors' approaches remain distinctly their own. For Eli Amir's protagonists and narrators, Zionism is the answer, despite the great contrast between former prosperity and present status and the hardships of acclimation.

40. See for example, Michael's novel *Ḥasut* (Tel Aviv: Am Oved, 1977), tr. Edward Grossman, *Refuge* (Philadelphia: Jewish Publication Society, 1988) about Arab and Jewish members of the Communist party in Haifa against the backdrop of the Yom Kippur War. The book opens with the character Mardukh proclaiming Israel's legacies as agricultural success and oppression of Arabs. By the book's end we come to understand that Israel's greatest achievement is in granting refuge. The questions of Israel, Zionism, and refuge are barely acknowledged in *Victoria*.

41. See for example Shalom Darwishe, *Phraim! Phraim!* (Tel Aviv: Kedem, 1986); Samīr Naqqāsh, "Laylat urābā"; and Bar-Moshe, *Bayt fī Baghdād*. These works present a mostly wealthy and secure Jewish community in Baghdad.

42. Nancy E. Berg, "*Victoria*: Answering the Ethnic Question," *Israel Affairs* (Summer 1996).

43. Dan-Benaya Seri, Ugiyot hamelaḥ shel savta Sultana (Grandma Sultanas salted biscuits) (Jerusalem: Keter, 1980; revised Jerusalem: HaSifriyah, 1988). Eliahu's father Yitzhak worked in the construction industry where his co-workers spoke frankly "and kept nothing from him." For whatever reason, he never thought to pass on this information to his own son.

44. A. B. Yehoshua, *Mar Mani* (Tel Aviv: Hakibbutz Hameuchad, 1990), trans. Hillel Halkin, *Mr. Mani* (New York: Doubleday, 1992).

45. A. B. Yehoshua *Hameahev* (Tel Aviv and Jerusalem: Schocken, 1977), trans. Philip Simpson *The Lover* (N.Y.: Dutton, 1977). Adam, the garage owner, is seen as the Israeli everyman, reduced to such impotence that he brings in a lover for his wife, inadvertently does the same for his daughter (and an Arab lover at that!), and becomes a lover himself when he takes advantage of his daughter's spacy girlfriend. Instead of getting his hands dirty and doing repairs himself, he is the bourgeois owner, manager, employer of Arabs. He is detached from friends and family, still mourning the death of his son Yigal.

46. Former Israeli; literally "one who descends," *yored* refers to an Israeli emigrant and carries a negative connotation.

47. A. B. Yehoshua, *Gerushim me'uḥarim* (Tel Aviv: Hakibbutz Hameuchad, 1982), trans. Hillel Halkin (Garden City, N.J.: Doubleday, 1984).

48. Yehoshua in Shmuel Huppert, "One Has to Fall in Love," *Modern Hebrew Literature* 13, nos. 1–2 (Fall-Winter 1987), pp. 7–11.

49. And elsewhere: "a 51-year-old man with grey but still thick curly hair and dark deeply set eyes" (p. 61, English tr.).

50. Huppert, "One Has to Fall in Love," p. 10.

51. Arnold Band, "Arkheologiya shel hona'ah 'azmit" (The archeology of self deception) in *Bakivun Hanegdi: Kovez mehkarim 'al Mar Mani shel A. B. Yehoshua*, ed. Nitza Ben-Dov (Tel Aviv: Hakibbutz Hameuchad, 1995) pp. 182–192, Gila Ramras Rauch, "A. B. Yehoshua and the Sephardic Experience," *World Literature Today* (Winter 1991), pp. 8–13.

52. *Mr. Mani*, p. 272.

53. Yehoshua differs from the Canaanites, however. While not denying the Arabs' rights to the land, the son in the fifth section looks upon the Arabs as

Jews who have gone astray, and tries to convert them. The book itself is undeniably Jewish in its orientation.

54. Shimon Ballas, *Heder na'ul* (A locked room) (Tel Aviv: Zemorah, Bitan, Modan, 1980); *Horef aharon* (The last winter) (Jerusalem: Keter, 1984); *Hayoresh* (The heir) (Tel Aviv: Zemorah, Bitan, 1987).

55. Shimon Ballas, *Vehu aher* (The other one) (Tel Aviv: Zemorah, Bitan, 1991).

56. See Orly Toran, "Ani Yehudi Aravi," *Kol ha'ir*, 15 March 1991, pp. 78, 80, 83.

57. Shaul was born 1904 in Hilla. He moved to Baghdad before World War I, where he worked as an Arabic teacher and lawyer, becoming important in the Jewish and literary communities. While he was best known for his poetry, he was also central to the development of modern Iraqi literature, especially in his efforts to promote short story writing. He founded the magazine *al-haṣid* (1929–37) and the publishing company (Shirkat al-tijarah wa-al-tiba'ah. He came to Israel in 1971 where his autobiography, *Qissat hayati fi wadi al-rafidayn* was published by the Association for Iraqi Academics in Israel.

58. See p. 56 in *Vehu aher*.

59. Compare to the statement by Anton Shammas: "The state of Israel, Jewish by its own definition, treats me as a Palestinian exile (*yored*) who is said to go up to his Palestinian state when and if it arises." ("Al galut vesifrut," Mishkenot Sheananim writer's conference, pub.)

60. Shimon Ballas, *Otot stav* (Signs of autumn) (Tel Aviv: Am Oved, 1992).

61. "The Making of a CounterNarrative: Two Examples from Contemporary Arabic and Hebrew Fiction," *Michigan Quarterly Review* (Fall 1992), p. 661.

62. Dalia Karpel, "Ani pohed rak meshedim," *Haarez* 9 February 1993.

63. See Siddiq, op. cit., Mordechai Shalev, "Hotem ha'akedah be'sheloshah yamim vayeled,' be'bethilat kayiz 1970,' be 'Mar Mani,'" and A. B. Yehoshua, "Hatimah: Levatel et ha'akedah 'al-yedei mimushah," in *Bakivun hanegdi: Kovez mehkarim 'al Mar Mani shel A. B. Yehoshua*, ed. Nitza Ben-Dov (Tel Aviv: Hakibbutz Hameuchad, 1995).

GILEAD MORAHG

Breaking Silence: Israel's Fantastic Fiction of the Holocaust

While other tragedies can be translated into the language of reality as we know it, the Holocaust cannot. —Ayala, in David Grossman's *See Under: Love*

I re-created these events and then I experienced them as any witness or victim.
—Steven Spielberg on *Schindler's List*

ISRAEL IS, in many ways, a consequence of the horrible events that have come to be called the Holocaust. Since it is also a country with a rich literature that is intensely preoccupied with questions of national origins and national character, one would expect the Holocaust to figure very centrally in the fiction that was written in Israel since its inception. But this has not been the case. The first four decades of Israeli writing have little to say on the subject. One clear exception to this are the stories and novels of Aharon Appelfeld, a highly accomplished writer whose persistent preoccupation with the Holocaust relegated his early work to the margins of mainstream Israeli literature.[1] But other than this lone and quietly powerful voice, there are only faint traces of the Holocaust experience in Israeli fiction written between 1948 and 1986.[2] Then things began to change, and Israel is now witnessing the emergence of a new literary preoccupation with the Holocaust.

The recurrence of the Holocaust theme in recent Israeli literature is a particular manifestation of a general cultural reorientation towards the Holocaust that seems to have begun in the late 1970s, and is also evident in many areas of Israeli popular culture, political discourse, educational policy, and academic research.[3] This new concern with the Holocaust is part of an increasingly intense national quest for a viable post-Zionist identity, and of the multifaceted public debate over the manner in which this identity should relate contemporary Israelis to their historical Jewish roots. But, as Tom Segev has observed, the recent eagerness to embrace the past is often no less problematic and charged with contradiction than the earlier tendency to deny it.[4] For what is at issue now is no longer whether or not to remember the Holocaust, but rather the nature of the personal and national lessons that are to be learned from it. Israel's political establishment has sought to press the heritage of the Holocaust into the service of its ideological agenda in the hope of forging a more unified national identity. Israel's literary community is at the forefront of a countereffort to explore the continuing impact of the Holocaust on the individual psyche and determine its relevance to a personal sense of Israeli identity.

A growing number of recent Israeli writers appear to have discovered that although they did not experience the Holocaust, the Holocaust is still very much a part of their experience. The work of these writers is marked by an acute sense that the wounds of history are hereditary and that Israeli identity is powerfully linked to Jewish calamity. Their stories and novels seek to penetrate the barriers of denial and to explore the impact of the Holocaust on the present lives of Israeli individuals and the current dynamics of Israeli society. These new works fall into two distinct categories. The first category is largely descriptive. It includes works that uncover and describe the deep residue of damage that permeates the lives of the Israeli heirs of the Holocaust generation. Most notable among them are the works of Savyon Liebrecht, Nava Semel, and Jacob Ya'akov Buchan.[5] These are works that seek to depict the varieties of social and psychological deformations incurred by the descendants of Holocaust survivors. Underlying many of these works is a strong suggestion that the individual instances they portray represent a broader social reality, and that every new generation of Israelis is a new generation of Holocaust survivors.

This sense of affinity between the Holocaust experience and the Israeli psyche is intensified in the second category of Holocaust-related novels, which includes David Grossman's *See Under: Love* (1986), Yitzhak Ben-Ner's *The Angels Are Coming* (1987), Dorit Peleg's *Una* (1988) and Itamar Levy's *The Legend of the Sad Lakes* (1989). These are more ambitious, exploratory works that confirm the psychological insights of the first category, but are much bolder in pursuing their existential implications. These novels are the focus of this study, which seeks to trace their narrative dynamics as they proceed from describing the damage to excavating its origins, considering its consequences, and exploring the possibilities of healing.

The central thesis of this study is that all four novels address the paradox of a culture that is predicated on a denial of its affinity with the Holocaust experience, but is obsessively conducting much of its life according to an ethos that was generated by this experience. They all involve lives that have been damaged by the denial of the Holocaust experience as an integral aspect of Israeli identity and by the emotional deprivations of an obsolete Holocaust ethos of survival. Three of the novels (*The Legend of the Sad Lakes* is the despairing exception) consider an unflinching encounter with the agonies of the concentrationary universe as an essential first step in the process of integrating the Holocaust experience into the identity of their protagonists and thus enabling healing to begin. Pursuing this project requires a radical departure from the prevailing cultural norms and the construction of what amounts to the beginnings of a new world of discourse. Consequently, all of these novels are characterized by iconoclastic postmodernist structures and, unlike the works of the first category, they regularly break with the conventions of realism by introducing powerful elements of the fantastic.

Thanks to the work of Tzvetan Todorov and the critics who have subsequently refined his thinking on this matter, we now have a fairly precise conception of the fantastic as a distinct literary mode.[6] The fantastic is defined by the antinomy of a simultaneous presence in the text of two conflicting, and mutually exclusive, discursive codes: the "realistic," or rational, code of nature, and the "unrealistic," irrational, code of the supernatural—or, perhaps more precisely, the unnatural. Each of these codes is obviously inconsistent with the other and the fantastic achieves both its defining structure and its narrative effects by projecting a wholly convincing realistic world and then injecting it with unnatural, or supernatural, phenomena.[7]

Since such use of the fantastic is unusual in Israeli literature,[8] there is a strong suggestion of a significant correlation between the desire to address the issues of the Holocaust and the inclination to engage the features of the fantastic. This correlation is evident in each of the novels included in the second group of new Holocaust works. Grossman's *See Under: Love*, for example, is the story of Shlomo Neuman, who grew up in Jerusalem surrounded by the silence and the madness of Holocaust survivors and became obsessed with the mysteries of the world they were trying to conceal. As an adult, Shlomo becomes an author who is trying to write the story of his grandfather, Anshel Wasserman, who himself was once a famous author of children's stories, but whom Shlomo knew only as a deranged and wholly inarticulate survivor of the Nazi death camps. In Shlomo's story, Anshel Wasserman appears as a death camp inmate who, fantastically, cannot die, even though he is subjected to the horrors of the gas chamber and is later shot repeatedly in the head. In an equally fantastic move, Shlomo transports himself to the death camp and joins his grandfather in witnessing the events that take place there. Later in the novel we are introduced to the baby Kazik, who completes an entire life-cycle in twenty-four hours. Out of context, such narrative devices may appear frivolous and contrived. But in the context of this extraordinary novel, they are sources of great power and profound signification.[9]

Ben-Ner's *The Angels Are Coming* constitutes a radical departure from its author's previous work, which established him as one of Israel's leading realists. Set in a postapocalyptic world of the mid-twenty-first century, *The Angels Are Coming* is a dystopian novel that depicts Israel as a country controlled by an oppressive theocratic bureaucracy, rife with clashes between gangs of militant religious fanatics, whose power is on the rise, and a waning minority of secular civil libertarians. Dystopian fiction seeks to persuade the reader of the plausibility of its futuristic vision by shaping its imagined world according to the conventions of the realistic novel. A modernist dedication to physical and psychological verisimilitude is one of the defining characteristics of the genre. Ben-Ner draws deeply on these conventions in shaping the features of his future society and in developing the character of his protagonist, David Halperin. He is well on his way to creating a compelling dystopian satire when he introduces a series of fantastic elements that defy the structural and thematic logic of the genre.[10]

One example of this deviant dimension is the blue Star of David that appears on Halperin's forehead a short time after he deliberately suppresses all memory of the terrible beating he received, for no apparent reason, from a trio of ultra-Orthodox thugs. Another fantastic element that is deeply disconcerting to Halperin is his discovery of a photograph of himself as a boy captured by the Nazis during the Holocaust, an event that took place long before he was born. Even more disconcerting is the appearance of the mysterious Dr. Zinderbaum, who makes a compelling claim to possessing magical healing powers and presents Halperin with the fantastic possibility of having an alternative identity and a double family history.

Dorit Peleg's novel *Una* is about a contemporary young woman who manages a travel agency in Manhattan and is haunted by the incorporeal figure of a girl who is living through the Holocaust. The girl, who first appears as a recurrent dream, eventually emerges from the dream and becomes a powerful presence that is gradually, and very deliberately, taking over Una's life and drawing it into the world of the Holocaust. What makes this novel fantastic, and not merely delusional, is the fact that it is told almost entirely from the point of view of the phantom girl who is encroaching on Una's life and who exists simultaneously in the past and in the present.

The protagonist of Itamar Levy's *The Legend of the Sad Lakes* is Arnon

Greenberg, a young Israeli whose father is accused of being a Nazi war criminal. Arnon sets out for Germany in order to prove that the accusation is false, but discovers conclusive evidence that it is actually true. The fantastic elements in this novel include Arnon's mother's return from the dead in order to tell her side of the story and to haunt her husband in prison. There is also a parrot who rallies the German crowds with cries of "Mein Kampf! Mein Kampf!" and leads them in mass denials of their complicity in the horrors of the Holocaust. This fantastic bird is a sentient being who is outlawed by the Munich police and who engages Arnon in provocative conversations.

The protagonists of the four novels under discussion are all young people who are struggling with the internal agonies that result from being descended from Holocaust survivors. This painful sense of a deeply damaged self is articulated with great intensity by Arnon in *The Legend of the Sad Lakes*. The style here is obviously his own, but the substance of his words is shared by the protagonists of the other works as well:

Why don't I listen to my heart as I have been told to do? Why do I evade, close doors, build walls, forget and remember and suppress and ask and erase the blue numbers that float up on my left skin? Why do I ignore the smells, and the sounds, and the colors? Why do I insist on listing you by your names and your professions but I never tell about the sorrow . . . and about the pain? . . . How do I tell about the fear of trains that I inherited? Why don't I mention my childhood battles against the Nazis? . . . With what do I blame myself? What haven't I done yet? Against whom haven't I taken vengeance yet? Why don't I tell about my work? Why don't I write poems about the Holocaust? Why don't I record my dreams? Why do I pray? Why do I close the shutters around me every night? Why do I leave the light on the porch? Who am I afraid of? Am I a "second generation"? . . . Don't know how to feel. Don't know how to cry. Don't know how to scream. Don't know how to explain . . . Do I hoard food? Can I throw away bread? Am I in dream therapy? Nightmare therapy? How am I affected by knocks on the door? Or by the sharp ring of the telephone? . . . Does everyone have a mother with a number on her arm? Who's asking? Who's crying? Who's lonely? Who hates? Who eats white meat? Who's afraid of dogs? Who am I named after? Is it after my grandfather who was murdered by the Nazis? Is it after my uncle who was murdered by the Nazis? Is it after my grandmother who was murdered by the Nazis?[11]

The fact that this searing outburst was written by an author who is not a child of survivors, is one of the many ways in which this novel suggests that all young Israelis are descendants of the survivors and that the experience of the Holocaust is an integral component of both their personal and communal identity. This is a view that contradicts the conventions of Israeli culture but is characteristic of Israel's new works of Holocaust fiction. These works are concerned with the Holocaust not as the historical reality of the horrible events that took place in the past, but rather as a psychological reality that is very much a part of their present. Consequently, the impetus of this literature is not towards "representation" or "understanding" of the "realities" of the Holocaust, nor is it an effort to commemorate or understand its victims. Each of these works is an attempt to confront the psychological consequences of the Holocaust as they affect the lives of Israelis today. Perhaps the most precise way of defining the distinction between the two categories of the new Holocaust fiction is that the first is concerned primarily with describing these consequences while the second seeks to come to terms with them by exposing their experiential causes and exploring their existential implications. This may well explain the additional concern of the works in the second category with the discursive barriers that have been placed in the way of the kind of exposition and exploration they seek to conduct.

"It's about him," says the narrator of *See Under: Love* about the protagonist of the story he is trying to write, "but it's also about me. It's about my family and what the Beast did to us. [It's] about fear. And about my Grandfather, whom I can't bring back to life, not even in a story. *And it's about being unable to understand my life until I learn about my unlived life Over There.* [my emphasis]"[12] Shlomo, like Una, is struggling with many of the same internal afflictions that were enumerated by Arnon in *The Legend of the Sad Lakes*, so his need to learn about their origins is understandable. The difficulty he encounters in learning about his "unlived life Over There" is not a lack of facts. Holocaust documentation is a pervasive Jewish obsession, and Israeli society is very much a part of the enterprise. As a child Shlomo spends long hours and many days poring over Holocaust books, documents, and photographs. He continues his study and research as an adult and, at one time, is involved in writing a Holocaust encyclopedia for children. But all of this does not suffice to make the necessary connection with the essential experience. One of the characters in *The Legend of the Sad Lakes* comes close to articulating the nature of the difficulty when he observes that

Our problem is that we treat the Holocaust like a history lesson. But that's not what it was. The Holocaust was a horrible crime . . . People were butchered in it, people were raped in it, people were starved to death in it. It wasn't history that did this to us. It was people who murdered us, and butchered, and raped, and starved other people to death. (p. 133)

The ability to connect with the human dimensions of this horrible crime or, as Shlomo has it, to experience the "unlived life Over There," is a fundamental requirement in any attempt to better comprehend and better integrate the life that is now being lived over here.

Our culture's most compelling means of providing access to the un-lived lives we need to experience in order to better live the life we have, is narrative fiction. Stories and novels are the best means we have to enter lives that are not our own. Yet this is precisely the area where, with regards to the Holocaust, Israeli culture fell short. For more than forty years there were virtually no literary texts that sought to actualize the human experiences of the Holocaust by transmuting them into a fictional discourse that would make them emotionally and intellectually accessible to those who, mercifully, were not part of these experiences, but were largely formed by them.

The virtual silence of Israeli literature on the Holocaust has been routinely ascribed to a traumatized culture's deep denial of its most horrible experience. But in view of the early proliferation of Holocaust references in a broad range of Israeli cultural contexts, and their obvi-ous prevalence in Israel's political and ideological discourses, it is evi-dent that the events of the Holocaust were actually very much a part of Israel's social consciousness. Hence, it is likely that the absence of the Holocaust theme from the literature is not a manifestation of a general national amnesia, but rather a specific consequence of a cultural code that controlled the uses to which Holocaust references could be put.

Israel's prevailing cultural code was, for many years, the discourse of ideological Zionism. Within this discourse, the Holocaust was regarded as the inevitable culmination of Diaspora conditions and the ultimate manifestation of the pathology of Diaspora mentality. In other words, the Holocaust was the epitome of everything that Zionism sought to re-ject. The new Jewish identity Zionism wished to forge was to be totally disassociated from the history and psychology of the Diaspora Jew. One of the basic tenets of the Zionist ethos was that the new life in Israel would bring about a healing psychological transformation of individu-als as well as of the Jewish people as a whole. It asserted that upon the resettlement in Israel of the Diaspora Jews, including the Holocaust sur-vivors, the conditions of their existence would be radically altered and the deformations of their psyche would be happily corrected. This be-lief in the transformative powers of life in The Land serves to define the particular kind of denial that informed the primary Israeli response to the Holocaust.

Zionist discourse did not deny the agony and the horror of the events of the Holocaust but it did deny the *relevance* of these events to the Israeli experience and to the formation of Israeli identity. "Everyone knows that they should get emotional over the news of the Holocaust," said Berl Katznelson, a leading Zionist ideologue. "Everyone knows that the situation is horrible, but people have trouble understanding these

stories as part of their personal experience."[13] And since Israeli literature was intensely preoccupied with matters of Israeli experience and
Israeli identity, the Holocaust was largely excluded from its domain.
It remained a dark and silent backdrop against which a brilliant new
reality was being etched. The Jewish victims of the Holocaust became
the objectified and internalized "others" that helped Israelis to consoli-
date their identities as "New Jews."[14]

The exclusion of the Holocaust experience from Israel's evolving
national metanarrative was reinforced by the emergence of a second discursive formation that was cultivated by the Holocaust survivors themselves. The mass transplantation of the survivors from the devastation of
Europe to the safe haven of Israel involved an abrupt transition from the
harrowing conditions of extreme cultural displacement to the benign,
but equally extreme, conditions of radical cultural replacement. Upon
their arrival in Israel, the survivors were engulfed by the imperatives of
integrating into a society that they were encouraged to call their own,
but that regarded their past experiences as irrelevant, if not shameful.
Their shame of being disdained outsiders was often compounded by the
guilt evoked by the actual experiences of survival. This involved not only
the often articulated guilt over having survived when so many others
perished, but also the hidden guilt and shame over what often had to
be done in order to survive. There was a powerful impulse to protect
themselves, as well as their children, from confronting the most painful
issues of compliance, collaboration, and the often savage selfishness that
were required in order to survive. Another factor that contributed to
the survivors' code of silence was the fact that the Nazi project of total
Jewish degradation and dehumanization was so effective that many of
its victims came to believe that the Nazi doctrine of Jewish subhumanity
was actually true. They felt they had to protect themselves against the
discovery of what they regarded as the shameful loss of their humanity.[15]

The combination of these external and internal pressures toward
protective denial generated the powerful paradigms of a new discourse
of Holocaust sanctity that was quickly and wholly embraced by the
Israeli community. Within this discursive domain, the lives of the Holocaust victims are sanctified and their experiences in the ghettos and
the camps are deemed inaccessible and incomprehensible to those who
did not actually live through them. Witness accounts by those survivors
who chose to provide them are permitted and even promoted. But any
attempt by a nonsurvivor to describe or explain these experiences becomes an intolerable violation of a sacred taboo.

The discourses of Zionist ideology and of Holocaust sanctity reinforced each other and quickly merged into a dominant national meta-

narrative that precluded the possibility of an imaginative engagement with the experiences of the Holocaust, and was a major cause of the long literary silence on the subject. Israel's new literature of the Holocaust reflects a fundamental challenge to the assumptions underlying the national metanarrative. Contrary to ideological expectations, a growing number of Israelis who were born after the Holocaust are discovering that they feel very deeply what the poet Nelly Sachs has called "the sealed pain" of the survivors. This pain belies the claim of the irrelevance of the Holocaust experience to Israeli identity and indicates the internal damage caused by the effort to suppress this essential aspect of the Israeli self. It also informs the growing number of recent literary works that attempt to expose and explore the impact of the Holocaust on the identities of their protagonists.

The constraints of the dominant literary discourse did not pose much of a problem for the writers of the first category of new Holocaust fiction. As mentioned above, these writers are primarily concerned with exposing and describing the psychological problems afflicting Holocaust survivors and, especially, their descendants. For this purpose, the familiar conventions of psychological realism are both sufficient and effective. By the late 1980s, Israeli culture was prepared to assimilate the notion that the Zionist experience was less successful than it would have liked to be in purging the identities of the survivors and their children from the consequences of the Holocaust experience. But it was not prepared to accommodate the desire of the works of the second category to actually integrate the Holocaust experience into Israeli identity. This desire encountered powerful cultural barriers, because it constituted an extreme violation of a fundamental Zionist tenet, and because it required an imaginative reconstruction of the horrors of the concentrationary universe, which was an extreme violation of the Israeli code of Holocaust sanctity. The writers who were impelled to reclaim and reintegrate the suppressed Holocaust experience were, in effect, working within a literary tradition that did not provide them with the means for carrying out their project. Traditional modes of Jewish literary response to catastrophe were no longer accessible or relevant to these writers.[16] And the secular, post-Holocaust, Zionist culture by which they were shaped had yet to generate a viable alternative.

On one important level, all of the novels in the second category are *about* the enormous difficulty of finding the literary means that would enable an imaginative engagement with the experiences and implications of the Holocaust. I believe that it is precisely this quest for a narrative mode that would subvert the impediments to such an engagement that led the authors of the novels under discussion to use the fantastic. For, as we have learned from Todorov, "The fantastic permits us to cross certain frontiers that are inaccessible so long as we have no recourse to it." It provides access to "certain taboo themes" that are prohibited by social norms, by psychological inhibitions, or by a combination of both.[17]

A number of critics have recently extended Todorov's investigation of premodernist fantasy to the postmodernist world of such writers as Franz Kafka, Julio Cortazar, Donald Barthelme, and Thomas Pynchon. Rosemary Jackson, for example, focuses on the ability of the fantastic to explore regions of experience that are outside dominant value systems. She shows how fantasy traces "the unsaid and the unseen of culture: that which has been silenced, made invisible, covered over and made 'absent.' "[18] And Jonathan Rabkin, who writes extensively on the fantastic, argues that fantasy represents an elemental mode of truth seeking and reality testing, which regards normative concepts of reality as nothing more than an arbitrary collection of perspectives and expectations that we learn in order to survive in the here and now.[19] In its quest for concealed or silenced truths, fantastic literature interrogates, and invariably subverts, the validity of these normative defense mechanisms. These attributes make the fantastic a natural, perhaps inevitable, choice for Israeli writers seeking to penetrate prohibited regions of the psyche and the culture and thereby reclaim the suppressed experience of the Holocaust, so they can integrate that experience as an essential component of their identity. The fantastic makes it possible for their narratives to confront the internal heritage of the Holocaust experience by breaking the barriers to the memory of this experience.

Memory was not useful to the inmates of the Nazi death camps who characteristically practiced functional amnesia in their struggle to survive.[20] The practice of this mode of protective forgetting was continued by many of the survivors. For, as Alan Mintz has observed, to remember would have meant to jeopardize the painstakingly constructed arrangements of the survivors' new life.[21] This is a heritage of denial that they have bequeathed to their descendants, who often cling to it with equal determination and fear. "We will protect our innocence at all costs," says Una as she recognizes her resistance to Holocaust memory:

Our innocence, like a cold flower, omniscient under its white petals. Carefully clenched, hiding the knowledge that was stored in its pollen from the day it sprouted forth . . . But is it possible to keep it there forever? Or at least for the duration of a lifetime? Are the petals strong enough, durable enough, sufficiently impermeable? Will it not break out one day from its prison of leaves, emerge into the daylight, and cover everything, every surface, corner, nook and cranny, with its silky golden powder that penetrates like poison? How can it be stopped? How can we control it, enclose it, put a lock on the doors of its prison once and for all?[22]

The futuristic Israel in Ben-Ner's *The Angels Are Coming* is a society founded on such suppression of memory. It is a debased and brutal society that has lost its capacity for cultural creativity and its sense of national identity. It is also a society from which all memory of the Holocaust has been eradicated. The dynamics of this monumental denial are reiterated and articulated by Halperin's suppression of a crucial experience that constitutes a personal parallel to the national trauma.

At the outset of the novel, Halperin is lured into the onrush of a civil rights demonstration and then plucked out of it, for no apparent reason, by three ultra-Orthodox thugs who vilify and beat him to the point of death (pp. 20–34). The grisly scene of Halperin's violent humiliation and abuse at the hands of his Jewish tormentors reverberates with ironic parallels to the Holocaust experience. The utter powerlessness of the randomly selected victim and the implacable, inexplicable violence of the victimizers; the placid indifference of the onlookers and the cowering betrayal of the friends; the denigration of the victim as inferior and debased, and the failure of all appeals to compassion and kindness; the terrible pain of mutilation and the equally terrible loss of human dignity, all coalesce into a paradigmatic encapsulation of the historical agony of the Jew. The underlying premise of *The Angels Are Coming* is that Halperin's mode of coping with this experience of ultimate agony is equally paradigmatic. He is determined to forget it.

Halperin is rescued, revived, and miraculously healed by a mysterious stranger who later identifies himself as Dr. Zinderbaum. In the aftermath of his miraculous recovery, Halperin is overcome by a searing sense of powerlessness and humiliation. Seeking for a way to cope with a life that will forever be tormented by the pain of this disgrace, his groping psyche eventually fixes on a solution:

I must forget. That's my only hope: to forget everything. As if nothing ever happened. Not to remember a thing. Not even in the deepest recesses of consciousness, so that the memory won't return as a nightmare . . . Only total oblivion will help. I must uproot everything. Erase every trace. So that they won't know. So that I myself won't know. So that it never will have existed.[23]

And, in an intense moment of superhuman effort, Halperin performs an incredible feat of psychological blocking that matches the miracle of his physical healing. He erases the entire experience from his memory (pp. 12–13). This fantastic feat of deliberate forgetting extends the analogical affinities between Halperin's experience of extreme violence and the nation's experience of near annihilation to the parallels between the personal and national modes of coping with the psychological effects of this shattering experience. But in the wake of his apparently successful attempt to reconstruct his life by suppressing all memory of its most traumatic event, Halperin is assailed by inexplicable intimations and fantastic apparitions that draw him back towards the event he was determined to forget.

The fantastic phenomena that disrupt Halperin's life finally coalesce around the mysterious figure of Dr. Zinderbaum and are fused into his outrageous story of five generations of Zinderbaum healers and marked men of which Halperin is purported to be the last. After repeated attempts to make personal contact with Halperin, Zinderbaum sends him a letter in which he reveals himself as his mysterious savior and makes the impossible claim of being his father. In support of this claim he recounts the Zinderbaum family history. This saga of impossible adventures and incredible survivals is the novel's definitive fantasy. It is a narrative that defies all reason and violates the accepted norms of both reality and realism. Yet its emotional force is undeniable, as is its ability to uncover suppressed truths. Zinderbaum is aware of the connection between fantasy and truth. His story, he writes to Halperin, is "a fantastic tale that is entirely true" (p. 204). And as this tale unfolds, it moves towards redefining Halperin's carefully constructed, and largely delusional, sense of self by shattering the intertwined prohibitions against personal and national memory.

Zinderbaum's story confronts Halperin with the suppressed memory of his personal trauma (pp. 209–10) and insists on reconnecting his individual experiences with the historical memory of his people. "Every word in this story is pure truth," says Zinderbaum. "The truth of the Zinderbaum family which is the truth of this nation, a nation that is always running away from itself but can never get away from itself" (p. 208). A key component of this fantastic truth is the claim that Halperin is a member of the Zinderbaum family and should therefore acknowledge "the connection between the mark on [his] forehead and the grand and terrible heritage of common blood and a common past" (p. 210). This claim, and the fantastic evidence that seems to support it, are not meant to dispute the facts of Halperin's biography, but rather to enhance the authenticity of his identity by revealing aspects of the self that had heretofore been suppressed. It is an invitation to explore a new contour of identity—not Halperin as an alienated individual and inventor of his self, but Halperin as a member of his nation and a product of its history.

The revelatory power ascribed to fantasy is dramatically confirmed by Halperin's response to Zinderbaum's fantastic text. His first reaction is

a mixture of confusion, disbelief, revulsion, and anxiety. But as he reads
on, he experiences a growing sense of internal penetration and reve-
lation of his innermost fears and hidden secrets (p. 213). This process
of self-examination leads him to acknowledge the heuristic function of
the inexplicable events that have been haunting him. "The mysteries
remain mysteries," he says. "But at least it's clear that they were all warning signals that were intended to shake me and awaken me from the
false tranquility that I imposed upon myself; so that I would remember, so that I would think about these things, so that I would search
for what they mean" (p. 214). Ultimately, Halperin comes to recognize
Dr. Zinderbaum's story as a deliberate device that was designed to pro-
pel him into "the unexplored darkness within." He understands that
Zinderbaum may well be "the key to everything that I have been hiding
by myself from myself" (p. 215). But then, in a reflex of anxiety and terror, Halperin recoils from the prospect of self-discovery. He rejects the
opportunity to use the evident connection between the fantastic manifestations of the Holocaust and the regained memory of his personal
violation as a means of reclaiming his connection with the historical and
moral legacy of his people. Instead, he chooses to pursue a path of violent vengeance against those who inflicted pain upon him. He sets out
to identify his tormentors, hunt them down, and kill them. This misuse
of memory turns out to be a tragic deviation, which eventually reduces
Halperin to a state of atavistic brutality and ultimately causes his demise.

The concern with the connection between communal memory and
personal identity is characteristic of all the novels under discussion. Unlike Halperin, the protagonists of the other novels come to acknowledge
this connection with varying degrees of willingness. Una is the closest
to Halperin in her resistance to memory. She is a contemporary young
woman who claims that the events of the Holocaust bear no relevance
to her present experience and insists on complete emotional separation
from them. But denial does not bring immunity. The phantom girl who
has emerged from Una's dreams seeks to impose her Holocaust experiences on Una's consciousness. When she introduces Una to a scene of
a great mass of men, women, and children who are being relentlessly
marched toward a death camp, Una attempts to deny any connection
with them. "I see them passing," she says,

wave after wave of grey, anonymous humanity, and I don't feel a thing; no terror, no pity, and no sorrow. Only a total detachment. I have nothing in common
with these grey people who are marching together with the infinite patience of
those who have lost everything . . . Yet sometimes, just for a few seconds, I am
overcome with a terrible fear that I hasten to suppress. Because we have nothing
in common, they and I. And there is no chance, no chance at all that the plague

that is devouring them will ever touch me. But there are also times, very rare occasions, in which I can't manage to crush the fear before it takes hold, and then I start hating. I start hating the very existence of these people. I hate their endless, submissive, marching. I hate the plague that they reveal by their very existence. And I pray that they would disappear, that they would all disappear, that they would sink in the sea, or be buried underground, or be covered with large stones, just so they wouldn't be here . . . so undeniably present . . . and with them their plague, their tragedy, the curse that they bear. (p. 74–75)

The struggle between Una and the girl who is seeking to inhabit her body and take over her life is an anatomy of the involuntary emergence of communal memory and the struggle to come to terms with it.

The growing presence of the girl makes Una's denial increasingly difficult: "I can't take it any more!" she complains. "I don't want to see the things she is forcing me to see . . . Since when did her over there become over here?" (p. 103). But challenging the distinction between here and there, now and then, us and them, is the precise narrative function of the girl's simultaneous existence in the past and in the present. Her atavistic encroachment upon Una's life demonstrates that this distinction is both false and damaging. It forces the realization that the Holocaust then and there are still very much a part of the contemporary now and here, and that the self will remain deformed and incomplete until it affirms its present affinity with the traumas of the communal past. Unlike Halperin, Una does not shrink away from this challenge and is ultimately able to recognize that "oblivion is the most expensive commodity in our generation. Perhaps it always was. You always had to pay a high price in order to hold on to it" (p. 125).

Unlike Halperin and Una, the protagonists in *The Legend of the Sad Lakes* and *See Under: Love* readily acknowledge their deep connection to the experiences of the Holocaust and become obsessed with recreating its events. After learning that his father was accused of being a Nazi war criminal who married a Holocaust survivor and passed himself off as Jewish, Arnon in *The Legend of the Sad Lakes* is compelled to recreate and articulate his mother's family history, including her experiences in the concentration camps. In *See Under: Love*, Shlomo's attempts to connect with the mysteries of what took place "Over There" date back to his early childhood. At that time he sought this connection in order to free his survivor parents from the tormenting consequences of their Holocaust experiences. But as his efforts continue into adulthood, it becomes apparent that the person who must be saved from the effects of the Holocaust is Shlomo himself.

All four novels seek to subvert the discourse of denial that has obscured the connection between the experiences of the Holocaust and

the shape of Israeli identity. They share the conviction that the Holocaust experiences of the Jews in Europe have had a profoundly damaging impact on the lives of their descendants in Israel, and that the only
way to address these consequences is to confront their causes. The difficulties of healing the heritage of Holocaust damage are compounded by
the fact that denial of memory is only one of many facets in a powerful
existential credo that evolved in response to the horrors of the Holocaust and was bequeathed to the descendants of its survivors. All the
novels suggest that one of the most pervasive, and most damaging, personal and national legacies of the Holocaust experience is an existential
ethos that is founded on fear and oriented exclusively towards survival.

Confronted with the implacable machinery of utter degradation, relentless extermination, and total absence of hope, the inhabitants of the
concentrationary universe were reduced to a condition in which all aspects of existence became subordinate to the sole purpose of preserving
life. It is little wonder that they developed an exclusionary ethos of survival, which those who emerged from the camps continued to practice,
and which they bequeathed to their descendants, often at the expense
of other ethical and emotional considerations. Shlomo, who insists on
regarding life as "a Darwinist existential process" in which "those who
cannot defend themselves will be wisely discarded" (p. 266/296), is a
characteristic product of this discursive dynamic. In his view, the legacy
of his survivor parents—and of the entire Holocaust generation—can be
summed up in one phrase: "Beware. So you'll survive." But, says Shlomo,
"his parents never explained specifically what it was he should beware
of and why. Nor was there ever any indication of the *purpose* of the life
he was instructed to protect so fiercely. Such discussions were regarded
as a useless luxury to be deferred to a time when things would be less
dangerous. A time that never came" (p. 258/287).
    Fried, the imaginary character who most fully embodies the ethos of
survival in the fictional reconstruction of Grandfather Wasserman's experiences in the camps, provides a succinct summary of the survivor's
credo: "Beware of strangers, and doubt your friends. Never tell anyone what you really think. Never tell the truth unless there's no choice,
someone is bound to use it against you. And don't love anybody too
much, not even yourself" (p. 316/354). The prohibition against love is
central to the survival ethos. It stems not only from the fact that love for
another diminishes the capacity to look after oneself, but also, perhaps
primarily, from the fact that the loss of a loved one is a cause of great
and enduring pain. Since such losses were a commonplace of Holocaust

existence, the ethos of survival precluded deep emotional connections to others as a way of defending against agonizing loss and unbearable pain.[24] A recurring perception in the new literature is that distrust and denial of emotion are pervasive and highly destructive legacies of the Holocaust experience.

In *The Angels Are Coming*, Ben-Ner presents the rigid denial of emotion as the main cause of the degeneration and brutalization of Israeli society in the twenty-first century. He textualizes this conception and explores its implications by making emotional denial a defining characteristic of his protagonist. David Halperin is a man who has programmed himself "to survive in an age in which the emotion that pulses in the soul is the source of all calamity and it is therefore best that emotions become dulled" (p. 319). The defining irony of *The Angels Are Coming* is that the failure to recognize and confront the emotional and ethical implications of the Holocaust experience has brought about the realization of the survivors worst nightmare: a recurrence of mass brutalization and dehumanization. Only this time it is the community of victims that is recreating the victimizing state.

Like *The Angels Are Coming*, *See Under: Love* is concerned with the detrimental consequences of projecting the survival ethos onto a reality to which it no longer applies. But while Ben-Ner's concern is, ultimately, political, Grossman's focus is essentially personal. His novel shows that the ethos of survival makes it impossible for a person to have an intimate, trusting, and emotionally fulfilling relationship with another person. It is a legacy that makes it impossible to love. The protagonist, Shlomo Neuman,[25] has inherited the survivor's dread of the inevitable recurrence of devastation and he is conducting his life in constant internal preparation for this event. "As you well know, Ruthie," he tells his wife, "one of these days we'll all be forced into the trains again. But unlike the rest of you, I will not be shocked or humiliated. And I won't suffer the pains of separation." In order to shield himself from this anticipated pain, Shlomo is determined to keep himself free from all emotional attachments, including those to his wife and young son, Yariv. "Look," he says to Ruthie, "I'm not absolutely sure that I'll be able not to hurt for you. But I'd like to believe that I'm strong enough for that. I'll be very disappointed in myself if, at the moment of separation, I'll feel unbearable pain" (p. 140/151–52).

Shlomo's commitment to the ethos of survival is evident in his determination to pass it on to future generations. Long before Yariv is born, Shlomo tells Ruthie that if he ever had a child, he would prepare him for life by slapping his face every morning, "Just like that. So he'll know there's no justice in the world, only war." He returns to this notion after his son's birth. And when Ruthie observes that the child may not love him very much for this, Shlomo's response is as chilling as it is telling: "Love? I said with a dark chuckle. I prefer a living son to a loving son" (p. 138/148).

A child of Holocaust survivors, Shlomo grew up in a household of unexpressed terrors and withheld affections. His father, who had been forced to transport the bodies of the dead from the gas chambers to the crematoria, never touched his son because he believed his hands were tainted with blood. As a child, Shlomo agonized over this deprivation. As an adult he appears to be destined to perpetuate the survivor's legacy of emotional denial by inflicting the same kind of loveless upbringing on his son. Yet, as his attempt to recreate the Wasserman story unfolds, it becomes increasingly evident that he also possesses a hidden desire for love which is resisting his craving for emotional detachment. *See Under: Love* is, in many ways, an ambitious narrative effort to explore and resolve these contradictory drives.

Like Shlomo, Arnon, the protagonist of *The Legend of the Sad Lakes*, grew up in a household in which "There was no love and no passion between [his parents] Naomi and Heinrich, only existential need. Only survival" (p. 53). This is a legacy that is about to be passed on to Arnon's offspring as well. His wife, Einav, is pregnant with a child she thinks of as "a third generation to the survivors and to the destroyers" and to whom she composes a poem that is yet another distillation of the survivor ethos:

My child
Hide in my womb
Do not lift your eyes to the danger
Your mother
Is warning you
My child
Hide in my cellars
Learn to adjust your height to the low walls
Train your eyes for darkness" (p. 72)

Although Arnon is different from Shlomo in many ways, his character also serves to thematize the question of whether the descendants of the survivors will perpetuate their parents' legacy of fear, or whether they will be able to break the barriers of denial in order to affirm and experience life, instead of merely preserving it.

The fantastic figure of the refugee girl in *Una* also acknowledges only one valid existential motivation. It is, as she says, "To survive at any cost" (p. 157). The girl also acknowledges that an essential component of this Darwinistic code of survival is the rigorous suppression of all emotion. "A person who does not cry is not alive," she says. "But a person who

cries has a good chance of dying" (p. 88). Hers is the clearest expression
of the toll that the ethos of survival takes on all other emotional needs.
And, as is often the case, it takes the form of a terse passage of poetry:

Who said you have to live in pairs
Who said you have to hold hands
Who said you have to stand back to back
In order not to fall. Lies. Lies upon lies upon lies
They fed us. We don't need
Anyone. We don't need
Anything. We don't need
What we don't need.
We don't need . . . (pp. 161–62)

What is at issue in this novel, as in all the others, is not the validity of
this ethos in the extreme conditions of the Holocaust world, but rather
the hold that it continues to exert in circumstances where physical survival is no longer a primal concern.

Contrary to traditional Jewish responses to catastrophe,[26] Israeli narratives of the Holocaust have typically been manifestations of what, in
a slight variation on Eric L. Santner's term, may be called narrative
displacement.[27] According to Santner, this is a mode of response to
traumatic loss that is the affective opposite to what Freud called *Trauer-
arbeit*, or the "work of mourning." Both mourning and displacement
are strategies employed by individuals and communities to reconstruct
their identities and revive their vitality in the wake of trauma. The crucial difference between these two modes of repair has to do with the
willingness or ability to include the traumatic event in one's efforts to
reconstitute identity. Narrative displacement is a response to traumatic
loss that involves the construction and deployment of a narrative that
is consciously or unconsciously designed to expunge the traces of the
trauma or loss that called the narrative into being in the first place. The
work of mourning, on the other hand, is a process of articulating and
integrating the reality of loss or traumatic shock by remembering and
repeating it in symbolically and dialogically mediated doses. This process of translating, troping, and figuring loss is essential to the dynamic
of healthy identity formation in a posttraumatic society. It is profoundly
different from narrative displacement, which is a strategy of emplot-
ting traumatic events in a manner that denies the need for mourning
by simulating conditions of intactness. Typically this is accomplished by
situating the site and origin of loss elsewhere, thus releasing the individual and the culture from the burden of having to reconstitute self-
identity in the context of posttraumatic conditions.[28]

The denial of the relevance of Holocaust events to the Israeli experience and the claim to wholesome normalcy that characterized Israeli
culture in the aftermath of genocidal trauma reflect a communal choice
of narrative displacement over the work of mourning. As a means of
reconstituting identity and attaining emotional viability, this was not a
wholly fortunate choice. For, as Santner (following Freud) points out,
it is the work of mourning that enables human beings to restore the
normal regime of the pleasure principle in the wake of trauma or loss.
Freud contended that it is the absence of appropriate affect (anxiety),
rather than loss per se, that leads to traumatization. Until such anxiety
has been recuperated and worked through, the loss will continue to
represent a past that refuses to go away. Only at the end of this process
of psychological recuperation does the individual become open to positive relations with himself and with others. Narrative displacement, on
the other hand, is a strategy whereby one seeks to reinstate normalcy
without addressing and working through those recuperative tasks that as
Freud insists, must be accomplished before the dominance of the pleasure principle can even begin. Instead of providing a symbolic space for
the recuperation of anxiety, narrative displacement offers reassurances
that there was no need for anxiety in the first place, thus perpetuating
the emotionally incapacitating effects of the trauma.[29]

Each of the novels under discussion may be understood as an effort
to subvert the discourse of narrative displacement and undo its delete-
rious effects. Each in its own way is an attempt to perform the necessary
work of mourning by reexternalizing the most deeply suppressed traumas of the Holocaust so as to recuperate their distressing impact and
ultimately reintegrate them into a national identity from which they
had been psychologically detached. Each performs the necessary work
of textualizing the context of this most horrific of historical events so as
to make it tangible to the imagination and thus accessible to emotion
and to thought. Textualizing the Holocaust experience in this manner
is a daunting project in many ways, not the least of which is that it requires the violation of one of Israeli culture's central taboos: the implicit
prohibition against imaginative representation of the concentrationary
experience itself.

Sidra DeKoven Ezrahi has accurately observed that in the history
of Holocaust literature there are relatively few stories that are actually
located in the camps.[30] This is particularly true of Israeli Holocaust literature, which, to the extent that it existed prior to the mid-1980s, was
the product of a cultural code that did not allow for imaginative entry
into the world of the Nazi death camps. Witness accounts and documented reports were permitted and, to some extent, encouraged, but
attempts to imagine the concentrationary experience by those who were

not there were considered an affront and an abomination. The effects of such suppression are apparent in *The Angels Are Coming*, where awareness of the Holocaust experience encroaches upon Halperin's consciousness and he is given the opportunity to explore his internal connection to the traumas of atrocity. But Halperin, whose laboriously constructed sense of self is a precarious edifice of evasive narratives, refuses to abandon his defenses and take the plunge into darkness within.

Unlike *The Angels Are Coming*, and in clear defiance of cultural convention, *See Under: Love, Una*, and *The Legend of the Sad Lakes* all take their narratives directly into the death camps. This incursion of the imagination into the heart of Holocaust pain and horror is driven by a sense that the need to advance the work of healing outweighs all ethical and cultural aversions to recuperating the traumas and losses of the victims. The narrative structure of each of these novels suggests that their imaginative engagement with the concentrationary experience was made possible by the impact of poststructuralist skepticism about attempts to recover "objective" historical "truth."

Accurate representation of historical truth has been the conventional prerequisite for stories of the Holocaust. Writers of Holocaust fiction characteristically felt compelled to assert the factual and wholly objective nature of their work because they were products of a cultural code that claimed that they had no ethical right to imagine the agony.[31] In their depictions of the Holocaust, most of these writers consequently refrained from entering the world of the camps, for no amount of factual and objective data could translate the essence of the concentrationary experience to the world of those who had not been there. Such refiguration and translation of experience is usually the work of the imagination and the primary domain of literary fiction. But according to the prevailing notion of Holocaust sanctity, the imagination has no place in representing the world of the camps.

The viability of this type of discursive restriction was called into question by such poststructuralist critics as Hayden White, who observed that "our discourse always tends to slip away from our data towards the structures of consciousness with which we are trying to grasp them."[32] This recognition opens the way for a shift away from the insistence on "authentic" representation of events to an expansion of the structures of consciousness that shape our perception of these events. In pondering what can truthfully be said about the natures of Nazism and its Final Solution, White suggests that the kind of anomalies, enigmas, and dead ends encountered in discussions of the representation of the Holocaust are the result of a conception of discourse that owes too much to realism, which is inadequate in cases such as the Holocaust. And, with a strong gesture towards the fantastic, he concludes that the best way to represent the Holocaust and the experience of it may well be by a different kind of writing "which lays no claim to the kind of realism aspired to by nineteenth-century historians and writers."[33]

The incorporation of fantastic elements into Israeli works of Holocaust fiction acknowledges the impossibility of an authentic representation of the concentrationary experience. At the same time, the fantastic enables an authentic response to this experience, which, although unrepresentable, continues to be powerfully present in the lives of Jews, including those who were not even born at the time. The primary objective of evoking the world of the camps in such works as *See Under: Love*, *Una*, and *The Legend of the Sad Lakes* is not representative or commemorative but rather therapeutic. All of these works employ the attributes of the fantastic in order to advance their project of healing recuperation and identity formation.

By contradicting the normative categories that control the narrative world in which it appears, the fantastic challenges the validity of the ideology that generates these categorical imperatives. It constitutes a counterforce to discursive formations that determine and constrain the forms of knowledge, types of "normalcy," and the standards of identity that prevail in the culture. Rosemary Jackson shows how fantasy can provide graphic images for expressing the problematic and very complex interaction between ideology and the unconscious life of the individual. Using Lacan's understanding of the ego as a cultural construction, Jackson also shows the capacity of the fantastic to depict a reversal of the self's cultural formation.[34] Such a reversal is necessary in order to accomplish the desired shift from the damaging metanarrative of Holocaust displacement to a healing narrative of Holocaust recuperation and integration into the identity of the new generation.[35] But the realization of this shift involves considerable risks.

To acknowledge an affinity with the Holocaust experience is to relinquish the heroic constructs of the conventional Israeli identity story and to experience an empathic connection with the extremes of human agony, degradation, and despair. The psyche recoils reflexively from the pain of such an experience and creates defenses against it. The fantastic has the capacity to breach these defenses without devastating that which they were designed to protect. By defying the codes of reality and reason, the fantastic may provide a protective measure of distance and alternative possibility that makes the horror bearable without diminishing its concreteness. At the same time, the attributes of the fantastic can also serve to recuperate the profound sense of unreality that assailed those who were cast into the concentrationary universe and discovered that all the normative categories that formed the world as they knew it had been horribly reversed.

Arnon, the Israeli-born protagonist of *The Legend of the Sad Lakes*, was not there. But his grandfather was, and his grandmother was, too. His mother and his father were also there, she as a prisoner and he as a concentration camp guard. Arnon, then, is the offspring of the terrible mating of Nazi atrocity and Jewish destiny. All four novels recognize the shaping influence of Nazi attitudes and actions on Israeli identity. But the shock of this recognition is the primary force of *The Legend of the Sad Lakes*. The discovery that his father had been a Nazi war criminal releases a devastating onrush of anguish, doubt, and outrage in Arnon. The foundations of his previous existence disintegrate and the assurance of his old identity dissolves. As he casts about for means to salvage his shattered sense of self, Arnon feels compelled to recuperate and re-articulate his family's Holocaust history. His struggle to find an idiom that would capture the agony and express the outrage brings the narrative to the brink of stylistic chaos. And it is, ultimately, his recourse to the fantastic that enables Arnon to bring the terrible events into emotional and formal focus.

The fantastic provides the figurative means that are needed for making the transition from the rationally constructed categories of the familiar world to the monstrous inversions of the concentrationary universe. This dynamic is evident in Arnon's depiction of what happened to his grandfather when he refused to collaborate in the building of a death camp:

Because Grandfather Greenspahn refused to build their city of death . . . the Nazis began torturing him. They whipped his back and his hands. They forced him to clean the pavement with a sulphurous fluid that burned his wounds. They told him they would kill him if he wouldn't sing "Heil Hitler" for them as he scrubbed. Then they shaved his Jewish beard with their daggers, ripping chunks of living flesh out of his face together with the hair. They ordered him to pray and to put on his *tefillin*, then they doused him with gasoline and threw him into the burning synagogue. Since the Jew emerged from there unharmed; since there was not even a trace of ashes on his skin, they accused him of separatism, i.e. Communism, and continued to torture him. They forced him to bend his knees over and over again, for six straight hours, under a constant shower of blows. They pushed pins under his fingernails, shocked him with electric currents. They handed him a postcard and a pencil and forced him to scribble a message to his loved ones: "I have arrived safely. I am healthy. I am happy and feeling fine." They crushed his testicles and welded his fingers together. They ordered him to carry rocks from here to there, without purpose. They forced him to dig holes and cover them up again. They used their pistols to practice marksmanship on the tip of his nose and his earlobes . . . And since none of this helped and the Jew continued to mock them and refuse, the soldiers tried new techniques. They tied his limbs to the device they called "the see-saw," which twisted and dismembered his body. They put starved rats inside his pants and shot at bottles they put on his head. Finally they dragged him into the forest and there—just for fun, because they had long forgotten what they wanted from him —they shot him in his neck and in his back and in his stomach and in his temples and in his mouth and in his heart. God made a miracle for my grandfather. When he died He did not allow his blood to flow from his body but created a miraculous blood that dripped only from the wounds of his pants and the gash in his shirt. His upper skin and his lower skin remained smooth and clean. (pp. 20–21)

This fantastic recapitulation and condensation of the extremes of the concentrationary experience, with its intimations of Jewish dignity and divine grace, may appear as an essential step in the imaginative work of mourning. But, in this case, recuperation does not lead to recovery and the fantastic does not provide sufficient psychic protection. Arnon's growing awareness of his intimate connection to the Holocaust horrors only serves to intensify his anguish and increase his sense of alienation. All that remains in the end is a consuming rage that drives him to become a murderer himself. He takes vengeance on an aging former S.S. officer and then drifts off to his own death. *The Legend of the Sad Lakes* is a novel of radical skepticism and overwhelming despair. The devastating consequences of its imaginary ventures into the world of concentrationary trauma challenge the notion that such acts of recuperation may actually have a therapeutic effect. Its myriad of styles and shifting modalities shape the novel into an unremitting scream of outrage over the defilements of the Holocaust which it presents as a heritage that cannot be healed. In this respect, *The Legend of the Sad Lakes* offers a view that is even more hopeless and helpless than the vision presented in *The Angels Are Coming*. *Una* and *See Under: Love*, on the other hand, offer a more positive perspective on the prospects of healing.

Una makes consistent use of the fantastic to express an unacknowledged desire to recuperate the experiences of the Holocaust so as to reconstitute a fragmented sense of self. One of the many mysteries of this novel is the precise relationship between Una and the chimerical girl that comes to haunt her. The blurred boundaries of their identities make it seem at first as if the girl is a delusional incarnation of Una's childhood self. It becomes increasingly clear, however, that the girl is not a suppressed biographical memory, but rather a fantastic cultural presence.[36] The girl's simultaneous existence in the world of the Holocaust and in contemporary Manhattan embodies the persistence of the Holocaust past in the modern present. The predatory nature of her encroachment on Una's life is a manifestation of the psychic damage that is incurred by denying the internal affinity of the present with this tragic and traumatic past. The fantastic conflict between the girl's Holocaust experiences and Una's contemporary experiences suggests that undoing this damage is contingent upon allowing these two worlds of experience to converge into a single sense of self. To overcome the constraints on this convergence, the cultural prohibition against any imaginary reconstruction of the camps and against any emotional affinity with their inhabitants must be subverted.

Like Anshel Wasserman in *See Under: Love*, the girl in *Una* is a miraculous survivor who moves unscathed through the world of Holocaust devastation. She is an immediate witness to the horror, but, like Una, she starts out by maintaining a resolutely detached attitude towards its victims. This is a stance that will be gradually altered and ultimately reversed as the girl's presence brings Una into increasingly closer communion with the Holocaust experience. In the course of her wanderings, the girl encounters a column of Jews who are being brutally marched towards Auschwitz. She is terrified and repelled by their ravaged bodies, oozing sores, and "the atmosphere of fear that has gone stale and turned into hard despair; a despair that encases them like a repulsive odor." Yet she is drawn to these people and is compelled to follow in their footsteps while adamantly denying all connection to them (p. 133). During this forced march, the girl witnesses a remarkable act of defiance and courage by a Jewish woman who saves the life of another woman by tripping up the Nazi guard who was about to crush her skull. The girl is powerfully drawn to this woman, who becomes the focus of her intense attention.

The column finally reaches Auschwitz and the people are marched through the iron gates into the yard where the selection begins. The girl does not join them. But she doesn't abandon the scene either. "I didn't go in," she says. "I don't belong to them. But I kept on looking from the outside, from behind the double fence, at the line that was being split in two" (p. 189). She decides to stay and observe the woman from her safe remove: "Just watching her day after day through the fence, walking, eating, carrying heavy rocks from the limestone quarry . . . and maybe one day I will cross the fence and go in and touch her hand." This is an unexpected and thoroughly terrifying thought and the girl immediately recoils from it. "These are nothing but dangerous daydreams," she says. "I must get away from the fence and from the camp and from everyone who is in it" (p. 193).

By leading its protagonist to the threshold of the concentrationary domain, and exploring the cross-currents of attraction and repulsion that this vantage point elicits, the narrative can bring the causes of these contradictory impulses into increasingly clearer focus. The emotional dissociation from the experiences of the victims and their denigration as tainted and inherently flawed beings is shown to be a consequence of the ethos of survival. It stems from the fear that an acknowledgment of common identity with the victims of the Holocaust would constitute an exposure to the contagion of the failings that caused their demise. The experiences of the victims are therefore relegated to the other side of a definitive human divide that separates those who have the capacity to survive from those who do not. "Two electrified fences are not enough to dispel my terrible fear that I will be tainted," says the girl. "That I, too, will be stricken by the plague that is infecting all those who are inside and I, too, will be declared unfit and will no longer be able to belong to the right side, the pure side, the side that survives" (p. 193).

Yet, despite her repeated self-admonitions to turn away, the girl stays at the fence, riveted by an initially inexplicable and ostensibly destructive desire to cross the line and join the woman and her companions inside the camp. It gradually becomes clear that this desire is actually a desire for comfort and completion, a desire for the integrating effect of breaking the experiential barriers between the victims and those who were spared. It is also a desire that defines the limitations of the survival ethos. "I yearn to finally take that last step," says the girl, and

> to cross the fence and go in and fall at her feet and curl up like a ball and cling to them weeping, to cling to them until I become part of them, of her, so that every step she makes will carry me with her. Because without her I am just a great big emptiness with two eyes and a mouth and a sophisticated network of signs and codes that will always, always, know how to survive, but is not smart enough to fill this great hole here, inside me. (p. 202)

The girl's desire to join the woman is soon extended to the entire community of women in the camp (p. 204). This indicates that it is, ultimately, a desire to recover an essential sense of identity that can be attained only by acts of belonging to a community of shared experience.

A voluntary entry into the world of the camps is the definitive act of acknowledging the personal connection to the communal experience. For the descendants of the Holocaust generation, such entry is possible only through acts of the imagination. The girl in *Una* is the creature of such an act of imagination. Yet despite the freedom that her fantastic mode of fictional existence bestows, the girl is immobilized by a powerful internal contradiction. She wants to join those "of her own kind" who are inside the camp, but she is afraid of the consequences of this desire. "I am too terrified," she says. "I am torn between the great fear that is consuming me from within [and] urging me to escape, and the great force that is drawing me in there, beyond the fence, to the heart of the matter . . . But when I reach the fence, always at the same place, I freeze" (p. 200). This immobilizing suspension between fear and desire links the girl's world to Una's world and defines the post-Holocaust dilemma of confronting the consequences of the trauma.

The process of overcoming the emotional paralysis caused by the ethos of survival must involve acknowledging and imaginatively revisiting the sites and experiences of the trauma that generated this ethos. But such a revisiting is prohibited by the taboos of Holocaust sanctity imposed by those who were part of the original experience. The turning point in *Una* occurs when this prohibition is removed and the girl's desire to enter the camp from the outside is recognized and affirmed by the Jewish woman within. The woman's gesture of acknowledgment and permission provides the girl with the necessary strength to overcome her fear and act on her desire. This is a taboo-shattering moment of mutual recognition in which the healing recuperation of the concentrationary experience is both actively pursued by someone who had heretofore denied it and morally sanctioned by a member of the concentrationary community that had heretofore prohibited it. "I stare at her straining face," says the girl, as she watches the woman dragging a cart of heavy rocks from the quarry to the camp.

I stare so hard that I'm sure that she must notice me, must notice this look that is slamming at her; knocking, seeking entry. And suddenly, with a feeling as piercing as pain, I see that she is smiling at me, right at me. She recognized me. *She recognized my right to be there, to be near her, and I know now that this is my place, this and no other.* And with great force I break the boundary of distance and take that one immeasurable step forward to reach her. Then the heavy carts smash through the force field that until now had always repelled me from the fence. They create an opening for me to go through. The force has been reversed and now it is drawing me in. I step forward, pass through the opening and join them, dragging and pushing the heavy white rocks and entering the gates of the camp alongside her, as one of them, and she is holding my hand. (p. 204. Emphasis added)

Once the girl is inside the camp, the horrors of atrocity and degradation are intimated rather than fully represented. It is clear that the novel assumes factual familiarity with Holocaust events and is less interested in the task of depicting the concentrationary experience than in the challenge of exploring the consequences of acknowledging and embracing this experience. Its primary concern is with the possibility of making the transition from horror to healing. Accomplishing this transition requires a transformation of the norms of the conventional Holocaust metanarrative. This convention determined the girl's original attitude of alienation and deprecation towards the concentrationary community. But once she is allowed into the camp, her experiences result in the creation of much more positive counter-narrative.

The same ineffable invulnerability that served the girl in her wanderings through the countryside accompanies her into the death camp
as well. She is a fantastic embodiment of the imagination that finally
has been permitted entry into the forbidden domain of the concentrationary universe without being bound by its constrictive rules. The
girl roams freely from barrack to barrack, attaching herself to different work crews, witnessing, learning, and changing. She discovers that
she had been mistaken in regarding the concentrationary community
as a depersonalized mass of compliant victims whose misery has erased
all their individual characteristics. The inmates are, indeed, emaciated,
oppressed, and withdrawn. But she soon learns that beneath their ex-
pressionless facade, many are alert, resourceful, and capable of acts of
humanity and courage. "I see all of this," she says, "and I still find it
hard to believe" (p. 205).

The girl also discovers that emotional denial is not the only way to
confront the horror and pursue survival. In the camp she befriends
Ruth, a radiant young woman whose ability to sustain her love for a man
who is imprisoned elsewhere enables her to "walk amidst the grey bar-
racks, the piles of excrement, and the terrible smell of smoke as if inside
a great halo that she carries with her wherever she goes" (p. 205). Ruth
believes that it is this love that makes it possible for her to survive the
horror (p. 207). But it is the love of the Jewish woman who embraces
and nurtures the girl that elicits the most powerful and transformative
response. It restores the girl's sense of communal identity as well as her
emotional capability. She is flooded by long-suppressed memories of a
happy Jewish childhood (p. 210) and is overcome with emotions she had
long denied. The girl who equated crying with dying learns to cry again
and, in an epiphanic moment of recognition, experiences a deep sense
of the need to replace her cold ethos of survival with an ethos of human
contact, compassion, and love:

And suddenly I began to cry . . . I was overcome with a great and terrible weeping which I couldn't stop and which dissolved the rock that had been frozen
inside me, that I thought I would preserve within me forever from the day I ran
on the forest path, the wind shrieking in my ears and the bushes rattling with
a thorny cackle . . . from the day I swore that I would never cry again. Because
only the weak and the vanquished cry, and those who are about to lose and to
give up. And I had no intention of being defeated by anyone. I was determined
never to weaken and therefore never to cry. Because I would belong to the other
kind, the strong, victorious kind who will survive. But after I saw [the Jewish
woman] pass the test of the icy eyes of the man at the gate, as tainted and full
of blemishes as she was, and after seeing that strong woman, Ruth, sitting on
the ground and weeping over that tangle of string, I knew that my calculations
had been wrong, and that I had been operating in error throughout my long
journey. But I also knew that all of this is not important now that I am here with

her and she is holding me and caressing my shoulder with a steady stroke that soothes the pain. (p. 210)

This renunciation of the ethos of survival, and the consequent affirmation of emotional expression and emotional connection, signal the possibility of a healing transition from the world of Holocaust victims to the world of their descendants. The girl's imagined experiences in the camp serve to redefine the implications of the concentrationary experience. They show that imaginative recuperation of the horror that often caused emotional death for its survivors may constitute a source of emotional rebirth for the descendants of these survivors.

Unlike the protagonists of *The Angels Are Coming* and *Una,* Shlomo in *See Under: Love* does not wish to evade his affinity with the Holocaust experience. He recognizes that this experience is a major shaping influence on his life and he wishes to gain a better understanding of it. Since childhood Shlomo had immersed himself in the study of what took place "Over There," but had not been able to find what he was looking for. "I know countless details [about the Holocaust]," he says. "The only thing that I'm missing is the essence" (p. 173/187). Eventually he concludes that the only way to attain the desired insight and understanding is by writing a fictionalized account of his grandfather's Holocaust experiences. But although Shlomo devotes himself to this project and attempts a variety of narrative approaches, he cannot get the story to take him where he wants to go. The essence of the Holocaust experience continues to evade him.

Shlomo's inability to create a narrative that would meaningfully re-articulate the Holocaust experience stems from the fact that he is very much the product of a culture that has placed such narratives outside the boundaries of its discursive domain. In the course of the novel's first two movements, Shlomo learns that he will not be able to attain his narrative objectives as long as he is bound by his culture's narrative conventions. He comes to recognize that, in order to be fully reclaimed, the Holocaust experience must be pursued to its utmost extremes of helplessness and horror. This requires breaking the primary cultural taboo of Holocaust sanctity by imaginatively entering into the world of the camps. And this is precisely what the third movement of the novel ("Wasserman") proceeds to do.

The "Wasserman" section opens directly on the concentrationary scene and locates both the character of Anshel Wasserman and the figure of Shlomo Neuman, the author who is creating Wasserman, inside the camp. This fantastic move, which dissolves the boundaries of time and space, enables the contemporary protagonist to enter into the heretofore forbidden world of the camps. It provides the narrative conditions for pursuing Shlomo's desire for empathic identification with his grandfather's concentrationary experiences. *See Under: Love* precedes *Una* in suggesting that such identification can begin to take place only when the outsider's desire to share in the concentrationary experience is recognized and sanctioned by a member of the concentrationary community.

Just as the Jewish woman's acknowledgment provides the girl with the strength to act on her desire to join the concentrationary community in *Una*, so Wasserman's look of recognition at his grandson who has suddenly crossed the boundary and appeared at his side, enables Shlomo to feel that he is finally capable of the narrative recuperation that had eluded him until now:

At this moment Anshel Wasserman turns his face and looks at me. It was only a quick glance, but I felt like a baby being born: because in the midst of all the anguish and confusion of the past few months his glance came through suddenly like a sobering slap on the back, and all the unmatched pieces of the puzzle fell at once into place. Grandpa Anshel recognized me and I felt him. His eyes were full of fear. (p. 173/187–88)

In addition to being gestures of deference to the right of the victims to control the story of their experiences, these recurrent moments of recognition suggest that the desire for recuperation may actually be mutual. They may be intimations of the possibility that, alongside the survivors' prohibitive stipulations of Holocaust sanctity, is a contrary desire that their story be recognized and rearticulated by a new generation of empathic listeners and tellers.

Anshel Wasserman is introduced into the camp scene after having miraculously survived the horror of a gas chamber killing in which all others perished. He is being hastened to the office of the camp commandant, Obersturmbann-fuhrer Neigel, who will try to accomplish with his pistol what his subordinates failed to achieve with the gas. Wasserman's liberating look of recognition towards Shlomo occurs while he is waiting on Neigel's doorstep. But he actually begins communing with his grandson only after Shlomo empathically shares in the experience of being a victim of a summary execution. Neigel steps forward and presses his pistol to Wasserman's temple. "And suddenly I hear myself screaming," Shlomo says. "Together with Grandpa Anshel I scream in terror and in humiliation, and the shot explodes in the room." Wasserman discovers, once again, that he cannot be killed. But he also discovers that he can now transmit his experiences to Shlomo, and it is at this point that he acknowledges his recognition and announces his decision to participate in the telling of his own story: "Sholem aleichem, Shleimeleh," he says, calling Shlomo by his Yiddish nickname. "I recognize you even though your appearance is greatly changed. Do not say a thing to me. Time is short and there is much to do. We have a story to tell" (p. 174/189).

His fantastic incursion into the world of the camps liberates Shlomo from the constraints of his culturally determined view of this world. By giving equal voice to the perspective of Wasserman, a death camp inmate, the narrative opens to dialogical figurations that will gradually come to include the voices of additional victims, as well as the increasingly distinctive voice of Neigel, the Nazi commandant. The result is a truly polyphonic narrative that is increasingly free of the constraining univocality of the dominant discourse. And because it gives voice to perspectives that have traditionally been suppressed, the narrative becomes increasingly unpredictable, often taking unexpected turns that are not always welcomed by Shlomo, who is no longer in full control.

The central story of the "Wasserman" section is the unfolding relationship between Wasserman, the former writer of the "Children of the Heart" adventure stories, and Neigel, the death camp commandant, who has made Wasserman his personal storyteller. On the surface, this is the story of Wasserman's storytelling efforts to humanize Neigel by awakening him to an awareness of the inhumanity of his deeds. But Shlomo gradually comes to realize that by venturing outside the narrative boundaries of his culture and subverting some of its most fundamental discursive structures, he has initiated a narrative dynamic that may also subvert some of the most cherished features of his own sense of self. He becomes increasingly aware that the story he is creating is actually an effort to humanize his own relations with the world around him by altering his perception of the correct response to what he regards as the key question of post-Holocaust existence.

"How," Shlomo says to Ruthie before writing the "Wasserman" section, "tell me how is it possible to go on living after seeing what . . . human beings are capable of doing" (p. 140/151). His answer at the time is a resolute commitment to the alienating ethos of survival. But the narrative he is creating now is motivated by an unacknowledged discomfort with this ethos and an unconscious desire for an alternative answer. The location and structure of the Wasserman section reflect an awareness that any viable alternative must be derived from the same experiential sources as the ethos that it seeks to replace. The alternative to the ethos of survival must therefore be pursued in the concretized context of the concentrationary world and in imagined dialogue with those who actually experienced its horrors.

Shlomo's fantastic presence within the camp and his empathic communion with the equally fantastic character of Wasserman enable the narrative to recuperate the concentrationary horrors from a position of immediate proximity and imaginative authenticity. But these same fantastic capacities also enable the narrative to safeguard both narrator and reader from the shattering effects of direct exposure to atrocity. Wasserman's situation places him in the very midst of the genocidal juggernaut. He witnesses the horror of the gas chamber, the bloody randomness of the executions, and the massive scale of dehumanization and extermination. He is there and his anguish is immense, yet there is never any real concern about his own fate. The fantastic quality of Wasserman's immortality provides a margin of emotional safety that protects Shlomo (and the reader) from being immobilized by terror, pity, and grief.

The ultimate purpose of Wasserman's project is not to represent the horror but to communicate an alternative existential vision from the world of the Holocaust victims to the world of their Israeli descendants. In order to communicate this, it is necessary to break the discursive barriers that separate these two worlds. Most formidable among these barriers is the inability of Zionist discourse to understand, accept, and condone the passivity of the Jewish victims in face of the Nazi onslaught. The question of why the Jews of Europe offered no resistance and went "like sheep to the slaughter" constitutes the defining divide between the generation of the Holocaust and the New Israelis. The image that shapes this question embodies the disdain of the latter and the shame of the former. It also designates their worlds as being mutually exclusive. This is a designation that must be undone if the recuperation of the Holocaust experience is to begin. The movement towards healing recuperation in *See Under: Love* is defined by its attempt to bridge the gap between these two worlds of discourse by reversing the context of their encounter.

Historically, encounters between Holocaust victims and other Israelis occurred after the liberation and, most often, in Israel itself. Literary representations of such encounters have usually followed suit. But, by its recourse to the fantastic, *See Under: Love* is able to disregard the order of events and pursue its project on other grounds. The novel textualizes the encounter between a Holocaust victim and his Israeli grandson in the imagined context of the *concentrationary world*, which it recognizes as the only context in which the critical issue of abject passivity may be legitimately engaged.

At one point in the narrative Wasserman notices that Neigel is about to replace the fifty members of the Blues, a team of Jews that was in charge of receiving new arrivals at the camp. As Neigel approaches them, the Blues realize that they are about to be sent to their deaths, yet they continue to perform their duties obediently, calming the terrified newcomers and guiding them to the selection lines. "Oh, God," Wasserman whispers to Shlomo. "Can you understand, Shleimeleh, why the Blues do not rise up now against their captors, and sacrifice their own lives at the cost of at least one of them? Now that everything is plain and clear to them? Let me explain this to you . . ." But Shlomo resists this attempted incursion into the sanctuary of his most cherished beliefs. Evading empathy, he refuses to hear Wasserman's side of the story and is determined to preserve the integrity of his own view. "I am not interested in hearing the answer from him," he says. "I have my own ideas about this matter of 'sheep to the slaughter'" (p. 234/259). But Shlomo's rebuff does not put the matter to rest. The issue of victim acquiescence is engaged again in the novel's fourth and final section, "The Complete Encyclopedia of Kazik's Life." It is in this section that *See Under: Love* attains its full polyphonic form. Shlomo's presence is greatly diminished and he no longer exercises control over the utterances of the other speakers.

The iconoclastic "Encyclopedia" devotes one of its entries to the matter of "Slaughter, Like Sheep To The." Here Wasserman's attempt to formulate an explanation for the victims' passivity, which he shared, is recorded in full. Wasserman acknowledges that when his group was being led to the gas chamber, accompanied by a single Ukrainian guard and knowing full well where they were going, there were no thoughts of resistance, or even of protest. "And even if not a real rebellion," Wasserman thinks in retrospective anguish, why not "at least a good slap in the Ukrainian's face . . . or at least a little spit, a small spurt of spit, one dribble of spit in all of Sodom? No?" (p. 319/357). No. Unlike *Una*, in which a quietly defiant Jewish woman saves a life by tripping up a Nazi guard, *See Under: Love* offers no heroic comfort. No one raises a hand in anger or spits in the guard's face. Wasserman struggles to explain this acquiescence and provide it with a measure of dignifying meaning. Recalling the moment of being herded down the corridor towards the gas, he says:

The same song, I believe, was playing inside all of us, a dazed lullaby of sorrow and despair. And the great metronome of Grandfather Death cranked out a dry, hypnotic rhythm; the rhythm of the gigantic jaws that were constructed here just for us and are sucking and grinding us in. Tick tock, tick tock, we become part of this machinery of death. Ai, yes. Because these are not human beings that are being marched to their death here. No, only that which remains of a person after being totally humiliated, after being robbed of self and left only with the metal scaffolds of human form, mechanical joints that have no soul and are common to all . . . This was all we could offer, in wretched and ironic defiance, to those who were killing us. And this, indeed, is the cruel reflection of their own image. Because it is not Jews that are being marched to their death here, but living mirrors, showing in a sad and endless procession the reflection of the world that is doing this to them . . . Thus they pass sentence upon it in their death. Ai, our mass death, our meaningless death, will be reflected from now to all eternity in the arid desolation of your lives. (p. 320/357–58)

But Shlomo, who serves as the editor of the "Encyclopedia," remains skeptical. "Wasserman's words have been recorded here in full," he says. "But still, for the sake of balance, let this also be said: Not even a curse? Really? Not even a slap in the Ukrainian's face? Like that? Like sheep to the slaughter?" (p. 320/358).

Shlomo is still disturbed and repelled by the victims' utter lack of re-sistance. But the narrative dynamics of his fantastic engagement with the world of the camps have created a space for the articulation of a con-trary, and heretofore suppressed, perspective that emerges from within this world. The incursion of the imagination into the concentrationary world gives a voice to the inhabitants of this world. It also creates the empathy that is necessary in order for this voice to be heard by some-one from the outside. While Shlomo may not agree with all that this new voice is saying, he no longer refuses to listen to it. This is a significant breach in the barrier between the two worlds of discourse and it opens the possibility for dialogue between them. Such a dialogue is essential for the process of healing because the two opposing worlds are actually contained within a single psyche. They are unreconciled aspects of the same self. The concentrationary world that Shlomo is now seeing and the victim's voice that he is hearing are a hidden world and a silenced voice that have been liberated from within himself.

In See Under: Love, as in Una, the crossing of discursive boundaries opens the way for a reassessment of the fundamental premises of a life that has been shaped by the demands of denying constitutive portions of the internal self. This reassessment accounts for the movement towards emotional affirmation and psychological integration with which both novels conclude.

Shlomo sets out to write the story of Anshel Wasserman in order to reclaim his grandfather's dignity and humanity. But as his project pro-gresses, he realizes that he is actually creating a story that is directed towards reclaiming his own dignity and humanity. Wasserman states re-peatedly that his purpose in telling his "Children of the Heart" story to Neigel is to defeat the Nazi officer by awakening him to his humanity. He is largely successful in this undertaking and regains considerable human and moral stature in the process. But as Wasserman's story un-folds, Shlomo begins to understand that the story of the character that he is creating is directed as much toward transforming him as it is toward transforming Neigel. He realizes that Wasserman's ultimate objective is to heal the psychological consequences of Nazi atrocity, which have co-alesced into an ethos of survival that makes it impossible for Shlomo to embrace life and experience love.

In accordance with the precepts of the survival ethos, Shlomo has always sought to divest himself of the potentially painful attributes of love, faith, trust, responsibility, choice, and hope. However, the more he insists on emotional self-sufficiency, the more difficult it is for him to carry on with the story he so desperately wants to write. He finally finds himself totally blocked. But there is another, hidden, side to Shlomo. The creative impasse he has reached is a result of the conflict between his ideological repudiation of emotion and his unconscious desire to affirm it. Wasserman embodies this desire and the objective of his nar-rative is to release the "great talent for love," which Shlomo has sought to suppress but which Ruthie, his wife, had long recognized in him (p. 142/153). His mission, says Wasserman, is to replenish the soul with "mercy . . . and love for other people and with the wondrously fool-ish capacity to believe in them, despite everything" (p. 217/239). He also proposes a narrative device that will break the creative deadlock and accomplish the humanizing transformation. "You know very well," Wasserman tells Shlomo, "that only my story, this one story, can show you the way . . . So please write the following: A baby will enter the story and he will live his life in it" (p. 251/279).

The "Kazik" section of See Under: Love interweaves the story of Wasser-man's concentrationary experiences with the story of baby Kazik and the personal stories of the aging members of "The Children of the Heart" group. This conflation produces a narrative that tests the viability of the ethos of survival against the emotional claims of an increasingly power-ful discourse of humanity. The organization of the narrative according to encyclopedic categories is part of Shlomo's strategy of resistance to Wasserman's storytelling powers. It is designed to objectify the narrated events and minimize their emotional impact. But the controlled cate-gories of the encyclopedia cannot contain the polyphony of characters who have emerged from Shlomo's story and who reflect the conflicting aspects of his fractured self. In the final movement of the novel, Shlomo no longer exists as a unified character and the narrative arena is given over to a multiplicity of figures who manifest his condition of fragmen-tation as well as his desire for integration.

One of the central oppositions in the "Kazik" section is between Otto, the leader of the Children of the Heart, who adheres to an ethos of human affirmation, and Fried, the physician, who, in his determination

to avoid pain after the death of his beloved Paula, has become a consummate disciple of the ethos of survival. Fried resolutely banishes all
wonder from his life and, like Shlomo, devotes himself to diminishing
and discarding all emotions (p. 242/268). Otto, who, like Wasserman,
"is infected with the disease of belief in man" (p. 378/427), is "always
trying to arouse [Fried] back to life" (p. 329/368). This proves to be
a futile undertaking until the baby, Kazik, is introduced into the story.
Once it is discovered that Kazik is doomed to live an entire lifetime
within the span of twenty-four hours, Otto delivers him into Fried's care.
Fried confirms the affective parallels between himself and Shlomo, on
the one hand, and Otto and Wasserman on the other, when he observes
angrily that Otto is using the child to "catch him in the trap of loving
life" (p. 241/267). He is right, of course. But once the trap is sprung, it
proves to be inescapable.

In the course of caring for Kazik and assuming increasing responsibility for his upbringing and education, Fried discovers that he is growing to love the child and that, contrary to all his convictions, this love
is a true source of fulfillment and joy. Throughout the "Kazik" section,
the brutal debasements of the Holocaust experience are counterpointed
with reverberations of Fried's emotional discoveries. He treats the numerous childhood diseases that rage through Kazik's tiny body, and
"through the child's suffering—more than through his joys and smiles—
Fried felt how much he was attached to Kazik and how much he loved
him" (p. 322/360). Later, Fried plays with Kazik and sings to him, and
"when Kazik laughed with pleasure . . . Fried felt that perhaps for the
first time in his life he had become a real healer" (p. 323/361). Fried's
movement from his life-negating ethos of survival to a recognition of
the healing value of such life affirming acts of love is the subject of the
"Education" entry of the encyclopedia.

When he realizes what a short time Kazik has to live, Fried decides to
devote himself to the child's education and finds himself compulsively
reciting the basic principles of the ethos of survival in accents passed
down to him by his own embittered father ("Beware of strangers, and
doubt your friends. Never tell anyone what you really think . . . And
don't love anybody too much, not even yourself" [p. 316/354]). But
as he reflects on the damaging effects of this ethos on his own life, he
realizes how much he actually despises it. It is then that Fried "stop[s]
talking about the foolish things he had been telling Kazik until now
and start[s] talking about what was is essential: about his beloved Paula"
(p. 317/355). Like Shlomo, Fried had never expressed his emotions
to his beloved, or to himself. When he does so now he is filled with
gratitude to the child whose unexpected presence provided for such

an emotional awakening. By the time the "Education" entry approaches closure, it is clear that the true beneficiary of the educational process that it traces is not the uncomprehending baby Kazik, but the newly revived Fried. The final movement of this entry marks the conclusive moment in Fried's transformation:

Fried suddenly opened his eyes. He looked at the child with **compassion** (*q.v.*) and saw how small and weak and miserable he was, and he fell into a sad silence. And so the two of them sat hugging each other for a long time. And the doctor knew that now, only now, he was doing the most important thing for his son (p. 318/355).

Fried, who initially embodied the credo of emotional denial and human disengagement passed down to Shlomo by his survivor parents, is now in accord with Wasserman, also a survivor, who embodies the alternative conviction that emotional affirmation and loving human contact are the necessary response to the internal ravages of the Holocaust experience. He believes that if a healing is to take place, the emotional capacities that were, of necessity, denied and suppressed during the Holocaust must be affirmed and reclaimed in its aftermath. "It's not miracles that we need," Wasserman tells Neigel. "What we need is to touch the flesh of the living person, to look straight into the blue of his eyes and to taste the salt of his tears" (p. 379/428). The reconciliation of Fried's perceptions with Wasserman's beliefs constitutes a healing integration of the conflicting elements within Shlomo's self. It marks the beginning of a new orientation towards the emotional heritage of the Holocaust and accounts for the hopeful note on which the novel ends.

In the encyclopedia entry that concludes *See Under: Love* ("Prayer"), Fried dedicates himself to becoming the kind of loving father that Shlomo never had and had not been able to become. He "vows to give the child that was sleeping beside him the best life possible; to be the best of fathers to him, and the best of friends." He declares his readiness to take action, even to fight, in order to provide Kazik with a meaningful life (p. 398/451). This is the final step in Shlomo's imaginative struggle to confront the internal heritage of the Holocaust and reconfigure its existential implications. It completes the process of recognizing that the psychological legacy of the Holocaust is not a set of categorical imperatives that are forever to be followed but a complex of psychic wounds that urgently need to be healed. Fried is now able to join Otto, Wasserman, and others in a prayer in which the previously fragmented and often discordant voices of survivors join together to wish such a healing upon their descendants:

And [Fried] looked at the child with pity that was now mixed with love, and blades of pain and pleasure plowed new furrows in the dry clods of his old heart. And again, as always, against his will, contrary to his resolve and to everything that he knew about this world and about its people and about life that is not life, fresh buds of hope sprung up within him. He prayed, Marcus: "That he will know how to preserve in the child this great passion for life, and this wondrous confidence, as he lies on his back, open to everything, believing in everything." Fried: "And that I won't poison him with all the hate that is in me," Marcus: "And with everything that I already know," Otto: "That I will be able to keep him manly and brave and willing to believe," Fried: "And that he won't be like me. Please let him be more like her. Like Paula." And Wasserman lifted his eyes to Neigel and said: "And all of us prayed for one thing: that he will live his entire life without knowing anything about the war. Do you understand, Herr Neigel? We asked for so little: that it would be possible for one person to live his entire life in this world, from beginning to end, without knowing a thing about war." (pp. 398–399/451–452)

The novel's conclusion constitutes a powerful repudiation of the ethos of survival. It marks the depth of the humanizing transformation that the narrative recuperation and integration of the Holocaust experience has effected in Shlomo. The man who started out believing that his legacy to his child should be that there is no love, value, or justice in the world, only war, can now affirm the value of hope and emotion and can believe in the possibility of a life that will never know war.

In *Una*, as in *See Under: Love*, the recuperation of the concentrationary experience is the necessary precondition for the integration of a dangerously divided self. Once the girl enters the death camp world of Holocaust victims and embraces it as her own, her obsession with possessing and destroying Una comes to an end. She concedes that Una "will manage to go on living, if I only let her be. And why shouldn't I leave her alone? Perhaps the time has come. The struggle is over and she has won" (p. 218). But as the girl prepares to release her grip and sink back into oblivion, Una asserts her grasp of the lessons learned from her fantastic encounter with the concentrationary experience. Having recognized the connection between emotional vitality and Holocaust memory, she now knows that oblivion is no victory. "I bought peace at the cost of total erasure," Una says. "And I bought the forgetting of the pillar of grey smoke at the cost of forgetting all the rest, and I bought the ability to forget the sunken faces marching in formation at the cost of the ability to really see any face at all . . . Not to feel too much, that was the watchword" (p. 219). But now, no longer willing to pay the high price of emotional curtailment extracted by the determination to deny the painful connection to the Holocaust experience, Una reverses her attitude towards the girl.

Instead of seeking to deny and suppress the Holocaust experiences that the girl represents, Una now acknowledges these experiences as important aspects of her self and seeks to effect an internal healing by integrating them with the rest of her life. "Don't go," she says to the girl whom she previously abhorred and who is preparing to depart.

> We can be here together. I will show you New York. We'll walk in the park together on Sunday, we'll sit on the couch in the evening and listen to music . . . I'll introduce you to Adam . . . Don't go, I call out to her again . . . I won't try to put you back in the closet . . . It has suddenly become very important for me that she stay. I know that if she leaves I will lose something, something that I no longer wish to live without. I don't want her to go. Because if she leaves I, too, will sink back into my shadow kingdom . . . It's true, I refused to see. I hated all the terrible pictures that she forced before my eyes. Yes, she forced me. But if she leaves, the picture will become blurred again . . . From now on I want to be able to see clearly. And I am willing to pay the price. (pp. 218–19)

As she concludes the process of Holocaust recuperation with a definitive move towards psychological integration, Una (her name is obviously significant) prepares to engage life with a greater degree of emotional openness and willingness to risk. Many of the old fears are still there, but they are countered by newly found measures of awareness and determination. When the prospects of what she has resolved to do threaten to overwhelm her with anxiety and dread, Una draws strength from an ancient message unearthed in the Naj Hamadi excavations. This message, which reverberates through *See Under: Love, The Angels Are Coming*, and *The Legend of the Sad Lakes* as well, articulates the fundamental premise that guides all of these novels in their efforts to recuperate the Holocaust dimension of the Israeli psyche: "The living god says, 'If you bring out into the light that which is inside you, that which you bring out will save you. If you do not do this, it will be your destroyer'" (p. 224).

Notes

1. For an excellent discussion of Appelfeld's early work, see Alan Mintz, *Hurban: Responses to Catastrophe in Hebrew Literature* (New York: Columbia University Press, 1984), pp. 203–238. Other useful studies of Appelfeld are Gila Ramras-Rauch, *Aharon Appelfeld: The Holocaust and Beyond* (Bloomington: Indiana University Press, 1994); Lily Rattok, *Bayit 'al blima* (A precarious house: The narrative art of A. Appelfeld) (Tel Aviv: Heker, 1989). Both books provide bibliographies of shorter studies of Appelfeld's work.

2. The waves of shock and recognition generated by the Eichmann trial, in 1961, brought forth three novels that attempted, largely unsuccessfully, to engage disparate aspects of the Holocaust experience: Yehuda Amichai's *Not of This Time, Not of This Place* (1963), Hanoch Bartov's *The Brigade* (1965), and Haim Gouri's *The Chocolate Deal* (1965). The appearance of these novels marks

a brief break in the literary silence surrounding the Holocaust. This silence, which was then to continue for yet another twenty years, was broken by Yoram Kaniuk's idiosyncratic novel *Adam Resurrected* (1969), which may well have been a harbinger of the change that was to come. With the early exception of Uri Zvi Greenberg's epic poetic cycle, *Streets of the River* (1951), the Holocaust theme also figured only marginally and very sporadically in Israel's poetic and dramatic literature until the mid-1980s.

For a discussion of Israeli fiction of the Holocaust during the 1960s, see Sidra DeKoven Ezrahi, *By Words Alone: The Holocaust in Literature* (Chicago: University of Chicago Press, 1980), pp. 103–107, 114–115; Mintz, *Hurban*, pp. 239–258; Gershon Shaked, *Gal hadash basipporet ha'ivrit* (A new wave in Hebrew fiction) (Tel Aviv: Sifriyat Poalim, 1971), pp. 71–86. For a discussion of the possible influence of Kaniuk's *Adam Resurrected* on later Holocaust literature, see Yael S. Feldman, "Whose Story Is It, Anyway? Ideology and Psychology in the Representation of the Shoah in Israeli Literature," in *Probing the Limits of Representation: Nazism and the "Final Solution,"* ed. Saul Friedlander (Cambridge: Harvard University Press, 1992), p. 235. For discussions of Israel's poetry of the Holocaust, see Hillel Barzel, "Shirat hasho'ah" (Poetry of the Holocaust) in *Hasho'ah bashirah ha'ivrit: mivhar* (Holocaust in Hebrew poetry: An anthology) (Tel Aviv: Hakibbutz Hameuchad, 1974), pp. 7–36; Mintz, *Hurban*, pp. 165–202; Hanna Yaoz, *Hasho'ah beshirat dor hamedina* (The Holocaust in modern Hebrew poetry) (Tel Aviv: Eked, 1984).

3. For a good survey of the evolution of Israeli attitudes towards the Holocaust, see Tom Segev, *The Seventh Million: The Israelis and the Holocaust* (New York: Farrar, Straus, & Giroux, 1993). The more recent changes in attitudes are discussed on pp. 386–517.

4. Segev, *The Seventh Million*, p. 513.

5. Savyon Liebrecht, *Tapuhim min hamidbar* (Apples from the desert) (Tel Aviv: Sifriyat Poalim, 1986), *Susim al kvish gehah* (Horses on the highway) (Tel Aviv: Sifriyat Poalim, 1988), *Sinit ani medaberet elekha* ("It's Greek to me" she said to him) (Tel Aviv: Keter, 1992); Nava Semel, *Kova zekhukhit* (A hat of glass) (Tel Aviv: Sifriyat Poalim, 1988), *Maurice haviv'el melamed la'uff* (The flying Jews or Hadara and Monsieur Maurice) (Tel Aviv: Am Oved, 1990); Jacob Buchan, *'Eever tsva'im* (Color blind) (Tel Aviv: Am Oved, 1990).

6. Tzvetan Todorov, *The Fantastic: A Structural Approach to a Literary Genre* (Ithaca, N.Y.: Cornell University Press, 1975).

7. In addition to Todorov's book, the following works have been most helpful in my understanding of the fantastic: Kathryn Hume, *Fantasy and Mimesis: Responses to Reality in Western Literature* (New York: Methuen, 1984); Rosemary Jackson, *Fantasy: The Literature of Subversion* (New York: Routledge, 1981); Eric S. Rabkin, *The Fantastic in Literature* (Princeton: Princeton University Press, 1976); Julio Rodriguez-Luis, *The Contemporary Praxis of the Fantastic* (New York: Garland, 1991).

8. For discussions of the fantastic in Israeli fiction see: Ortsion Bartana, *Hafantasia besipporet dor hamedina* (Fantasy in Israeli literature in the past thirty years [1960–1989]) (Tel Aviv: Hakibbutz Hameuchad, 1989); Hillel Barzel, *Sipporet ivrit metarealistit* (Metarealistic Hebrew prose) (Ramat-Gan: Massada, 1974).

9. A fantastic aspect of *See Under: Love* that requires a separate discussion involves the character of the Polish writer Bruno Schulz. In reality Schulz was murdered by the Nazis. In the novel he is given an alternative life in which he

fantastically joins a school of salmon making their way in the sea. Another fantastic character in this novel is the Sea herself. A robustly feminine entity, the Sea has a significant speaking part and enters into a complicated relationship with Shlomo.

10. The discussion of *The Angels Are Coming* in this chapter often draws on my "Subverting Dystopia: Ben-Ner's Fiction of the Future," *Prooftexts* 13, no. 3 (1993): 269–287.

11. Itamar Levy, *Agadat ha'agamim ha'atsuvim* (The legend of the sad lakes) (Tel Aviv: Keter, 1989), p. 53–54. All subsequent references to this book are in the text. The translations are mine.

12. *Ayen erekh: 'ahava'* (See under: Love) (Jerusalem: Hakibbutz Hameuchad, 1986), pp. 100–101. Parenthetical page references in the text will be to this book/followed by the reference to its English translation: David Grossman, *See Under: Love* (trans. Betsy Rosenberg) (New York: Washington Square Press, 1989), p. 109. Although this book is more successfully translated than most Hebrew novels, I often found it necessary to provide my own translations. Consequently, the second page references indicate the places in which a different version of the quoted text may be found in the English translation.

13. Segev, *The Seventh Million*, pp. 76–77.

14. As I was preparing this chapter for print, I came upon the work of the historian Moshe Zuckermann, whose conclusions on this matter coincide with mine. See Moshe Zuckermann, *Shoah baheder ha'atum* (Holocaust in the sealed room) (Tel Aviv: Hamehaber, 1993), pp. 19–22. An earlier, but conceptually identical, English version of Zuckermann's argument appears in Moshe Zuckermann, "The Curse of Forgetting: Israel and the Holocaust," *Telos: A Quarterly Journal of Critical Thought*, no. 78 (Winter, 1988–89): 45–47. For an illuminating discussion of the cultural dynamics that affected Israel's literary response to the Holocaust until the early 1980s, see Sidra DeKoven Ezrahi, "Revisioning the Past: The Changing Legacy of the Holocaust in Hebrew Literature," *Salamagundi* (Fall-Winter 1986): 245–269.

15. This sense of belonging to a "secret order" of those who had lost their humanity is discussed by Dori Laub, a psychotherapist who has worked extensively with Holocaust survivors. Shoshana Felman and Dori Laub, *Testimony* (New York: Routledge, 1992), p. 82.

16. For an illuminating reading of Israel's emergent literature of the Holocaust against the background of its traditional antecedents, see Mintz, *Ḥurban*, pp. 157–269.

17. Todorov, *The Fantastic*, pp. 158–159.

18. Jackson, *Fantasy*, p. 4.

19. Rabkin, *The Fantastic in Literature*, p. 227. For a complementary perspective, see T. E. Apter, *Fantasy Literature* (London: Macmillan, 1982), pp. 6–11.

20. Ezrahi, *By Words Alone*, p. 81.

21. Mintz, *Ḥurban*, p. 223.

22. Dorit Peleg, *Una* (Tel Aviv: Hakibbutz Hameuchad, 1988), p. 126. All subsequent references to this book are in the text. The translations are mine.

23. Yitzhak Ben-Ner, *Mal'akhim ba'im* (The angels are coming) (Tel Aviv: Hakibbutz Hameuchad, 1987), p. 11. All subsequent references to this book are in the text. The translations are mine.

24. As is often the case, the insight of the writer coincides with the observation of the psychoanalyst. Dori Laub, a psychotherapist who has worked exten-

sively with Holocaust survivors, notes a recurrent lesson passed down by survivor parents to the next generation: "not to love, not to dare fate, not to risk having a family . . . (for such family and such loved ones were only destined to be taken away again)" Felman and Laub, *Testimony*, p. 67.

25. The name, Neuman (new man), must be an ironic allusion to the Zionist notion of the New Jew.

26. For excellent studies of traditional Jewish response to catastrophe, see Mintz, *Ḥurban*, pp. 1–154; David Roskies, *Against the Apocalypse: Responses to Catastrophe in Modern Jewish Culture* (Cambridge: Harvard University Press, 1984).

27. Santner employs the useful, but infelicitous, term "narrative fetishism." Eric L. Santner, "History Beyond the Pleasure Principle: Some Thoughts on the Representation of Trauma," in Friedlander, *Probing the Limits*, p. 144. My discussion of narrative displacement is drawn from this article.

28. Santner, "History Beyond the Pleasure Principle," pp. 144–152.

29. Ibid., p. 147.

30. Ezrahi, *By Words Alone*, p. 52.

31. James E. Young, *Writing and Rewriting the Holocaust: Narrative and the Consequences of Interpretation* (Bloomington, Ind.: Indiana University Press, 1990), p. 53.

32. Raman Selden, *A Reader's Guide to Contemporary Literary Theory* (Lexington: University Press of Kentucky, 1989), p. 95.

33. Hayden White, "Historical Emplotment and the Problem of Truth," in Friedlander, *Probing the Limits*, pp. 50, 52. White was preceded in this thought by Lawrence L. Langer who was one of the first critics to recognize that a full literary engagement with the experiences of the Holocaust exceeds the capacities of an art devoted entirely to verisimilitude. Lawrence L. Langer, *The Holocaust and the Literary Imagination* (New Haven: Yale University Press, 1975), p. 43.

34. For further discussion of these attributes of the fantastic see: Jackson, *Fantasy*, pp. 62–89, 175–177; Rabkin, *The Fantastic in Literature*, pp. 4–8, 189–216.

35. The prospect of recuperation and more authentic identity formation is also extended by the fantastic healing powers of Dr. Zinderbaum in *The Angels Are Coming*. But Halperin fails to embrace it. It is important to note that the figure of the healer also recurs in the two novels that do pursue the possibilities of Holocaust recuperation and integration. Una benefits greatly from the guidance of her psychiatrist. Fried, who is entrusted with the care for Kazik in *See Under: Love*, is also a doctor.

36. The story takes place in the late 1970s or early 1980s. Una is in her late twenties or early thirties. The girl was twelve years old (p. 38) at the outset of her ordeal, which took place during the last two years of the war. This means that the girl was born around 1930, much too early to be Una herself.

Notes on the Contributors

ROBERT ALTER is Professor of Hebrew and Comparative Literature at the University of California at Berkeley, where he has taught since 1967. His two most recent books are *Hebrew and Modernity* (1994) and *Genesis: Translation and Commentary* (1996).

NANCY E. BERG is Assistant Professor of Hebrew and Comparative Literature in the Department of Asian and Near Eastern Languages and Literatures at Washington University in St. Louis. Her book *Exile from Exile: Israeli Writers from Iraq* has recently been published by SUNY Press. She is currently working on a study of Sami Michael's writing and its reception.

YAEL S. FELDMAN is Associate Professor at NYU, Associate Editor of *Prooftexts*, and Cultural Editor of *HaDo'ar*. She previously taught at Columbia and has been a visiting professor at Yale (1993) and Princeton (1996). She completed her postdoctoral training at the Columbia University Center for Psychoanalysis. She has received fellowships from the Fulbright Foundation, the NEH, and the Oxford Center for Hebrew Studies. Her publications include three books and scores of articles; she is currently working on *A Woolf in the Holy Land: Israeli Women Novelists Between Nationalism and Feminism*.

ANNE GOLOMB HOFFMAN is Professor of English and Comparative Literature at Fordham University in New York City. She is the author of *Between Exile and Return: S. Y. Agnon and the Drama of Writing* (SUNY Press, 1991), and co-editor with Alan Mintz of *"A Book That Was Lost" and Other Stories by S. Y. Agnon* (Schocken, 1995). Her essay in this volume forms part of a longer study titled *Inscriptions of Difference: Gender and Body in 20th-Century Jewish Writing*.

ALAN MINTZ is Joseph H. and Belle R. Braun Professor of Modern Hebrew Literature at Brandeis University. He is co-editor (with David G. Roskies) of *Prooftexts: A Journal of Jewish Literary History*. His books include *Hurban: Responses to Catastrophe in Hebrew Literature* and *"Banished From Their Father's Table": Loss of Faith and Hebrew Autobiography*.

GILEAD MORAHG is Professor of Hebrew literature at the University of Wisconsin-Madison. Prior to his work on Israel's new literature of the Holocaust, he published studies on A. B. Yehoshua, David Shahar, Amos Oz, Yitshak Ben-Ner, and on images of Arabs in Israeli fiction. He is President of the National Council of Organizations of Less Commonly Taught Languages, Executive Vice President of the National Association of Professors of Hebrew, and Associate Editor of *Hebrew Studies.*

Index